Chaucer from Prentice to Poet

UNIVERSITY PRESS OF FLORIDA

Florida A&M University, Tallahassee
Florida Atlantic University, Boca Raton
Florida Gulf Coast University, Ft. Myers
Florida International University, Miami
Florida State University, Tallahassee
New College of Florida, Sarasota
University of Central Florida, Orlando
University of Florida, Gainesville
University of North Florida, Jacksonville
University of South Florida, Tampa
University of West Florida, Pensacola

Chaucer from Prentice to Poet

The Metaphor of Love
in Dream Visions and *Troilus and Criseyde*

EDWARD I. CONDREN

University Press of Florida
Gainesville/Tallahassee/Tampa/Boca Raton
Pensacola/Orlando/Miami/Jacksonville/Ft. Myers/Sarasota

Copyright 2008 by Edward I. Condren
All rights reserved
Published in the United States of America

First cloth printing, 2008
First paperback printing, 2025

30 29 28 27 26 25   6 5 4 3 2 1

Library of Congress Cataloging-in-Publication Data
Condren, Edward I.
Chaucer from prentice to poet : the metaphor of love in dream visions and Troilus and Criseyde / Edward I. Condren.
p. cm.
Includes bibliographical references and index.
ISBN 978-0-8130-3241-2 (cloth) | ISBN 978-0-8130-8079-6 (pbk.)
1. Chaucer, Geoffrey, d. 1400—Criticism and interpretation. 2. Love in literature. 3. Chaucer, Geoffrey, d. 1400. Troilus and Criseyde. 4. Metaphor.
5. Visions in literature. 6. Dreams in literature. I. Title.
PR1875.L6C66 2008
821'.1—dc22   2008014468

The University Press of Florida is the scholarly publishing agency for the State University System of Florida, comprising Florida A&M University, Florida Atlantic University, Florida Gulf Coast University, Florida International University, Florida State University, New College of Florida, University of Central Florida, University of Florida, University of North Florida, University of South Florida, and University of West Florida.

University Press of Florida
2046 NE Waldo Road
Suite 2100
Gainesville, FL 32609
http://upress.ufl.edu

For Gail —

ещё раз . . .

Первая мая любовь,
Тогда обещаемая,
В конце концов,
Любимая жена мая --

my cherished, loving wife

Contents

List of Illustrations ix

Abbreviations xi

Acknowledgments xiii

1. Introduction 1

2. *Book of the Duchess* 8

3. *Parliament of Fowls* 63

4. *House of Fame* 96

5. The Missing Tidings of the *House of Fame* 125

6. *Troilus and Criseyde* 140

Appendix A: Parallel Structures of *Duchess, Fowls,* and *Fame* with its Tidings of Love 189

Appendix B: The Golden Proportion 193

Notes 197

Works Cited 223

Index 235

Illustrations

Figures

Figure 2.1. Golden proportion with its self-contained next step made explicit 58
Figure 3.1. *PF* complete with parts 1–3 in geometric harmony 83
Figure 3.2. *PF* part 1 in arithmetic harmony 85
Figure 3.3. *PF* part 2 in harmonic proportion 86
Figure 3.4. *PF* part 3 in golden proportion 92
Figure 6.1. Pythagorean triangles: rational and irrational 141
Figure 6.2. Pythagorean triangles: equal hypotenuse 144
Figure B.1. Divine proportion 194

Tables

Table 2.1. *BD* 1309–17 in its four exemplars 25
Table 2.2. Proposed sequence of selected events, 1350–1380 33
Table 2.3. Man in black echoing words of dreamer/narrator 39
Table 2.4. *BD* 514–1310 apportioned to dialogues and monologues 56

Abbreviations

BD	*Book of the Duchess*
Ch L-R	*Chaucer Life-Records*, ed. Crow and Olson
ChauR	*Chaucer Review*
CT	*Canterbury Tales*
HF	*House of Fame*
Inf	Dante, *Inferno*
LGW	*Legend of Good Women*
PF	*Parliament of Fowls*
PMLA	*PMLA (Publications of the Modern Language Association)*
Riv Ch	*Riverside Chaucer*, ed. L. D. Benson
T&C	*Troilus and Criseyde*

Acknowledgments

Attraction to Chaucer usually begins with the *Canterbury Tales*, an anachronistic introduction still honored in undergraduate curricula. By a quirk of fate, I came to know Chaucer as he perhaps came to know himself, during a maturing process that grew from energetic attractions and false starts into more thoughtful engagements with the internal world in which he chose to live. His dream visions captured my interest first, for they showed an acolyte kneeling at the steps, impatient with what he had been and eager to discover what he would become.

This book had its beginnings many years ago under the guidance of Father Laurence K. Shook during his tenure as president of the Pontifical Institute of Mediaeval Studies at the University of Toronto. His early interpretation of the *House of Fame* was the first to show a Chaucer profoundly concerned with the nature and craft of literature, an interest that appears repeatedly throughout his poetry. Other scholars, friends, and students had further influence as this project was developing. Both Chauncey Wood and J. Stephen Russell, who read the manuscript for the Press, provided judicious advice that made the book more cohesive and persuasive. Robert E. Bjork, director of the Arizona Center for Medieval and Renaissance Studies, kindly invited me to give a formal lecture on the thesis appearing here as chapter 3. The stimulating Q&A following that lecture contributed much to its final form. Chuck Berst and Dick Lanham, friends and scholars whom I much admire, became accomplished listeners during this project's long gestation. Several laymen, too, brought large measures of wit and sanity to my endeavors: Bob Greer, Bob Gebhardt, Stan Colbert, and a numerous, congenial "dawn patrol," golf addicts who have long been good friends.

For copyediting of exceptional substance and detail, I am indebted to Ann Marlowe. I also wish to express gratitude to several presses for permission to republish material previously in print: to Pennsylvania State University Press for sections of my articles "The Historical Context of the *Book of the Duchess: A New Hypothesis*," *ChauR* 5 (1970): 195–212, and "Of Deaths and Duchesses and Scholars Coughing in Ink," *ChauR* 10 (1975): 87–95; to the same press for permission to adapt two figures from Thomas Elwood Hart, "Medieval Structuralism: 'Dulcarnoun' and the Five-Book Design of

Chaucer's *Troilus*," *ChauR* 16 (1981): 129–70, appearing as figures 6.1 and 6.2; to Southern Illinois University Press, Edwardsville, for a passage from my article "Transcendent Metaphor or Banal Reality: Three Chaucerian Dilemmas," *Papers on Language and Literature* 21 (1985): 233–57; and to Peter Lang Publishers for sections of my article "The Disappointments of Criseyde," in *Chaucer and the Challenges of Medievalism: Studies in Honor of H. A. Kelly*, edited by Donka Minkova and Theresa Tinkle (2003).

To the extent that this book's ideas and theories are accessible, its style and tone agreeable, and its love of subject obvious, I acknowledge my deepest debt in the dedication, to my wife, Gail, whose editorial patience and generous labors with proofing and indexing deserve enormous credit.

1
Introduction

"What is truth? said jesting Pilate, and would not stay for an answer." Bacon's swift indictment of Pilate—that quintessential symbol of postlapsarian man, frivolous in the divine presence and smug in the belief that neither Christ nor truth matters—emphasizes the enormous difference between absolute reality and man's flawed perception of reality. Long before Bacon quoted Pilate's supercilious inquiry, put to Truth's face, the same biblical scene came to Chaucer's mind as he was advising a friend that a flawed perception of love might be leading him to marriage.[1] Unlike Pilate viewing truth skeptically, Chaucer apparently understood love to subsume all things true, beautiful, and harmonious, although the precise meaning he attributed to the word may be difficult to grasp. His dream visions and the *Troilus and Criseyde* studied in the following chapters are often said to be about love, but the texts of these works do not support the claim. When a line in the *Parliament of Fowls* states unambiguously, "Al this mene I by Love" (4), the phrase "Al this" refers to some unnamed craft or skill, and leads directly to a philosophical treatise on the harmony of the universe. If the usual understanding of love is not, then, the actual subject of Chaucer's poetry, literature is immeasurably richer that he stayed a lifetime to discover what love is, to understand its various forms, to show it in his poetry, and to show it *as* poetry.

Ockham argues that love, like every abstraction, can only exist in concrete demonstrations, in the variety of details that enrich the portraits of persons who love. The dress and trappings Chaucer gives his characters may reflect their values, as their oblique speeches perhaps reveal what their literal words are often meant to conceal. But that "faire cheyne" (*CT* I.2988) he names again and again takes us higher, away from these characters and their accoutrements, away from ourselves, to love's wider context, the eternity on which all his works subtly focus.[2] He keeps this context at a less intense level than the immediate attention he gives to life's surfaces. His particular subject, then, is the sum of all the objects and sounds in his poetry, while this wider love remains as a remote, yet ever present, implication.

A second allusive context, influencing almost everything in the foreground of Chaucer's poetry, gives the works studied here still another facet of meaning. Each of the poems discussed in the following chapters reveals Chaucer's concern with matters that challenge him as a practicing poet. To begin, he focuses in the *Book of the Duchess* on the practical matters of winning patronage and achieving an acceptable poetic form. The *Parliament of Fowls*, while displaying a variety of subjects explored by prior poets, virtually defines poetry as a subset of universal harmony whose unwitting seekers show varieties of chaos more often than the understanding Chaucer promotes. And in the *House of Fame*, he worries about the genus and species of this thing called poetry. One of *Fame*'s characters, a wittily energetic eagle, spreads a complicated series of syllogisms across 173 lines (*HF* 711–883) to demonstrate that, since poetry is speech, and "spech is soun" (762), and "Soun ys noght but eyr ybroken" (765), poetry must be nothing but broken air. Putting aside olfactory sensibilities, the insufficient definition possesses enough truth to include the broken air that offends Lady Nature in another of his poems (*PF* 568–617). Elsewhere, *Fame*'s professorial eagle, still lecturing on the standard fare of poets, pronounces harshly on typical audiences, "Loo, ys it not a gret myschaunce / To lete a fool han governaunce / Of thing that he can not demeyne?" (*HF* 957–59). The eagle's judgment much concerns the subject of the final chapter. *Troilus and Criseyde* profoundly inquires into events of the past—an insoluble question, since recorded history itself often bears a dubious relation to facts. What then of the opinions of audiences? True, audiences are important, Chaucer maintains through his horseback editor of the *Canterbury Tales*, for if a man lacks an audience there is no point in his airing his thoughts (*CT* VII.2801–2). All of these ruminations appear again and again in the poetry examined here.

The suggestion that Chaucer has a main subject, the daily lives of the men and women he creates, and two surrounding contexts of uncertain relation to this subject—macrocosmic love and the creation of poetry—implies different authorial methods. With his main subject, Chaucer invests his stories and scenes with specifics that make his characters palpably present. But with the latter two, he only dots his poetic landscape with loosely connected allusions that suggest both a much larger universe created and presided over by an intelligent, just, and omnipotent deity and a smaller universe created by his own imagination whose aesthetic ideals give these works their final form.

A parallel series of creators and the worlds they fashion emerges before us. As the Creator is to Creation, so Chaucer is to the poetry he creates, so his characters are to the dreams, tales, and reports they share. One would expect such a plan to be impossibly complex and confused, yet it miraculously unfolds with charming simplicity and success.

Not everyone agrees. Where one reader finds charming simplicity, another sees long, vacuous rhetorical passages. Critics used to assume these incompatible opinions referred to the terminal points of Chaucer's "French romance period" and his "English period." A better description might be his "beginning period," when he hardly knew what he was doing poetically, and his "period of poetic maturity," when he knew more about literary creation than we have yet realized. We know much, that is, about Chaucer before he matured as a poet, and by slow degrees we are learning much about his later achievement. What we seem to pass over are the specific literary epiphanies that contributed to this growth. By focusing on these subtler implications in Chaucer's poetry—the allusions that are often missed as we marvel at the fully realized details dominating the surface—this book attempts to explain some of the maturing processes that took him from his earliest extended poem, the *Book of the Duchess*, where I shall argue a persona of the poet lampoons a younger image of himself, to his fullest maturity in *Troilus and Criseyde*, a poem he executes, and then must defend, with all his poetic might.

Several compositional strategies contribute to this maturity, techniques recognizable in poetry he wrote throughout his lifetime. The *Book of the Duchess*, while very decidedly establishing Chaucer's commitment to the career of poet within a climate of patronage, also implies the interchangeable nature of love and poetry since both of these activities depend on versions of harmony. Not that they do not naturally recommend each other, but for Chaucer poetic creation is an act of love in the same way that love is a creative act. In this earliest extended work we also see Chaucer's first experiments with two techniques he retained throughout most of his career, self-dialogue and numerical construction, the latter a technique he may have learned in some formal curriculum, or perhaps informally from one of the Schoolmen, who may also have introduced him to Virgil. In the *Duchess*, we see self-dialogue as a confrontation between two dissimilar representations of his own poetic voice, in the language of the dreamer and in the monologues of the Black Knight. One of these representations he underscores with a numerical design, the divine proportion (or the "golden section," to use Kepler's term), as a way of endorsing the voice he would cultivate for the remainder of his poetic life. Decimals are more familiar to the twenty-first century than would be the unit fractions Chaucer had to use before Indian decimals were introduced to Europe in the fifteenth century. Boyer (1989, 174) gives a sense of how awkward unit fractions must have been by summarizing a computation of Heron of Alexandria (fl. 100 A.D.). "In dividing 25 by 13 [Heron] wrote the answer as $1 + \frac{1}{2} + \frac{1}{3} + \frac{1}{13} + \frac{1}{78}$." To discuss Chaucer's computations, the present book uses the decimal system without further comment.

Chaucer's multilevel strategy guides each of the poems studied here, although he expresses this method less obviously as his poetic maturation acquires increasing subtlety. By the time he writes the *Parliament of Fowls* he has learned to cast his internal debate as if it were successive symphonic movements on the same theme, the first presented allegorically, the next represented as living action. His mathematics, too, remains out of sight, but encodes *Fowls*'s entire seven hundred lines in a mathematical tour de force that embraces the four most prominent numerical proportions to show all varieties of harmony as products of number. The *House of Fame*—argued here as the prologue to Chaucer's story of Troy—offers still another internal conversation between the accretions of history and the creative imagination, all in preparation for a man of great authority to recite Chaucer's most accomplished work, *Troilus and Criseyde*. This poem's internal dialogue pits unattainable ideals against practical needs, while a numerical context alludes to the incompatibility of rational and irrational magnitudes, representing the tension between the ideals humanity wishes it could reach and the errant lives its human subjects must live because they *are* human.

Since three of the poems studied here belong to a varied genre called "dream visions," it may be useful to identify a feature that perhaps sets these poems apart from other vision poetry; it could well be their most important characteristic. In a very thorough discussion of the dream visions from *Gilgamesh* through the fourteenth century, J. Stephen Russell suggests that all known examples of the genre may be found between "the two apprehensible poles of dream-as-narrative-event and apocalypse" (1988, 22). Although he defines more precisely than is needed here several categories of vision between these poles, three points along the continuum he presents may clarify a progression in the concerns these visions address. In the most visionary category, at least for the tradition in which medieval English poetry descends, the Book of Revelation introduces each new image with the formula "I, John, saw . . ." Dazzling images of walls, towers, gates, gemstones, and much more enrich our sense of the New Jerusalem and leave no question that the struggle between good and evil will earn salvation for some, while others will be lost. But the struggle itself is largely left to the imagination of an audience whose members have for a lifetime been well aware of the quotidian moral dilemmas all humanity faces. Even more important as a distinguishing feature of apocalyptic literature, adds Russell, is this: "The visionary is never depicted as distressed or anxious; in fact, he is always represented as worthy, pure, and totally free from worldly cares" (39–40). As a result, apocalyptic literature has no need to resolve dilemmas, for only the reader, or listener, would be numbered among the troubled.

A second category of dream vision features a central figure poised at the dividing line where eternal reward will be judged. The *Dream of the Rood*, for example, visualizes a dreamer wounded by sin, as he readily admits:[3]

>   ond ic synnum fah,
> forwunded mid wommum.
>   (13–14)
>   [and I, stained with sins,
> utterly wounded with evil.]

The poet's use in line 30 of bivalenced *stefne* ("voice"; "stem, stump") reinforces the notion that a moral condition both results from and causes the absence of light and voice. The dreamer's surrogate, the cross, realizes

> þæt ic wæs aheawen   holtes on ende,
> astyred of stefne minum
>   (29–30)
> [that I was hewn   at the edge of the wood,
> cut from my stem-voice]

Despite once being severed from its stem and its voice, the cross now speaks, though it first saw its sinful state

> to midre nihte,
> syðþan reordberend   reste wunedon!
> (2–3)
>
> [in the middle of the night
> when speech-bearers   were at rest!]

Newly committed to a salvific path, and newly blest with a forceful voice, the dreamer too engages his listeners in the proselytic mission the cross has urged him to accept.

A dream vision of this nature, touching both the temporal and eternal realms, would seem to be excluded from the purely apocalyptic type. But the dreamer of *Rood* exhibits characteristics of a true visionary, "empty of earthly concerns" and thus able to "accept the indwelling of the Divine Presence" (Russell, 40). We neither see this visionary during temptation nor feel the poet's need to resolve the anxiety that inspired his poem.

A similar division accounts for Boethius's *Consolation*, a meditation on the rival views held by Lady Philosophy and Boethius's fictive persona, views that only approach, never reach, the point at which all struggle ceases as profound understanding arrives. Among the works in this middle group of vision poems, *Pearl* perhaps affects readers most deeply. Here the confrontation between the recently deceased maiden and the dreamer, cast as a grieving father, cannot overcome the impasse that keeps the temporal world from possessing by will alone the metaphysical world beyond. Hindered by his limited imagination, the dreamer simply cannot apprehend infinite measurement, when his every instinct imagines a measured world. Thus the dreamer may be as ignorant by the end of the poem as he was at its beginning, despite his believing otherwise. The difficulty of facing questions of eternity with a limited capacity, certainly not original to the *Pearl*-poet, has been explored in nearly every significant poem and treatise produced in the high Middle Ages. But the authors of poems in this category apparently feel no need to resolve in their poems the struggles that inspire these compositions in the first place.

Chaucer's dream visions typify a third category, creating figures who face dilemmas well known to modern readers. In contrast to apocalyptic visions that suspend their central figures between this world and the next, thoroughly examining their concerns from sophisticated points of view, yet leaving them largely unchanged, these dream visions work their way dynamically and relentlessly toward resolution. A reader experiences the struggles these central figures face, and the release they feel as they progress toward understanding. That understanding may only be partial, perhaps even unrecognized by the central figure, who may have been looking for something altogether different. But readers understand that the poem has provided sufficient answers.

The chapters that follow examine the texts of these poems very closely to understand the dynamic ways they use to reach their resolutions and the connections they make to Chaucer's progress as a poet. This critical method, inviting readers to view the small differences between scenes that otherwise seem similar, will show, I contend, a stronger coherence among these early poems than among the tales of Canterbury, even as that awkwardly beautiful collection of twenty-four disparate pieces also rises above several varieties of *discordia*. Chaucer's dream visions and *Troilus and Criseyde*, though alluding to each other only rarely, nevertheless present explicit subjects and parallel structures that imply a more obvious unity than does a pilgrimage. To suggest the basis of this unity, appendix A presents a chart of Chaucer's three dream visions showing the similarities they share. It also includes in brackets the proposal—noted above and argued in chapters 4 and 5—that Chaucer understood the *House of Fame* to be completed by the "love-tydynges" (2143) now known as *Troilus and Criseyde*, told by the poet himself, wittily described as "a man . . . [who] semed for to be / A man of gret auctorite" (2155–58).

2
Book of the Duchess

Readers in every age have as broad a range of motives for taking up a book as signs of enrichment when they finally put it down, yet they share one feature without question. To be told, at the outset of reading a mystery, say, that the butler did it would ruin their pleasure. The fascination of viewing a drama for the first time would almost disappear if an audience were told to watch that military fellow who murders his beautiful wife at the end of the play and executes himself, as he once smote "a malignant and a turbaned Turk" (*Othello* V.ii.363).

Critics must assume that readers of the *Book of the Duchess* are of a different sort. Nearly every study of this fascinating poem begins by announcing an interpretation of the poem based on lines that appear only at its end. Never mind that among the four exemplars used by all modern editors—three manuscripts and a printed edition, all of which date from after Chaucer's death—the only complete text, Thynne's edition of 1532, and the manuscript with the fewest omissions, Tanner 346, do not point to this interpretation in their titles. Thynne names the poem *The Dreame of Chaucer* and Tanner 346 calls it *Chaucer's Dream*. Moreover, the author himself apparently refers to the poem, or to a part of it, when he has his Man of Law refer to it thus: "In youthe he made of Ceys and Alcione" (*CT* II.57). Granted, the two remaining exemplar manuscripts, Fairfax 16 and Bodley 638, show at the head of the poem "The Boke of the Duchess." And two works written late in Chaucer's life, the *Legend of Good Women* and the *Retraction*, name it, respectively, "the De(e)th of Blaunche the Duchesse" (F 418, G 406) and *the book of the Duchesse* (*CT* X.1086).[1] On the evidence of the titles, then, at least this much is clear: the poem was not always known as "the book of the duchess."[2] At some point after having his Man of Law call it "Ceyx and Alcyone" and after scribes copied Chaucer's original sources for Tanner 346 and Thynne's edition, but before he composed the prologues to the *Legend of Good Women*, and the *Retraction*, Chaucer apparently began thinking of the poem as related to the duchess. Even exercising maximum caution, we can still say that when Chaucer referred to the poem as "Ceys and Alcione," and when scribes wrote "The Dreame of Chaucer" and "Chaucer's Dream," the figure whom critics now assume to have been the poem's inspiration must not have been emphasized strongly enough to demand explicit identification in the poem's title. We shall return in due course to the subject of the poem's origins.

Critics have every right, of course, to rest their work on long-accepted interpretations, and may even be excused for referring to them as if they were fact.[3] In the case of the *Duchess*, however, this practice makes severe impositions on the poem. For example, absolute certainty leads Gwen M. Vickery to identify the man in black in a mere parenthesis, "[the] comfort and consolation given to the Black Knight (John of Gaunt) . . . seems negligible . . . ambiguous and ineffective," leading her to suggest the poem is "a carefully argued justification of Gaunt's second marriage," rather than a pure elegy (1995, 161). See also the recent book by Susan Schibanoff, where again Gaunt's identification appears in a confident parenthesis, "the Chaucerian narrator of the *Book of the Duchess* adopted the stance of the weak, puerile, and loveless poet . . . as a way of inoculating his courtly superior, the Black Knight (the historical John of Gaunt's alter ego), against the contemporary moral censure" (2006, 12). David Lawton explains the missing consolation somewhat differently: "Chaucer does not presume to console Gaunt for his loss but presents him with a poetic monument to his grief" (1985, 56). And a similar belief regarding Gaunt's surrogate forces the poem's most recent editor, Helen Phillips, to accept Skeat's century-old claim that line 455 contains an error:

> Than found I sitte even upryght
> A wonder wel-farynge knyght—
> By the maner me thoghte so—
> Of good mochel, and ryght yong therto,
> Of the age of foure and twenty yer,
> Upon hys berd but lytel her,
> And he was clothed al in blak.
>
> (451–57)

When all exemplars of the poem agree on the wording of line 455, one would think there was no reason to imagine it contained an error, as Phillips (1982, 153) apparently assumes:

Since John of Gaunt was born in 1340, it has been argued that *foure and twenty* arises from a scribal misunderstanding of xxviiij as xxiiij or of xxix as xxiv. . . . This argument is not destroyed by recent evidence for 1368 as the date of Blanche's death: twenty-nine could be the age of Gaunt as a mourner, at the time the poem was written. Medieval statements about age are often approximate.

Perhaps Phillips is right, that Chaucer could have been referring to this "wel-faryinge knyght" whenever Gaunt actually was 29. The "recent evidence" to which she refers is a November 1368 letter to Queen Philippa from Louis de Mâle of Flanders tactfully rejecting Philippa's offer that her son, John of Gaunt, marry Louis' daughter Margaret. Before 1974, scholars assumed Blanche died in 1369. Louis de Mâle's letter makes it plain, however, that she must have died before Philippa offered Gaunt to Louis' daughter. Further evidence demonstrates conclusively that she died in 1368, not 1369 (J. Palmer 1974). Chaucer, who was virtually on the scene, certainly knew that Blanche died in 1368 when Gaunt was 28, not 1369 when he was 29. Thus, when scholars explain how xxiiij (or xxiv) could be a misreading for xxviiij (or xxix), they ought to be explaining how a scribe could mistake 24 for 28, that is, read xxiiij for xxviij. The misreading would require converting a "v" into a minim. But surely, a discussion of Roman numerals misses the point, for it hardly explains how a poetic line that spells out its numbers, "foure and twenty yer" (455), can be a mistaken copying of an imagined "nine and twenty yer."

Would it not have been more logical for scholars to inquire into plausible persons to whom the extant line could refer, than to force an illogical defense of a supposed 29 by assuming that the four exemplars have made an error, as now seems to be the consensus? The implication that the scribes who produced these four exemplars, which descend from a stemma with at least two very different branches,[4] were all guilty of the same scribal misunderstanding greatly weakens the entire suggestion. If an error is to be ascribed, it is more likely that utter conviction of Gaunt's presence as the man in black—to be contested below—has erroneously persuaded, not defenseless scribes who can too easily be accused of blotting their copybooks, but scholars, editors, and everyone else who assumes a mistake must have been made either by Chaucer or by all of his editors unwittingly acting in concert.

To begin his very thorough discussion of the poem, Robert R. Edwards points to a more serious kind of error, a literary disconnect. He points out that the well-documented sociopolitical context of the poem, connecting it to "the death in 1368 of Blanche of Lancaster, the wife of Edward III's son and Chaucer's patron, John of Gaunt," would naturally respect "the gravity of the presumed occasion." But the poem's style reflects "the poet's seemingly desultory manner of exposition and his ironic self-presentation."[5] Though Edwards attempts to reconcile this inconsistency by posing a deliberate collaboration between an older style and Chaucer's new mode of expression, the present chapter sees not a reconciliation but a rejection of that earlier style. My intention is to note the paucity of evidence on which the current critical understanding has long been based, and to subject to fresh scrutiny the circumstances of the poem's composition. The result, I believe, will reveal the poem as a much richer work than current opinion acknowledges.

Sorrowing Insomnia

In subtle ways, the opening lines of the *Book of the Duchess* lay out the thematic strategy governing the whole poem. The first twenty-nine lines attempt to describe the narrator's complex medical condition—indeed to do so twice, as all modern editions indicate by dividing these lines into two paragraphs. John M. Hill (1974, 39–43) calls this condition "head melancholy," a name gleaned from medieval medical treatises. This unwanted condition receives several names in the first paragraph: life-threatening sleeplessness, idle thought, lack of care, inability to discriminate, sorrowful imagination, and an incapacity to feel anything save as a blob about to fall. Except for two references to sleeplessness (3, 5), the symptoms of this malady wander from the concrete to the abstract.

However much the narrator despairs of his physiological or mental condition, he confines to vague hints and shapeless implications the internal condition he would much prefer. Concern that sleeplessness could bring death (1–3) quickly yields to a lengthier complaint of other effects that seem to concern him more than the threat to his life. His illness affects him in two almost entirely unrelated ways that begin to particularize the sound health he would prefer. Lack of sleep produces "ydel thoght" (4–5), while the comment "sorwful ymagynacioun / Ys alway hooly in my mynde" (14–15), introduced by the word *For* (14), seems to identify the origin of the conditions listed from line 6 through line 13. These internal conditions, all similar to each other at some level, make him incapable of discriminating between opposites—coming and going, desire and abhorrence, joy and sorrow.

If "thoght" and "ymagynacioun" differ from each other such that the latter, based mainly on the passive experience of the senses, leads to the active cerebration of the former, the narrator has described in reverse order a series of causes and effects. All his mental images are of sorrow, making discrimination impossible and, in turn, causing idle thought. Yet he earlier named the cause of this idle thought "defaute of slep" (5). In other words, lack of sleep may metaphorically represent the sluggish mental life the narrator would very much like to energize.

The second paragraph (16–26) restates much of the first paragraph's complaint of sluggishness, noting again the danger to health that insomnia and a feeling of heaviness can cause. Mainly the narrator has lost vitality and zest, although it takes this paragraph eleven lines to restate these symptoms. It concludes, however, with a significant new detail. Whereas the previous paragraph ended lamenting the mere fact of "sorwful ymagynacioun" without commenting on whatever restriction that condition causes, the final comment of this second paragraph regrets that "Suche fantasies ben in myn hede / So I not what is best to doo" (28–29). These "fantasies" apparently prevent the narrator from knowing as well as accomplishing some particular activity. "Fantasy,"[6] though not identical to the first paragraph's "ymagynacioun," is close enough in meaning to suggest that "sorwful ymagynacioun," too, must be preventing the narrator from going about whatever activity he has a mind to pursue—for example, turning "ydel thoght" into something more constructive. The first paragraph's language of a passive/active dichotomy appears again in the second, implying the narrator's desire for some active engagement, while explicitly revealing the passive *lugubrium* that prevents it.[7]

Thoughts of a precise diagnosis cannot rise to the practical level of a cure, the third paragraph laments, for two reasons. Not only does the narrator's "eight yeer" (37) malady suggest an entrenched condition, but the only cure he knows cannot be reached. The adversative clause "but that is don" (40), referring to a remedy curiously figured as a "phisicien" (39), does not flatly state that no cure exists. The words rather imply that at one time a cure did exist, was available to him, perhaps regularly offering the sort of medicinal care that could forestall the condition now plaguing him. That is, though effective at one time, a cure is available no longer. The past participle "don" implies finality, yet the subject to which it belongs does not vanish from the poem. On the contrary, the lines referring to the physician/remedy metaphor combine several subjects whose cryptic relation to each other conveys much of the poem's organization:

39 For there is phisicien but oon
40 That may me hele; but that is don.
41 Passe we over untill eft;
42 That wil not be mot nede be left;
43 Our first mater is good to kepe.

However straightforward in appearance, these artful lines participate in two worlds and two periods of time while faintly suggesting a third. Line 39 and the first half of line 40 obviously refer only to the narrator's personal history up to the poem's present time. Line 43, on the other hand, clearly refers to a decision concerning how the present account should parcel out its information, especially since "mater" often refers to verbal expression, written or spoken. The line may also allude to imagined listeners implied by the word *Our*. Transparency suddenly becomes opaque when we try to understand how much of lines 40b–42 refers to the narrator's past history, how much to the report he is shaping of a single event in his very recent past, that is, to the poem we know as the *Book of the Duchess*, and whether any part of these middle three lines contributes to both. To wit, the first half of line 41, "Passe we over," sustains the finality of the last four words of line 40, "but that is don," and seems therefore to refer to the narrator's remote past. But the tense and mood of "Passe" (present, hortatory subjunctive) implies a decision affecting his immediate present, while the final two words of line 41, "untill eft," extend this present into an unidentified future, compromising the finality with which line 40 ends. And yet, "Passe we over untill eft" may refer neither to the remote past nor to a very recent time, but only to the narrator's present time currently being poetically re-created. The same ambiguity affects the words in 40b, "but that is don," which certainly refer to the narrator's remote history but may also allude to the poem now being created, with the sense "I have already covered that." Thus the concluding words of line 42, "mot nede be left," are ambiguous as well. Either they mean "must be left behind," particularly when taken with the finality of "that is don" and "wil not be," or they mean "must be put aside" until the indefinite future implied by "eft." Perhaps both meanings should be retained, despite apparently precluding each other.

Readers who reach line 43 and pause before continuing may well be as perplexed by "ydel thoght" (4), "sorwful ymagynacioun" (14), and "fantasies" (28) as the narrator has long been. If, however, a reader senses the narrator's two points of reference in these opening lines—his personal situation over the preceding eight years (37)[8] and a very recent sequence of events that ended with sleep and a wondrous dream—some tentative conclusions would probably come to mind. On the question of his preceding eight years, the word *phisicien* (39) hints strongly of a woman, for this word and others associated with it appear explicitly in troubadour and French poetry as a metaphor for a cherished lady whose mere presence cheers those who cherish her.[9] The intensity of the narrator's emotion on this subject further suggests the typical symptoms of mourning, while the words "Passe we over untill eft" (41) perhaps refer to the causes of sorrow. If they refer as well to a deceased lady, as the "phisicien" borrowed from French love poetry implies, the word *eft* could also call attention to life after death. Appearing later in the poem to reinforce such thoughts are a number of subtle images of immortality, as Rodney Delasanta persuasively calls the "transition from the Seyx and Alcione story to the Dreamer's own awakening into his dream by the device of the birds whose absence in the first story is gloriously supplied at the very outset of the second.... the sounds he hears are otherworldly: of 'the moste solempne servise,' 'a thyng of heven,' surpassed only by a 'toune of Tewnes'" (1969, 249). The deceased Ceyx, apparently speaking to Alcione from the afterlife, similarly suggests immortality, as does the poem now being read that will confer literary immortality on a woman who might otherwise have simply passed away. Let us add as well the "stor[ies] of Troye" (326) by Guido delle Colonne and Benoît de Sainte-Maure, whose personages disappeared from the world leaving scarcely a trace, yet still appear alive on the walls of the narrator's sleeping chamber and in the lines of the story he tells. The success of these allusions and others depends, of course, on their being just that, subtle allusions left in the margins of the poem.[10]

On the question of the most recent past, the arrangement of material the narrator decides to use in presenting his account commands his immediate attention. Though his two reference points may be unavoidably intertwined in his mind, he separates them now to show each one more clearly, as a teacher of literature might do with students as they trace simultaneous themes in a literary work. He elects to postpone the matter of his remote past, the event that has produced his unhappy condition, while he takes up some "first mater" (43). Apparently a two-part sequence is proposed, with this first matter followed by the story of his missing physician. It is left to the reader to determine where, among the remaining 1,291 lines,[11] the division between these two subjects may be found. There would be no difficulty had the narrator mentioned a three-part sequence, for the poem's natural divisions would then reveal (i) the narrator's reading and responding to one of Ovid's stories, (ii) the early parts of his dream (his sleeping chamber, a hunt for the hart, a little whelp who guides him, and an appealing forest), and (iii) the conversation with the man in black. But only two parts are referenced, not three. Since the conversation with the man in black differs so greatly from other material in the poem and lasts so long that it must be called a matter unto itself, we are left to conclude that the first matter covers everything from line 44 to a point just before the first appearance of the man in black at line 445. The second matter, though never named such in the poem, must then refer to the ensuing conversation between the narrator and the man in black, lines 443 to 1310, revealing a pitiable story of sorrow and a remembered lady who could have assuaged that sorrow, had she lived longer. This second matter evidently expands the narrator's account of the "phisicien" who is no longer available. Completing the poem, the final twenty-four lines recall his first matter by briefly alluding to the hunt and its leader (1311–23), remembering his session with Ovid (1324–29), and reminding readers it has all been that "queynt...sweven" he promised himself he would put into meter and rhyme and is now finished (1330–34).

Before looking closely at the narrator's first matter, we should not fail to notice the strategy Chaucer employs to effect a transition from his narrator's personal condition to his first matter, for the same strategy will recur at every important step in the poem. He has the narrator turn away from certain scenes in favor of others he apparently finds more appealing or more urgent. After having his narrator describe a passive psychological condition in the opening paragraphs, Chaucer has him choose something noticeably active. While this is not a "strategy of rejection," simply put, implying the narrator's distaste for what he leaves behind, Chaucer clearly turns him away from one situation in favor of another that raises his enthusiasm to a higher level. Throughout the poem each transition shows the narrator choosing some active engagement he finds more compelling than what he leaves. The narrator's decision to read Ovid initiates this strategy.

Reading Ovid's Ceyx and Alcione

One of the earliest modern critics of the *Book of the Duchess*, Wolfgang Clemen, whom Robert R. Edwards (1989, xiv) credits with establishing "the dominant mode of aesthetic criticism" of Chaucer's early narrative poems, was correct in cautioning that our long interest in Chaucer's literary sources—a simple recognition of parallels between Chaucer's lines and those of early continental poets—has misled us into believing that such influence accounts for more than can justly be claimed for it. Instead, he urged readers to be attentive to a poem's response to borrowed passages, including those borrowed passages "to which [Chaucer] was consistently resistant or unresponsive" (4). As a case in point, Ovid's tender story of King Ceyx and Queen Alcione, the anodyne to which the narrator says he turned "To rede and drive the night away" (49), has been discussed most often as a parallel to the circumstances later described by the man in black. In Ovid, Alcione mourns the death of her husband Ceyx; in Chaucer, the man in black mourns at length the death of a lady. While this similarity cannot be ignored, the parallels between them tend to be overemphasized or assumed. For example, the switched genders—from a sorrowing woman in the Roman story to a mournful man in black in the narrator's dream—could possibly offend. A grieving male, especially one of royal blood whom current interpretations assume the man in black represents, may not appreciate being foreshadowed by a saddened woman who learns of her husband's death and then dies within three days. Even more revealing of his literary purpose, Chaucer summarizes Alcione's mourning for her husband very differently from the Black Knight's protracted description of his mourning for an absent lady. Alcione's anxiety and a yearning to receive news greatly outweigh the few references to her sorrow and mourning. In fact, the great sorrow that might have been expected after the queen learns of her husband's death never materializes. Nor do we hear from Alcione a profession of "that specifically connubial 'bliss' she has supposedly enjoyed" (Hansen 1992, 70). Rather, "sorwe" appears only in a subordinate phrase (213), overshadowed by the spare remark that she "deyede within the thridde morwe" (214). Such as it is, sorrow shrinks to "swow" (215) two lines later, as the narrator's words ignore Alcione's suffering to explain why he has taken time with this Ovidian introduction to his "first matere" (218):

For I ne myghte, for bote ne bale,
Slepe or I had red thys tale
Of this dreynte Seys the kyng
And of the goddes of slepyng.

(227–30)

To advance one of Chaucer's narrative threads, where a variety of images imply life after death, these gods seem to resurrect Ceyx, as it were, evoking a scene more vivid and moving than anything the narrator's idle thought and sorrowful imagination have yet been able to bring to his mind. But they also contribute a narrative thread the dreamer considers more important. They provide Alcione with information about the fate of her husband. The dreamer, wanting to make his narrative more compelling than a reminiscence about Ovid, turns immediately to his own appeal, a wittily crafted *reductio* to initiate the same steps that brought information to Alcione. Not precisely the same steps. Whereas Alcione prays to Juno for sleep and the informative dream she longs for, the narrator thinks immediately of the god who actually brought Alcione her dream. As a result, he prays directly to Morpheus, only adding "hys goddesse, dame Juno, / Or som wight elles, I ne roghte who" (243–44) as a playful afterthought. He may claim it is sleep he longs for, yet, as Lisa Kiser (1991, 16) points out, drawing on another influential early critic, Bertrand Bronson, the narrator partly projects himself into the man in black as "the alter ego of the poem's narrator ... a version of the poet himself."[12] Sleep as metaphor presents the condition that produces a dream and the eagerly sought images a dream can bring. The underlying logic of the poem's opening lines suddenly becomes clear. The mutually causal relation between sleeplessness and failed powers of thought and imagination implies a positive equation between sleep and productive powers of discrimination. If Morpheus has the power to re-create an image of Ceyx, such that the king's wife accepts the image as reality, then surely Morpheus can help the narrator re-create an image of the woman he seems to be mourning. The emphasis, therefore, is not on sorrow but on re-creating an image heretofore blocked by "ydel thoght" and "sorwful ymagynacioun" (4, 14), conveyed metaphorically as insomnia.[13]

The appearance of this pseudo-Ceyx before the worrying Alcione and its relation to the fascinating lines in *House of Fame* where a written or spoken word, no matter how long ago, assumes the very form it refers to or emanates from (*HF* 1074–82), has attracted a good deal of attention. The subject has lately centered on whether ancient or medieval thinkers had addressed sufficiently the subject of memory, in particular as it appears in Cicero's *Rhetorica ad Herennium*. See, for example, Frances Yates (1966), Mary Carruthers (1987, 1990), and Beryl Rowland (1993). Minnis hesitates to accept Kolve's influential suggestion (1984, esp. chaps. 1–2) that the medieval mind habitually recalled image clusters, like those found in many a fifteenth-century manuscript painting, rather than mythological terms, since he cannot find this idea discussed in such a way by any writer before or during Chaucer's lifetime (Minnis 1995, 199).

Perhaps the discussion should be reconceived as a conflation of two different kinds of thinking, the way a scholar explores philosophically every avenue and byway brought to mind by some abstract subject, and the way every human being experiences mental activity in the immediacy of a given moment. For Chaucer's poetry, the crucial question should not be whether a thought is, or is not, too refined for the medieval mind, but whether a given passage should lead to the philosophical thought of its day, rather than remain in its own context as a necessary contribution to the poem's overall coherence. The former certainly has importance for those studying medieval philosophy on its own terms. At times Chaucer was one of these; if he had not been, Macrobius's *Commentary* would never be mentioned. But for those seeking the principles that led Chaucer to make poetic decisions, pure philosophy can be a red herring. Indeed he affirms in various places that the pursuit of philosophy as a subject in its own right is not his primary interest at a given moment: the Nun's Priest, despite obviously knowing much about free will, predestination, and conditional necessity, prefers to leave these subjects to those who can "bulte it to the bren" (*CT* VII.3240); in the *House of Fame* Geffrey professes ignorance of the causes of dreams, willingly leaving the subject to others, "But why the cause is, noght wot I. / Wel worthe of this thyng grete clerkys / That trete of this and other werkes" (*HF* 52–54); and later, in the grip of a golden eagle, this same Geffrey prefers to leave Martianus and Alanus to "Hem that write of this matere" (*HF* 1013).

A connection between the appearance of drowned Ceyx and the gods of sleeping, neither of whom has anything to do with mourning, obviously interests the narrator more than the sorrow of Alcione or a meditation on the hereafter. Moreover, had he merely been reading Ovid for pleasure rather than utility, he would certainly have noted the satisfying and deserved metamorphosis of Ceyx and Alcione into seabirds, a serene reference that would make the narrator's induced sleep entirely natural. But Ovid's ending would also have distracted the narrator from the first matter. Accordingly, the narrator pursues the gods of sleeping, not as a "trumped-up suggestion" (Strohm 1989, 54–55), but as the logical connection to the strategy that has been unfolding since the poem's opening lines.

A Dream World

When sleep finally comes to the suffering narrator, it brings a dream whose scenes and rapid transitions carry symbolic meaning. The first of these, a sleeping chamber where he awakens to the exquisite songs of birds clustered on the roof tiles outside his tightly shut windows, catches musically the thread conspicuously dropped from the retelling of Ovid's account of Ceyx and Alcione. These birds and the heavenly harmony their songs produce (301–20), while suggestively recalling the metamorphosed Ceyx and Alcione, set vocal music as the sustained context for whatever direction the rest of the dream will take. As Denis Walker has pointed out, "art . . . survives—in the birds that waken the narrator, not warbling native woodnotes wild but taking pains, like fine musicians, 'to fynde out mery crafty notes'" (1983, 15, quoting line 319).

Sunlight, too, quickens the day and the dreamer:

> the sonne shon
> Upon my bed with bryghte bemes,
> With many glade gilde stremes
>
> (336–38)

Before reaching the dreamer in his bed, these sunbeams pick up "al the story of Troye" (326) and "al the Romaunce of the Rose" (334) as they pass through glass windows and reflect from walls where these works appear. The general notion of vocal harmony arrives first in the matins music of birds, then in music better suited to human ears, the vocal music and harmony of literary art. Like the opening of a blossom summoned by the rays of a literal sun, the narrator awakens to literature, specifically to the matter and form of the works mentioned. Even more, no equivocation weakens his certainty of the weather outside his room, "ful attempre . . . nother to cold nor hoot yt nas" (341–42), a detail he cannot possibly know, for he twice says that the windows are shut tight (322–25, 335). The literary beams from the *Roman de la rose* and the story of Troye have become more certain realities than his sleeping chamber. A parallel with Chaucer's own career, where the *Roman* and Troye hold prominent positions, cannot be coincidence. The dreamer inescapably reminds us of Chaucer himself, surrounded by the Old French allegory that shaped him when he was beginning to study this new art form called poetry, and by the most sustained love story he would celebrate in his later career, *Troilus and Criseyde*.

It has been customary for critics to imagine the walls and windows of the dreamer's chamber as a kind of art gallery crowded with visual images inspired by the *Roman de la rose* and the story of Troy. But the word *ywroght* (327) that undoubtedly influences this assumption may not refer only to crafted shapes that visually resemble figures and objects. The parallel sounds of *wright* and *write*, *wrought* and *wrote*, though doubtful cognates, suggest the parallel sense that a piece of writing, originally something produced by scoring wood or stone, may also have been crafted, especially if accompanied by illuminated borders and decorations. Indeed, when speaking exclusively of literary art, one can hardly avoid using a vocabulary normally associated with the plastic arts. Authors paint pictures, craft scenes, construct plays (*playwright*), create lives, and do a dozen other things whose verbs would imply actions other than writing if ink and paper were not already in a reader's mind. That Chaucer's word *ywroght* may include here the literary sense of written strokes shaping the letters of the alphabet, as well as painted strokes tracing visual shapes, receives confirmation a few lines later where "text and glose" (333) bring to mind a vellum folio. V. A. Kolve in his study of the pictorial imagery in which, he suggests, the medieval mind habitually thought, implies that authors would have proceeded from such images to the texts they then composed.[14] The *Book of the Duchess* appropriates the same art forms but creates an opposite sequence, at least to the extent that it chronicles the narrator's awakening to textual lines projected on his walls and eventually becoming an author of powerful visual imagery. Proceeding very like a scholar, whose habits Chaucer's self-portraits often display (cf. *HF* 629–33, 652–58), the narrator begins his dream with books, acquires the energy of an active life, and then returns, as we shall see, to the literature he is now prepared to create and in which he is eager to take part.

For all its intoxicating beauty, this opening scene of the narrator's dream lacks an important dimension. Save for its sounds, nothing animates the scene.

Everything is passive, more inviting certainly than the passive condition described in the poem's opening lines, but still awaiting some positive act from the dreamer. Not unexpectedly, his dream turns him away from inactivity for something more intriguing, a horn being tested for a hunt. Although he describes with enthusiasm his joining the hunt and learning that "th'emperour Octovyen" (368) leads it, his interest in this kind of boisterous activity lasts only thirty lines before he leaves to chase a fawning whelp "Doun by a floury grene wente" (398).

As when the narrator turns away from Ovid's story of Ceyx and Alcione before it comes to an end, and later leaves his sleeping chamber for the energetic bustle of a hunt without saying more about the literature on his walls and windows, neither can this turning away from the hunt be called a rejection, for he is much moved by Ovid, thrilled by the *Roman* and Troye, and strongly attracted to the hunt. Rather, he has been ascending several plateaux, adding dimensions, narrowing his focus, to find the particular combination of circumstances best suited to him. To leave his sleeping chamber implies a need to add to his passively absorbed literary surroundings an active participation under the lead of a noble figure, "th'emperour Octovyen," whose name in this literary context reminds readers of Caesar Augustus, the patron of Virgil. Next, having responded to the palpable appeal of an active life with a noble patron, he shortly finds the hunt unsuited to him (or he to it) and shifts his attention from horns, horses, and hounds, men literally hunting a hart, to a diminutive animal that happily leads him to a wooded paradise. He has now symbolically replaced the idle thought and sorrowful imaginings of the poem's opening three paragraphs with a taste for literature, an urge to engage it actively, and a reminder of the literary patronage that could make it possible. The new landscape to which the dreamer's sensibilities lead him proclaims that Chaucer's persona has found his métier at last. He has become active in an unmistakable world of artifice,

> Ful thikke of gras, ful softe and swete.
> With floures fele, faire under fete,
> And litel used.
>
> (399–401)

Flora and Zephirus dwell here. Earth competes with the heavens "To have moo floures, swiche seven, / As in the welken sterres bee" (408–9). Branches thick and plentiful cast refreshing shade everywhere. All species of animal move about freely and peacefully, not merely eating but feasting (402–33). Delight in the scene may be measured by the narrator's alliterating sounds of "softe and swete" and especially by the languid consonants of "floures fele, faire under fete."

This route from debility to enthusiasm is in fact circuitous. Already an obvious persona of Chaucer, the narrator will shortly meet another version of himself, "a man in blak" (445) who represents the mournful sufferer described at the poem's opening.[15] A bold claim, this. Not only does it run counter to the dominant critical belief that the man in black represents John of Gaunt, but it also presents the unusual prospect of a character having a conversation with himself. And yet, this technique has a long tradition. In addition to literary debates between self and soul, which are thinly veiled internal conversations,[16] Guillaume de Machaut frequently employs a similar strategy. As R. Barton Palmer notes, "Machaut was very much concerned to establish a 'poetic identity' for himself by . . . often making a fictional alter ego into a main character" (1993, xii). Palmer comments further on how Machaut, who "was not well born," presented himself: "This social status is consistent with the self-portrait that emerges from the poetry, in which Machaut often makes his diegetic alter ego a humble or even cowardly clerk who moves uncertainly among his betters, the butt of mild class humor" (xiii).[17] Let us examine closely, then, this long-assumed identification of Gaunt as the man in black and propose the more probable identification of a Chaucerian persona after Machaut's lead.

The Man in Black

The consensus now surrounding the historical context of the *Book of the Duchess* and governing the critical discussion rests on four main points of interpretation: (i) the "man in blak" whom the dreamer meets at line 445 represents John of Gaunt; (ii) the ensuing exchanges between the dreamer and this man in black afford Gaunt an opportunity to eulogize his deceased wife Blanche of Lancaster; (iii) this same conversation gives the narrator/ dreamer a means to draw Gaunt from his grief, to help reconcile him to his wife's death, and to enable him to get on with his life; (iv) following this conversation, the "kyng" observed riding to a castle (a) is obviously John of Gaunt, and (b) must therefore also be the Black Knight with whom the narrator has been conversing.

I list these four points in the sequence dictated by the poem's events. In critical discussion, however, the fourth point, especially its part b, always occurs first to enable each of the three preceding items to flow from it. Let us recognize, therefore, that point iv(a) is the only authority from which points iv(b), i, ii, and iii derive. But despite the obvious clarity with which the puns in lines 1318–19 identify Gaunt, nothing flows from this identification, apart from its implication for the poem's date of composition (discussed below), for Gaunt used the title "kyng" only between 1372 and 1388.[18] Most especially, Gaunt's presence as "this kyng" (1314) riding to his castle provides no authority for assuming he is also represented by the "man in blak" (445).

That the current consensus relies exclusively on point iv(b) cannot be overemphasized. Belief that "this kyng" is the same figure as the "man in blak" grows from a tenuous line of reasoning that begins with those famous lines near the end of the poem, lines whose allusions are more bluntly obvious than Chaucer's usual subtlety, as if he wanted to be certain that no one, not even a dull-witted sleepy courtier at an evening's recitation, could miss the reference to John of Gaunt.

> With that me thoghte that this kyng
> Gan homwarde for to ryde
> Unto a place, was there besyde,
> Which was from us but a lyte—
> A *long castel* with *walles white*,
> Be Seynt *Johan*, on a *ryche hil*,
> As me mette; but thus hyt fil.
>
> (1314–20, emphasis added)

There can be no doubt that lines 1318–19 unambiguously refer, first, to Blanche who inherited the surname Lancaster ("long castel") from her father and to whom "walles white" allude, making the line almost literally "a Lancaster with [the name] Blanche," and, second, to her husband John of Gaunt, identified by his given name Johan and his title Earl of Richmond ("ryche hil"). This unassailable reference has encouraged critics to fill out the whole of the fourth point of interpretation and then leap to the first three with such ease it makes one wonder why the narrator thought his dream would be beyond the interpretive powers of a Joseph or a Macrobius (280–89).

Received opinion notwithstanding, nothing in the poem justifies extending the valid equation between Gaunt and "this kyng" to include a second, invalid equation between Gaunt and the man in black with whom the narrator has been conversing for eight hundred lines.[19] Indeed, in his 1974 article announcing discovery of the letter from Louis de Mâle of Flanders, John N. Palmer seems to accept the argument that "the king referred to in these lines is not the Black Knight but the leader of the hunt, Octovyen, that the end of the Knight's lament is separated from the reference to 'this king' by three lines which recall the reader to the hunt with which the dream sequence had opened, and that 'this king' is therefore more naturally identified with the leader of the hunt, Octovyen, than with the Black Knight" (259).[20]

In support of Palmer's summary of this argument, table 2.1 shows the arrangement of lines 1309 to 1317 in all four exemplars.[21] Though the three manuscripts rarely indent for a new paragraph, Thynne's printed text has ninety-five paragraph indentations, marking each new speaker or new topic.[22] But Thynne also reinforces the indentation at line 1311 with a single paragraph sign, ¶, undoubtedly on the authority of his copy text, to show that the shift from one subject to another at this point is more important than a simple indentation would indicate by itself. No other ¶ appears in the whole of Thynne's *Duchess*.

The current standard edition, *The Riverside Chaucer* which succeeded F. N. Robinson's 1957 edition, follows very closely Robinson's practice of setting paragraphs where Thynne set them. It is difficult to understand, therefore, why the editors of *The Riverside Chaucer*, and Robinson before them, fail to show a paragraph break at line 1311 where Thynne's ¶ and indentation direct a new paragraph to begin:

> "She ys ded!" "Nay!" "Yis, be my trouthe!"
> "Is that youre los? Be God, hyt ys routhe!"
> And with that word ryght anoon
> They gan to strake forth; al was doon,
> For that tyme, the hert-huntyng.
> With that me thoghte that this kyng
> Gan homwarde for to ryde
>
> (*Riv Ch* 1309–15)

By neglecting to show a new paragraph at line 1311, the Robinson and *Riverside* texts give the impression that lines 1311–13, though referring to the

Table 2.1. *BD* 1309–17 in its four exemplars

Thynne, A.D. 1532	Fairfax MS 16

She is deed: Nay / Yes by my trouthe
   Is that your losse / by god it is routhe.
¶ And with that worde right anone
They gan to strake forthe / al was done
For that tyme / the hart huntynge
   With that me thought that this kynge
Gan homwarde for to ryde
Vnto a place was there besyde
Whiche was from vs but a lyte
	She ys ded / nay / yis be my trouthe
	Is that youre losse / be god hyt ys routhe
	And with that worde / ryght anoon
	They gan to strake / forth al was doon
	For that tyme / the herte huntynge
	With that me thoght / that this kynge
	Gan homewarde / for to ryde
	Vnto a place / was there besyde
	Which was from vs / but a lyte

Tanner MS 346	**Bodley MS 638**
She is dede / nay / yis bi my trouth Is this youre los / be god hit is routh And with that worde righ[t] anon Thei gon to strake ~~right~~ al was don For that tyme the herte huntynge With that me thoght that this kinge Gan homewarde for to ride Vn-to a place was ther be-side Which was from vs but a lite	She ys ded . nay . yes be my trouth Is that your losse bigod it ys routh And with that worde right anon They gan to strake forth all was don ffor that tyme the harte huntynge With that me thought that this kynge Gan homeward for to ryde Vn to a place was there bisyde Which was from us but a lyte

hunt with which the dream sequence began, somehow belong to the account of the conversation between the narrator and the man in black.[23] Thus the "kyng" in the next lines can easily be mistaken as a reference to the man in black from that same account. If *The Riverside Chaucer* had followed Thynne's direction to begin a new paragraph at line 1311, doubly enforced by a paragraph symbol, ¶, having followed Thynne almost everywhere else, the recollection of the hunt would be understood to introduce a subject very different from the conversation between the man in black and the dreamer, whose last words, "Be God, hyt ys routhe!" have an appropriate note of somber finality. The "kyng" would naturally belong to this new subject. In short, had the editorial direction provided by Thynne's text been followed, line

1311 would not refer to the man in black who disappears from the poem at the end of the previous line. It would refer to the leader of the hunt, called at first "th'emperour Octovyen" (368) to remind listeners of Virgil's patron Octavian. At the end of the poem this leader is seen mounted, riding home, almost literally identified in lines 1318–19 as John of Gaunt, making his first appearance in the poem *in propria persona*. Gaunt became Chaucer's historical patron in 1374.[24]

Evidence within the poem, as well as the historical circumstances of Chaucer's royal patronage before his connection with the House of Lancaster, make it highly unlikely that Chaucer would create the man in black as a fictive representation of John of Gaunt. Let us consider a few factual details pointing to this conclusion. The *Duchess* records two immature poems (475–86 and 1175–80) composed by the man in black, who ultimately explains very thoroughly how he took up poetic composition in a serious way (1155–82). There is no evidence that Gaunt had any fondness for poetry, much less attempted to compose poems. The suggestion that the duke would have been flattered at being cast as a poet, particularly one of such meager power, disregards the social structure of fourteenth-century England. To demote a king's son to the rank of a mere knight, when this son held ranks of earl and duke, and then to show this "knight" in the role of a poet, an entertainer, in need of tutelage from the young wife of this king's son, would be a triple insult. Does it not also strain credulity to suppose that Chaucer would imagine Gaunt, England's second most prominent hunter after his father, preferring to sit on the ground, lean against a tree, and compose a pedestrian poem, rather than join a manly hunt nearby? Nor is it likely that a twenty-eight-year-old man, the age of Gaunt when his young wife died, would have "Upon hys berd but lytel her" (456) or, if Gaunt's beard actually was sparse, that it would be noted in a public poem by the otherwise adroit Chaucer, who later uses a missing beard as a mark of effeminacy in the Pardoner (*CT* I.689).[25] Moreover, this "crossing and blurring of gender lines and the feminization of the court poet," as Elaine Tuttle Hansen calls the depiction of the man in black, seriously undercuts his grief: "If we wish to speak of this dream-vision as a poem of consolation, it may be more accurate to say that it works to console men not for the loss of the perfect woman but for the loss of their own solid sense of masculinity, the gender identity that is put at risk by both the pursuit and the attainment of heterosexual love" (68). No, the young age, the indifference to a hunt, the struggle with poetry, the absence of a retinue, the demotion to a knight, the missing beard, and the hint of effeminacy would be reckoned ridicule, if this figure in the poem were meant to represent John of Gaunt. No one, least of all Chaucer, would have had confidence that the volatile John of Gaunt would take such ridicule in good humor. Finally, the horse. The poem gives no indication that the man in black has a horse, but Octovyen certainly leads the hunt on horseback, and "this kyng / Gan homwarde for to ryde" (1314–15). Even if these minor inconsistencies were the only evidence available, they would make it extremely unlikely that the man in black represents John of Gaunt. Other evidence makes the claim even less likely.

Chaucer's limited, albeit well-documented, associations within the royal family give no authority for inferring a relation between Chaucer and Gaunt close enough to justify a claim that the man in black represents Gaunt.[26] While the documents collected in *Chaucer Life-Records* provide more information for the late 1360s than for the early 1360s, they offer no basis whatever for assuming a relationship between Chaucer and Gaunt earlier than 1374. From April 1357 to June 1367, Chaucer was employed by Elizabeth, Countess of Ulster, and her husband Lionel, Duke of Clarence (*Ch L-R* 13–18). "He was most probably a page . . . a boy or youth anywhere between about 10 and 17 years old who was engaged as a servant and personal attendant in the household of a person of rank, to work there, in many quite menial kitchen and household tasks" (Pearsall 1992, 38). That he received a small sum for Christmas necessities in 1357 suggests that he was present when Gaunt visited his older brother Lionel at Hatfield during that same season (*Ch L-R* 18). Whether Chaucer was present or not, he undoubtedly knew Gaunt by sight. It is uncertain, however, that Gaunt knew Chaucer or, if he did, that he had anything more than a royal's awareness of a menial. Lads of seventeen, Gaunt's age at that Hatfield Christmas, rarely have much in common with boys of thirteen—Chaucer's age that year.

Opportunities for further contact certainly broadened within a few years, though we may doubt a close association developed between the page and the duke. Having transferred to Lionel's retinue in time to serve as his *valletus* (attendant) at Reims during the campaign of 1359–60, Chaucer was taken prisoner and ransomed by the king for £16 (*Ch L-R* 19–20). Gaunt was also in this campaign, leading part of the combined units that totaled more than a thousand men (Pearsall, 41), among whom the fifteen- or sixteen-year-old Chaucer would hardly have stood out. That he was still with Lionel in October of 1360 (*Ch L-R* 19–20) suggests he was probably in the entourage that traveled with Lionel to Ireland in 1361, although no record confirms this assignment. And six years later when Gaunt was at the battle of Najero, Chaucer may also have been in Spain, though it is doubtful he was at the battle (*Ch L-R* 64–66).[27] These slight opportunities for contact do not support the claim Pearsall makes, that Chaucer "is likely to have met [Gaunt] on some of these and many other occasions" (83). The verb *met* misleads by promoting the improbable image of a formal introduction, "My lord, I'd like you to meet young Geoffrey Chaucer." The more probable view Gaunt had of Chaucer in 1368, if he had any view of him at all, is well described by Pearsall on his next page, "A young pipsqueak of an esquire" (84). Even Paul Strohm, who argues for Chaucer's widening circle in the late 1360s and early 1370s, suggests that the confidence with which Chaucer approaches his audience in *Duchess* argues "for greater social equality than that existing between Chaucer and John of Gaunt" (1989, 55). As far as historical records indicate, the Hatfield Christmas of 1357, the only occasion when Chaucer and Gaunt were known to be within the same household at the same time, is the most plausible occasion for Chaucer to have "met" Gaunt. If, however, Chaucer would "not have presumed to write" about Gaunt and Blanche in 1368, when he was in his midtwenties (Pearsall, 84), he would have been much less likely, as an even more insignificant page in his early teens, to take up the duke's time at Hatfield in 1357. Apart from the unconvincing claim that Gaunt is pictured as the man in black in the *Book of the Duchess*, there is neither record nor likelihood that Gaunt and Chaucer ever met prior to 1374.

Despite these attempts to speculate, and even presume, that a relationship existed between Chaucer and Gaunt, undoubtedly to make Chaucer's writing the *Duchess* seem less improbable than it would otherwise, the available facts suggest that Chaucer's attention was directed elsewhere. After serving in Lionel's household in the early and middle 1360s, he was continuously in the king's service and on his payroll from June 20, 1367 (*Ch L-R* 123) until at least 1374 when he was made a customs controller and given a home over Aldgate.

That a representation of John of Gaunt as the man in black has no support either in the lines of the *Duchess* or in the historical circumstances of Chaucer's life does not mean that I accept, with Huppé and Robertson, this mournful figure as a surrogate "of all those who have honored and loved Blanche and lost her in death" (1963, 52). The clearest indication of whom he represents may be seen in the very words Chaucer gives him to describe himself, "For y am sorwe, and sorwe ys y" (597). Expressions like this were heard earlier. In the first two paragraphs of the poem, Chaucer the poet gives Chaucer the narrator the same word, "sorowe" (variously spelled), three times in quick succession (10, 14, 21). He then has the narrator call upon the same word twice again (547, 555) to describe the man he has just met, before the man himself pronounces the word six more times (563, 567, 576, 592, 593, and 596) prior to uttering the quoted line 597 where the word appears twice more. The narrator and the man in black, I am convinced, are two slightly different representations of the same historical figure, Geoffrey Chaucer. Earlier we heard only of diagnoses and symptoms, including insomnia and an inability to distinguish the mundane from the remarkable. These conditions, though unexplained earlier, are about to be represented before the dreamer's very eyes, showing not only the result of a literal event, the death of a patroness, but also the cause of a subsequent eight-year inability to bring life and feeling to a tribute for a cherished lady as convincingly, for example, as Morpheus brought apparent life to Ceyx. The next nine hundred lines bring face to face two versions of Geoffrey Chaucer, one a twenty-four-year-old apprentice poet trying desperately, but unsuccessfully, to create a poetic tribute to his recently deceased patroness, the other an image of the same man, better skilled by as much as eight years, who, with the help of an Ovidian tale he may have adapted "In youthe" (*CT* II.57), finally completes the tribute he has long been unable to compose.

Let us consider the evidence that the dreamer is eight years older than the man in black's "foure and twenty yer" (455). Of the extant copies of this poem used by all editors, none of which dates from Chaucer's own lifetime, only one, Thynne's edition of 1532, as remarked in note 8, calls the narrator's condition "a sicknesse / That I have suffred this eight yeer" (36–37). Neither Fairfax 16, Bodley 638, nor Tanner 346 includes lines 31 to 96, although Fairfax originally had a sixty-six-line gap after line 30, filled in from Thynne in the seventeenth century. But nothing can be inferred either from the gap in Fairfax or from the missing lines in Bodley and Tanner except that Thynne must have had access to at least one copy that was unavailable to the scribes of Fairfax, Bodley, and Tanner. No one has flatly denied the authenticity of lines 31–96, and only N. F. Blake (1986) regards them skeptically. It is fair to assume, however, that if Chaucer actually composed these lines, he must have done so at a later date, though not more than eight years later than the original manuscripts from which Fairfax, Bodley, and Tanner descend. This assumption could well affect our understanding of the date of Chaucer's final version of the *Duchess*.

The kind of representation we have been considering foreshadows a technique that will become a Chaucerian staple. In every other poem in which an obvious persona of the poet has a speaking role—*Fame, Fowls, Legend of Good Women, Canterbury Tales*, and even *Troilus and Criseyde* where Pandarus is an undoubted persona of the poet—we see the same kind of self-disparagement that appears for the first time in the *Book of the Duchess*. It is by no means irrelevant that Chaucer's principal model for many of the lines of the *Duchess*, Guillaume de Machaut, used the same technique of placing a slightly ridiculed figure of himself in his poems. Not only do marks of gentle ridicule undercut the man in black—the distracted scribbler oblivious to the narrator's approach, the scant beard, the humble posture sitting on the ground leaning against an oak, and the undistinguished poem just completed—there is also the transparent attempt to gain some little dignity for the man by having the dreamer infer from his manner "A wonder welfarynge knyght... Of good mochel" (452–54). These "marks of distinction" are meant as obvious fetches, ploys as ludicrously inappropriate and pathetic as the attempt to make Thopas seem admirable for his skills at archery and wrestling—fitting for a foot soldier, not for a knight—and for wearing cordovan shoes and imported socks. We should not have been surprised if, on being interrupted, the man in black had replied, "why wiltow lette me... Syn that it is the beste rym I kan?" (*CT* VII.926–28). Let us hold in abeyance this hypothesis of the man in black as a surrogate of Chaucer, while we consider a set of parallel circumstances that ought to have cast the traditional interpretation into further doubt.

Another great lady, indeed a lady more highly honored than Blanche, also died during this period. Eleven months after the death of Blanche, the same plague that claimed Blanche's life also brought down Edward III's wife, Queen Philippa. As Chaucer was a resident employee in the king's household in the late 1360s, in fact on the queen's staff at the time she died, one suspects the fledgling poet would have written an elegy for her, as did another sometime resident in Philippa's household, Jean Froissart,[28] to show the surviving members of the royal family his indebtedness to the queen for retaining him and his gratitude for the kindness she showed him. How odd that such an elegy from Chaucer seems not to have survived. One can hardly believe that Chaucer would have ignored the death of a woman of lofty rank to whom he owed everything, when a year earlier in the highly crafted elegiac *Book of the Duchess* he is assumed to have eulogized a woman to whom he was not in the least indebted, perhaps did not even know. Worse, would not the poem, according to its current interpretation, be a grave insult to Edward III and his deceased queen if Chaucer in 1368 commemorated Blanche, who was never a queen, with a poem that clearly refers to her as a queen, while ignoring Philippa, who actually was the queen and for whom Chaucer was working both in 1368 when Blanche died and in 1369 when Queen Philippa herself died? Nevertheless, such has been assumed by nearly all Chaucerians, apparently ever since someone in the sixteenth century wrote a marginal note in a manuscript of the *Duchess* asserting that the poem was written at the request of John of Gaunt for the memory of his dear deceased wife, a claim for which there is no earlier evidence.[29]

Difficult as it may be to accept Chaucer's failure to eulogize his recently deceased patroness, as most Chaucerians silently assume, an equally surprising omission must be charged to us, the professionals who pore over the works of great authors and claim to understand the circumstances that bring literature into existence. The full impact of this scholarly omission should have been even more obvious before 1974 when John N. Palmer, combining a fortuitous discovery and a brilliant argument, demonstrated that many chronicles had kept the duchess alive a full year after she died. Before 1974, Blanche was thought to have died on September 12, 1369. Why did we not notice that Chaucer neglected the death of his patroness, Queen Philippa, in whose household he then lived, yet wrote an elegy for a woman of lesser nobility who died (we then thought) twenty-nine days later? The corrected date of Blanche's death, now conclusively established by Palmer as September 12, 1368, eleven months before the queen died, hardly diminishes the scholarly oversight. A poem as long as the *Book of the Duchess* would take the most efficient poet several months to complete. If the *Duchess* were finished by late February, say, who could believe that six months later its poet would not have recognized an obligation to compose another elegy, even more splendid, for his queen and patroness? Why have we overlooked Chaucer's apparent neglect of such an obligation?

Scholarly indifference to what seems to be Chaucer's oversight may be difficult to excuse, but Chaucer's own neglect is easily answered. He did not forget his queen at all. His lines commemorating Philippa, who died when Chaucer was either very close to or exactly at "the age of foure and twenty yer" (455), survive in the poem we now call the *Book of the Duchess*, as the ur-*Duchess*, one might say. It is significant that Crow and Olson have several pages quoting the records awarding a clothing allowance for "liverees de drap noir . . . a cause de la mort nostre treschere compaigne la roine" (*Ch L-R* 98). There are no comparable records of mourning clothes granted for the death of Blanche of Lancaster. It was Queen Philippa's death, not Blanche's death, that made the mourner in Chaucer's poem a "man in blak" (445).

It may be useful here to suspend discussion long enough to summarize the thesis of the present chapter (see table 2.2). In September 1368, when Blanche of Lancaster died, Chaucer probably let her death pass without attempting a poetic tribute of any kind. When Queen Philippa died eleven months later, Chaucer was very likely twenty-four years old, having given no, or at most scant, indication of the literary distinction he would later achieve. Despite this lack of skill, he attempted to commemorate his deceased queen with a poetic tribute indebted to the conceptions and very words of poets whose works were then much revered. Perhaps he composed a dream vision whose opening lines included references to Ovid's tale of King Ceyx and Queen Alcione, accounting for the Man of Law's reference to a work he made "In youthe" (*CT* II.57). As an undistinguished member of the royal household, there is little reason to suppose this poetic tribute, regardless of its merit, was known to any but his immediate friends and relatives. It is unlikely he would have hired professional scribes to make copies; nor should we imagine it existed in any form other than in Chaucer's own working pages. There was, after all, no such thing as "publication" in the modern sense; it would not have been available to Chaucer had there been one. The poem languished, one may assume, in Chaucer's private possession for several years.

In the mid-1370s, the expected dynastic succession in England found itself in sudden turmoil. Edward III, still reigning, had fallen into poor health—and poor favor as well, to judge from the unpopularity of his mistress Alice Perrers. His heir apparent, the Black Prince, also became ill, dying on June 8, 1376, and leaving as his heir a ten-year-old son, the future Richard II. It was evident that Richard, while a juvenile, would be obliged to rely on advisors,

Table 2.2. Proposed sequence of selected events, 1350–1380

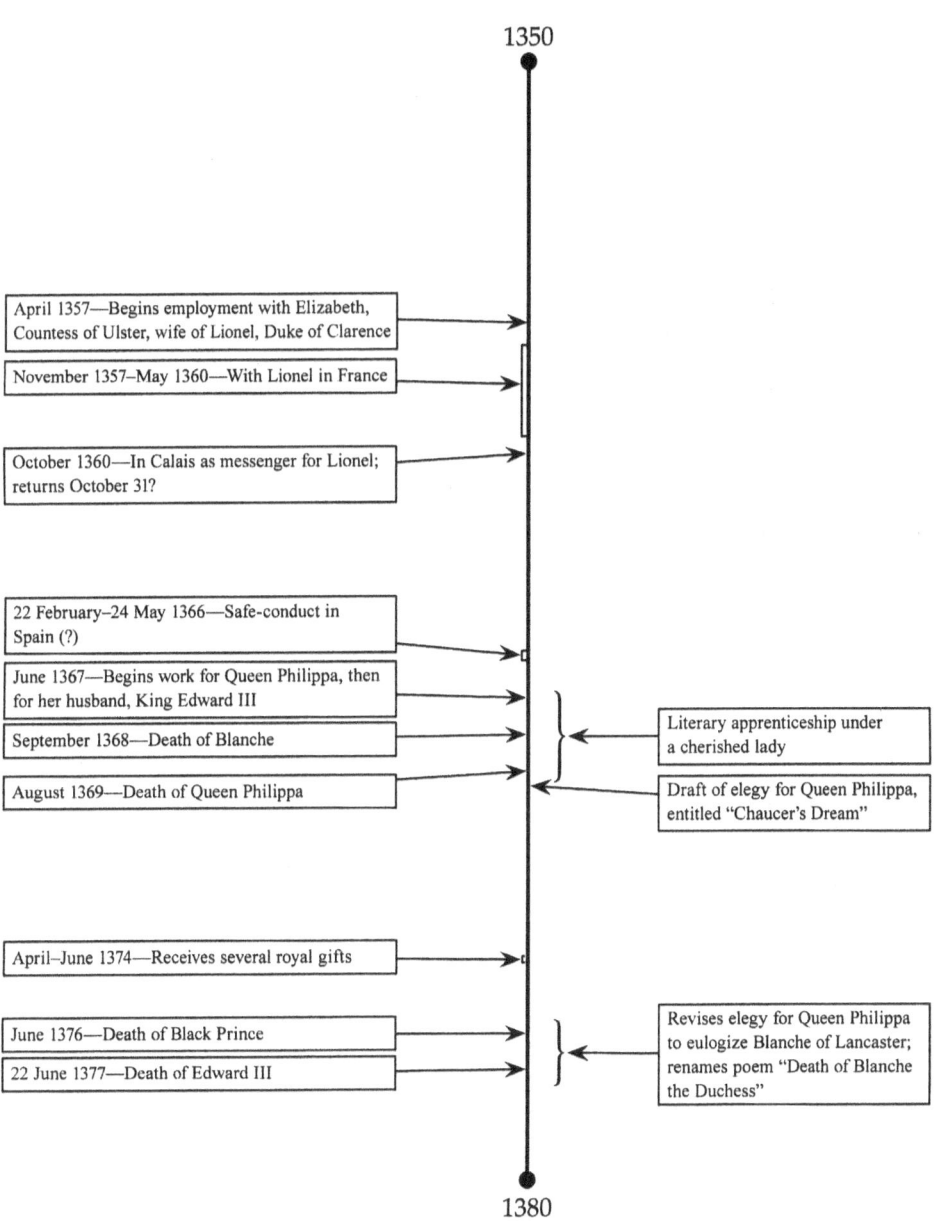

the most prominent of whom would be John of Gaunt. Thus, from the time Richard's succession seemed probable, all those who depended on royal preferment naturally sought ways to ingratiate themselves with Gaunt to remain in the crown's continued favor.

Chaucer was one of those whose preferment needed reconfirmation. For this purpose, I suggest, he broke out his old manuscript, originally written to commemorate Queen Philippa, and revised it to sound like the product of an eight-year struggle to complete a poem in tribute to Gaunt's wife Blanche.[30] Though it would be fruitless to speculate over which lines are revisions and which original, we may assume he had much to draw upon from the time he was teaching himself how to make poems by translating works of Machaut and Froissart. Little would be absolutely necessary to accomplish the redirection. A couplet near the end would immediately identify Gaunt and Blanche, reinforced by a few puns on the name White which obviously identify Blanche. The whole of lines 31–96, undoubtedly added very late and literally referring to an event that occurred eight years earlier, would bring listeners back to Blanche's death and extend the seven years since the poem's original composition to eight years, since Blanche died. A precise reference to the age of the man in black would identify him as the young Chaucer, who was probably twenty-four years old when Blanche died. A few references to the former queen may still have remained in Chaucer's text: the word *fers*, referring directly to the queen on a chessboard, could allude to the queen herself, and the comment that the deceased lady "loved so wel hir owne name" (1018) could be a reference to the name Philippa, since Greek φιλος (love) echoes the first syllable of the queen's name. Yet these small details do not compel an audience to think of Philippa and therefore undermine the poem's new purpose, when they can serve as admiring metaphors for any lady. Nor would listeners be reminded of Chaucer's earlier effort, for it is highly doubtful anyone at court would have heard the earlier attempt, despite the suggestions of scholars that by this time Chaucer would have had an audience.[31]

Since the "troubled history of the title of the poem lends support to the hypothesis that the poem had existed in several versions" (Thundy 1995, 99),[32] we might consider how well this hypothesis agrees with an ancillary argument. If Chaucer's acquaintance with Blanche dates from the time he began his employment in the king's household, June 20, 1367, her occasional visits to the royal family would have spanned only a fifteen-month period before she died. If, on the other hand, the original honoree of the poem was the queen, which seems to me more likely, Chaucer would not only have been in daily contact with his lady, but his friendship with her would have spanned twenty-six months at the time Philippa died, making Chaucer's commitment to compose a long poetic tribute easier to understand.

For our purposes here, another important question concerns the Black Knight's "age of foure and twenty yer" (455). To test the hypothesis of Chaucer's presence in the *Book of the Duchess*, let us see if he would fit the facts we know. If Chaucer, as represented by the man in black, was twenty-four years old when Blanche died on September 12, 1368, he would have been born on any date between late 1343 and, say, the end of August 1344. If he was twenty-four when Philippa died on August 14, 1369, his birth year would have been 1344 or 1345. Though all these dates are a little later than has been assumed, the earlier ones seem preferable, for they agree more closely with the record of testimony Chaucer gave on October 15, 1386, at the Scrope-Grosvenor trial, which identifies him as "Geffray Chaucere esquier del age de xl ans et plus *armeez par xxvii ans* product pur la partie de Monsieur Richard Lescrop jurrez et examinez" (*Ch L-R* 370, emphasis added). To subtract twenty-seven years (the "xxvii ans" since he first bore arms) from 1386 takes us back to 1359, which happens to be the year in which Chaucer's first military campaign began, on November 3, 1359, the campaign against Reims (*Ch L-R* 23–27), when Chaucer would have been fifteen if his date of birth were 1344. Chaucer's precise date of birth is difficult to pinpoint because the vague phrase "del age de xl ans et plus" could mean any age from a few months over forty to about forty-three, yielding a birth date anywhere from 1343 to 1346. But this range decidedly includes 1344, the year that would make him "foure and twenty yer" when Blanche died in 1368.

It may appear that an inconsistency in reasoning has not been accounted for. Would not the theory that the queen was the original honoree of the poem fail, if the date of the death mourned in the poem pointed to Blanche? Not at all. If the original poem had been designed to honor Philippa, whereas the poem we now have unquestionably honors Blanche, a date pointing to 1368 would constitute strong evidence of revision. To boot, the eight years of elapsed time from Blanche's death would agree perfectly with the time when Chaucer may have been concerned over the continuation of his royal appointments, that is, when the Black Prince's death was imminent, perhaps had already occurred, and near the actual death of Edward III on June 21,

1377. Such a revision would affect only that part of the poem identifying its historical context. Other parts, those having nothing to do with a fixed date, could remain as they were first written, an especially appealing consideration if haste was advisable. Chaucer's insertion of a precise age for the mourning man in black emphasizes that it is he, the twenty-four-year-old prentice poet, whom the man in black represents, an insertion that would certainly have taken less time than to rewrite major portions of the poem. Equally convenient revisions for identifying Blanche, lest anyone assume Chaucer was mourning his actual patroness when he was twenty-four, namely Queen Philippa, are the poem's four plays on the word *whit*. Two of these (905, 942) may be one-word additions, to judge from the extra beat these lines now have. The other two involve only the four lines at 948–51 and the two painfully obvious punning lines at 1318–19 identifying the first wife of the man whom Chaucer perhaps hoped to gain as a patron. In general, every other line attributed to the man in black could have been written for Queen Philippa and still have been appropriate for Blanche several years later.

Let us conclude this discussion of identities, dates, and honorees with a small aside, not precisely on the subject at hand, but potentially too significant to risk losing in an unread endnote. If 1344 were to be accepted as Chaucer's date of birth, another uncertainty about Chaucer's life could possibly fall into place. Scholars have long wondered at the reason for the spate of gifts Chaucer received beginning in April of 1374. In quick succession over a two-month period he received: a daily gallon of wine for life; a rent-free home over Aldgate; appointment as collector of customs and subsidies on wool, sheepskins, and leather passing through the Port of London at an annual salary of £10; and a life annuity of £10 for himself and his wife. That these gifts commenced in April invites speculation about an earlier April, in 1357, when he began working for the countess Elizabeth (*Ch L-R* 13–18). If April is not a mere coincidence, it may indicate a significant advance in age, as for example a major birthday. Perhaps he began his employment in April because he turned thirteen in that month (assuming he was born in April 1344) and became eligible for employment. Perhaps, too, a decision had been made later in his life to promote him to a significant role in the conduct of royal affairs, and his thirtieth birthday in April 1374 may have been chosen as the occasion for the promotion. An array of gifts, commencing in April 1374, could have expressed the king's gratitude for Geoffrey's prior service and for his future willingness to accept new responsibilities.

Conversing about the Deceased

Let us begin our discussion of the verbal exchanges between the dreamer and the man in black by reviewing the situations of these two men who meet each other within the poem, and offering an overture to what their exchange signifies. The dreamer presents himself as mourning the loss of (probably) a lady, whose absence has thrown him into an eight-year (37) undiminished sorrow that seems still in force when the first lines of the *Duchess* begin. This tale-telling event, however, including its account of Ovid's story of Ceyx and Alcione and the dream that follows, eventually becomes the means by which he is able to work his way beyond the bitter sorrow that has prevented him from completing his poem. The man in black, though representing a condition and process identical to the dreamer's, presents a somewhat different perspective. Placed in a single scene that lasts no longer than it would take to recite lines 445 to 1310, he provides a flashback that compresses the eight years during which the dreamer has been a suffering insomniac who is incapable of achieving some desired activity but who eventually arrives at the threshold of a cure. The exchanges between the two men, therefore, enact the internal deliberations the dreamer has had with himself to overcome his long lethargy or, put less kindly, his indifference to a poetic obligation he should have discharged long ago.

   The dissimilar concerns of the two men imply an interesting paradox. The man in black summons the cadences and expressions of traditional French love poetry to pay tribute to his lost lady, yet remains incapable of producing fresh, vivid expressions. The dreamer and to a certain extent the poem as a whole focus on the craft of storytelling, thus distancing themselves from the hyperbolic language of courtly literature and coming ever closer to the direct expressions of unadorned meaning. As a result, the dreamer apparently experiences the healing process that has long eluded him. Regarding the poem's literary meaning, the *Duchess* may be even less complex. The exchange between dreamer and man in black reconstructs the maturing of a poet, his emancipation from a clichéd genre that had long since lost its vitality and now invites comment normally reserved for the deceased. His initial efforts to create a new genre sound close to the experience and language of life as it is actually lived. Governed by a startlingly original confrontation of the old and the new, the poem presents a contemporary *ars nova*, free at last from the lifeless lines of an outmoded tradition.

The influential studies of this poem by C. S. Lewis and Wolfgang Clemen apparently agree with this low opinion of the poetic skill evident in the *Duchess*. At the same time they lend coincidental support for the suggestion that Chaucer revised only some parts of his original writing. Lewis calls lines 985–93 "the old bad manner," saying, "A man could forgive, as mere honest debility, the lumber of expletives—'as ever had Hester'—'and more, if more were possible'—'by the rode'; what is radically bad is the fussy prolixity, the air of saying so much while so little is said, the pseudo-legal or pseudo-logical pretentiousness" (1936, 164). Clemen echoes this critique: "There is the oxymoron at lines 599–616, where an antithesis is as it were flogged to death. Elsewhere, too, repetition and variation, climax and contrast are overdone; clearly Chaucer is still keen to parade his knowledge and rhetorical skill" (1964, 60). Neither critic points out that every blemish cited comes from the lines of the twenty-four-year-old man in black, not the dreamer. In the revision I suggest Chaucer made in later years, he had only to recraft the lines of the dreamer, for the speeches of the man in black could remain as he originally wrote them, when he was incapable—for whatever reason, inability or sorrow—of distinguishing "leef" from "looth," "Joye" from "sorowe," for "Al [was] ylyche good to [him]" (8–10).

My earlier remarks on the beauty of a forest to which a small whelp leads the narrator deferred an important detail. Like the wooded scenes of a Georges Seurat painting set on La Grande Jatte, the wood in the *Book of the Duchess* is both appealing and strangely artificial. Every tree stands ten or twelve feet from its neighbor, rising forty or fifty fathoms high, clean of boughs until the crop where its foliage stretches less than an inch from the foliage of neighboring trees (419–26). However much this locale charms the narrator-turned-dreamer, it is not his neighborhood. This atelier belongs to the man in black. Whereas artifice dominates this habitat, the scenes in the dreamer's locale—his sleeping chamber, the hunt he joins briefly, the episode with a whelp—come vividly to life. And yet, so much of this Black Knight's demeanor recalls earlier language in the narrator's description of himself that Chaucer must have wanted to call attention to their similarity: Both men suffer a severe sorrow. Both think of Ovid, the narrator summarizing

Table 2.3. Man in black echoing words of dreamer/narrator

Dreamer/narrator	Man in black
I have gret wonder, be this lyght, How that I lyve (1–2)	And in hys wyt disputed faste Why and how hys lyf myght laste (505–6)
I have so many an ydel thoght (4) Al is ylyche good to me (9)	Yowthe, my maistresse, Governed me in ydelnesse (797–98) Al were to me ylyche good (803)
For nature wolde nat suffyse To noon erthly creature Nat longe tyme to endure Withoute slep and be in sorwe. (18–21)	Hit was gret wonder that Nature Myght suffre any creature To have such sorwe and be not ded. (467–69)
For there is phisicien but oon That may me hele; but that is don. (39–40)	Ne hele me may no phisicien, Noght Ypocras ne Galyen (571–72)

the story of King Ceyx from the *Metamorphoses* (44–217), the man in black doubting Ovid's *Remedia Amoris* could cure him (567–68). Even the psychological language describing each man, apart from a shared use of the word *sorrow*, echoes the condition of the other. Table 2.3 compares the narrator's self-description (left column) with the impression he has of the man in black and with that man's own self-portrait (right column).

Identical with respect to their circumstances, they are quite dissimilar in their expressions of these circumstances. In contrast to the narrator's compelling description of himself, his lively summary of Ovid, and his lines describing the beginning scenes of his consequent dream, the first words from the man in black amount to a "brief undistinguished lyric" (Phillips, 12), a short poem he has apparently just composed from sentiments felt equally by the narrator:

> I have of sorwe so gret won
> That joye gete I never non,

> Now that I see my lady bryght,
> Which I have loved with al my myght,
> Is fro me ded and ys agoon.
>   Allas, deth, what ayleth the,
> That thou noldest have taken me,
> Whan thou toke my lady swete,
> That was so fair, so fresh, so fre,
> So good that men may wel se
> Of al goodnesse she had no mete!
>
> (475–86; see note 11)

Surrounded by the dreamer's interesting narrative, these banal, end-stopped verses by the man in black may well be "rym dogerel" (CT VII.925). As the halting attempt by the pilgrim Chaucer in the *Tale of Sir Thopas* annoys Harry Bailly, these lines too stand in discomforting relief, almost as lamentable as the death of a great lady. We admire the man's noble impulse to create a tribute as beautiful and fitting as the forest where the dreamer finds him. But his stilted result mirrors the regularity and artificiality of the trees found there.

To appreciate the incongruity between the intention of the man in black to express a lament and the actual words he chooses for it, we might call again upon the Ovidian story of Ceyx and Alcione. Chaucer edits Ovid's version to show Alcione praying to her goddess Juno to gain information about her husband. Information appears immediately in the dreamed image of Ceyx, who explains clearly and unambiguously, "I am but ded. / Ye shul me never on lyve yse" (204–5). In the narrator's dream immediately thereafter, this same scene is reenacted with different characters. Now it is the dreamer who asks for information from the man in black whom he has just met:

> But certes, sire, yif that yee
> Wolde ought discure me youre woo,
> I wolde, as wys God helpe me soo,
> Amende hyt, yif I kan or may....
> And telleth me of your sorwes smerte;
> Paraunter hyt may ese youre herte,
> That semeth ful sek under your syde.
>
> (548–57)

Unlike the prompt reply Alcione receives in Chaucer's retelling of Ovid, here 750 lines will pass before the narrator receives an intelligible answer to his question. Not for want of trying. After listening to an overdrawn metaphor of chess, the narrator asks again:

> Good sir, telle me al hooly
> In what wyse, how, why, and wherfore
> That ye have thus youre blysse lore.
>
> (746–48)

On assuming the dreamer must not have been listening attentively, the man in black exacts a promise that "thou shalt hooly, with al thy wyt, / Doo thyn entent to herkene hit" (751–52). The dreamer agrees, but hears another inflated circumlocution instead of the direct answer he asked for. Once again he asks plainly and directly:

> "What los ys that?" quod I thoo;
> "Nyl she not love yow? Ys hyt soo?
> Or have ye oght doon amys,
> That she hath left yow? Ys hyt this?"
>
> (1139–42)

Alas, the dreamer "[l]eseth his asking trewely" (33). Another long monologue details the history of the man's relationship with his admired lady—covering the beginning of his attempt to "make songes" (1157); quoting the first of these songs about his lady; recounting the failed progress of his declaration to her; recalling how he eventually explained that he "ne wilned thyng but god ... and to kepe hir name" (1262–63); and finally delighting to report that "My lady yaf me al hooly / The noble yifte of hir mercy" (1269–70). Not until the dreamer asks a direct question the grieving man must think insensitive, "where is she now?" (1298), does he get the straightforward answer he has patiently awaited. To no surprise, it is much the same answer Alcione received from the image of her husband, "She ys ded!" (1309). But what a difference in style. The impasse in communication has nothing to do with the dreamer's inability to concentrate on the words used by the man in black, everything to do with the man's own inability to speak in a direct, intelligible way.

I dwell on these insistent questions by the dreamer, and the perverse indifference to them by the man in black, because the exchanges between these two men may be instructive in noting how the *Duchess* plays at the border between artifice and literal speech, making it difficult for readers to be certain of the poem's stance at any given moment. With relative ease we recognize the knight's many borrowed passages from the love visions of Machaut, but we are less certain that Chaucer also follows the compositional strategies of Machaut and endorses the style of his *dits*. For example, Kathryn L. Lynch (1988a, 280) expects the poem to rely on "what we know about how communication by genre operates, for although genres may form mixtures and hybrids, at any given time a single recognizable type provides the condition for meaning and interpretation." Though potentially valid, her claim closely approximates an assumption of literary predestination. In philosophical visions, great ladies—personifications such as Philosophy in *Consolation*; Nature in *Parliament*; Reason in the *Roman de la rose*—lead their interlocutors to truth. The *Duchess*, lacking such a guide, is thus prey to a further assumption, this time a construct of critics rather than a consequence of genre. Lynch, alleging a dull wit in both the "uncomprehending dreamer" (285) and the knight, concludes that the poem's main theme is a frustrated quest for knowledge. These, I believe, are incorrect assumptions and conclusions. The dreamer is not more "uncomprehending" than the man in black; he is merely struggling with a man too enveloped in a particular genre and style to engage in normal conversation. Nor is the man in black incapable of understanding; he is simply a very bad poet. Though able to speak "nouther towgh ne queynte" (531), he seems eager to try out his literary style in his narrative responses to the dreamer.

Two instances of uncertainty in the poem regarding whether a genre should (or should not) be imported for interpretive purposes tend to confirm that the borrowing of mere passages implies nothing about the borrower's attitude to the passages borrowed. When the dreamer hears the words "my lady bryght . . . Is fro me ded and ys agoon" (477–79), he certainly understands their literal meaning. But he would also recognize the genre and style of a troubadour's typical love lyric and that genre's frequent use of hyperbolic similes and metaphors. Indeed, he will shortly listen to a lengthy monologue farced with the same language and style. Led by his understanding of this genre, the dreamer may believe the overheard poem is a literary work in progress, not an autobiographical effusion. Nevertheless, a majority of critics, ignoring genre in this instance and assuming the dreamer should certainly have understood the literal meaning of these words, take his persistent repetition of the same question as evidence of either obtuseness or artful attempts to ease the man's grief—the two preclusive interpretations that have defined critical positions for decades. I contend, on the contrary, that the dreamer's subsequent remarks reflect his increasing exasperation at the man's reluctance to give a direct answer to his initial request, "telleth me of your sorwes smerte" (555). Had the man in black a mind to do so, he could untangle his artful speech from his literal meaning and resolve the dreamer's confusion.

A second passage, later in the poem, reveals the same dilemma. The man in black, painstakingly explaining how he failed to progress in love, and employing the much-used convention where love and poetic creation are synonymous, explains the lady's reply to one of his personal declarations of affection for her: "And whan I had my tale y-doo, / God wot, she acounted nat a stree / Of al my tale" (1236–38). Though he had been declaring his personal love for her, he represents this declaration as a "tale," surrounded by literary conventions that fetched from the lady a plain-language evaluation of his literary effort. His *poetry*, not his attempt at romance, is not worth a straw.

The dreamer undoubtedly perceives all of this, for the ensuing conversation eventually weans the sorrowing man away from his indirect expressions and borrowed lines, toward the poetic style we uniquely associate with the mature Chaucer. "Conversation" may be too ambitious a word to describe what takes place between line 445 where the dreamer becomes aware of a man dressed in black and line 1310 where their exchanges come to an end and the man disappears. More accurately, the man in black gives four separate performances—let us call them monologues—bracketed and interleaved by conversational dialogues between the two men.

The bracketing by two of the young man's poetic compositions unmistakably indicates that these monologues and dialogues constitute a well-designed unit unto itself. The first of these poems happens to be the first words we hear from this grief-stricken man (475–86, quoted above), a poem still in the process of being composed. Though undistinguished, its literary merit is less important for the structure of *Duchess* than for its comparison to another of his poems, the "firste song" (1182) he composed:

> Lord, hyt maketh myn herte lyght
> Whan I thenke on that swete wyght

That is so semely on to see;
And wisshe to God hit myghte so bee
That she wolde holde me for hir knyght,
My lady, that is so fair and bryght!

(1175–80)

Fashioned from nothing but the clichés of the lovelorn and without a hint of death, this little song was apparently composed while the lady was still alive, indeed when its author began composing songs "to kepe [him] fro ydelnesse" (1155). This startling use of a word we heard from the narrator at the very beginning of the larger poem, "ydel" (4), makes us compare not just two poems from the man in black but the two interlocutors as well, for the man in black moves ever closer to the dreamer in sentiment, if not in time. Even if a reader had not noticed the similarity of structure, rhymes, and simple thought between this song and the one quoted earlier, the author of this little song invites his listener to assess its quality: "this was [the] altherferste—/ I not wher hyt were the werste" (1173–74). With only one other lyric by the man in black with which to compare this initial effort, the available evidence suggests there has been no progress between this earliest poem and the one he just finished composing—more lines, but not a better song.

The first monologue by the man in black (558–709) differs from the scene introducing it in the same way the man's recent lyric differs from the scenes that precede it. As his undistinguished lament, "a lay, a maner song, / Withoute noote, withoute song" (471–72), follows the narrator's intriguing words setting the forest scene (443–74), the man's deadening first monologue follows the dreamer's gracious invitation to tell "of your sorwes smerte; / Paraunter hyt may ese youre herte" (555–56). The next 152 uninterrupted lines by the man in black have only four movements, each hyperbolic in its own way. He gives the extent of his sorrow (558–97), its effect on his power to discriminate (599–617), its cause allegorized as a chess game he lost to Fortune (618–69), and a final movement that carries over some metaphors of chess but also sounds like a resolve to commit suicide (670–709).

This long tale of woe reduced to superlatives elicits from the dreamer responses to only two points. He remarks the silliness of paying attention to Fortune and the futility of risking damnation by committing suicide for losing a trivial chess game to her. The dreamer's pithy response (714–57), lasting less than a third the space allotted to the younger man's first monologue, reaches perhaps the most crucial moment in the entire exchange, for with one stroke the dreamer challenges both the allegorical way the man reduces death to a chess game and the hyperbolic way he inflates sorrow to justify suicide. On overhearing the young man's lament, the dreamer may have wondered whether "death" had a literal or metaphoric sense. A protracted use of hyperbole, however, and especially a long excursion into a chess game would confirm a metaphoric sense. But the man in black concludes his riff on chess with a line he may intend as an explanation of his sorrow, "[Fortune] staal on me and tok my fers" (654). The dreamer has no indication these words mean "my lady died." The insistence by critics that even the dull wit of this dreamer cannot doubt the lady's death, since he heard the man's lament, would demand that the dreamer shift from metaphoric to literal language as quixotically as the man in black does.

Of course the dreamer heard the lament, well enough to quote it, well enough to know he was hearing a paraphrased translation of some lines in Machaut's *Le Jugement dou Roy de Behaingne*,[33] as later in this first monologue he hears more paraphrases from the same poem (599–617), the very lines Clemen (60) cites to accuse Chaucer of flogging to death a series of antitheses.[34] The lines of *Behaingne* have apparently not improved in two score years, at least not for David Lawton, who calls them a "slick and rather repugnant denigration of bereavement" (52). No surprise that the dreamer ignores the cause of the man's sorrow; he has no way of knowing the poem attempts to describe reality. The dreamer becomes a literary critic, calling specific attention to the man's manner of expression in the only endeavor at which he unambiguously applies himself, *poetic* expression, not only in the eleven-line lament we overhear but also in the poetry he chooses to emulate. The long debate, then, over whether the dreamer lacks intelligence or possesses tact, may be entirely irrelevant if the dreamer sees the man in black as simply struggling to translate Machaut and to produce a competent little poem, one that has nothing to do with his own emotion.

The implicit shift that the man in black makes between metaphoric and literal senses forces attention on another word. While sustaining his chess allegory, the man indulges himself in a phrase that has much significance for the poem as a whole:

> At the ches with me [Fortune] gan to pleye;
> With hir false draughtes dyvers
> She staal on me and *tok my fers*.
> And whan I sawgh my fers awaye,
> Allas, I kouthe no lenger playe,
> But seyde, "Farewel, swete, ywys,
> And farewel al that ever ther ys!"
>
> (652–58, emphasis added)

Among the many scholars who have researched the game of chess in connection with *Duchess*, no one doubts that the term *fers* signifies the queen, despite its Arabic origin, *firzan*, meaning "wise man" (*Riv Ch* note to lines 652–71).[35] Donaldson even provides a paraphrase of the line in which the term first appears, underscoring his view that a reader with wit as slow as the dreamer's would need a secondary meaning clearly spelled out, "in a game of chess Fortune has captured the Knight's queen" (1975, 1116). Certainly "fers" denotes a playing piece in chess, in keeping with the already overly drawn allegory. It also thinly veils a metaphorical reference to a woman who has recently died. In view of arguments already advanced in this chapter, "fers" could well have a third meaning drawn from the man's actual situation in life, an unambiguous reference to Queen Philippa, the literal queen of England in whose service, under whose patronage, and in whose household the author of this poem worked, flourished, and was still living when the queen died in August 1369. It is more than likely, then, that the original draft of the eulogy we know as the *Book of the Duchess*, the draft Chaucer probably composed to honor his queen and patron shortly after her death, survives in parts of this and the three succeeding monologues by the man in black.

Eager to bring the conversation back to the subject *he* considers most important, the man in black bristles at the dreamer's assumption he had a literal chess match in mind: "Thou wost ful lytel what thou menest; / I have lost more than thow wenest" (743–44), a thought he will repeat twice more (1137–38, 1305–6) before the two men finally reach the same level of meaning at line 1309. The dreamer chides the man in a gentle way, taking a cue from his hyperbole to point out how silly it is to let a chess match bring him to the dire remedies of Medea, Phyllis, Dido, Echo, and Samson (726–38), whose overpowering loves caused their deaths, when the man himself is in no such danger, despite his echoes of Machaut.[36] The dreamer's subtle point makes no impression on the man, who accuses the dreamer of a failure of attention. Accordingly, on being asked again, "telle me al hooly / In what wyse, how, why, and wherfore / That ye have thus youre blysse lore" (746–48), the man agrees in the reply we saw earlier, on "condicioun / That thou shalt hooly, with al thy wyt, / Doo thyn entent to herkene hit" (750–52). Agreed (753a, 754a, 755–57). Good (758a).

They reach a meaningless agreement at best, for the man's second monologue is as much indebted to French love poetry as is his first, and equally void of literal meaning. At once the longest and most admiring of his monologues, this second attempt also has a number of inappropriate, ludicrous patches. Consider the lines where the man in black means to praise his lady's eyes: "And whiche eyen my lady hadde! . . . noght to wyde. / Thereto hir look nas not asyde / Ne overthwert" (859–63). It is difficult to be kind to praise of this sort, which must mean she was neither walleyed nor cross-eyed. Continuing to use a clinical vocabulary while striving to praise his lady's physical person, he sounds like a horse broker proud of the flanks and withers of a beast standing at auction:

> Ryght faire shuldres and body long
> She had, and armes, every lyth
> Fattyssh, flesshy, not gret therwith;
> Ryght white handes, and nayles rede;
> Rounde brestes; and of good brede
> Hyr hippes were; a streight flat bak.
> I knew on hir noon other lak
> That al hir lymmes nere pure sewynge
>
> (952–59)

These descriptions are so inappropriate, so inelegant, they obscure minor infelicities, like his gratuitous swearing, "by the roode . . . by the masse" (924–28), which ironically precedes and follows praise for the lady's "eloquence [her] . . . swete . . . sownynge facounde" (925–26). Chaucer obviously intends his audience to notice the startling incongruity between these expressions and the sincere admiration the man in black has for his lady. Perhaps this was the kind of jejune poetry the youthful Chaucer was writing at the time Queen Philippa died, when he was still assiduously teaching himself how to compose poetry by translating French love poetry, "Be the werkes never so queynte" (784). His younger surrogate, the Black Knight, admits as much when he describes giving himself over "To Love, hooly with good entente, / And throgh plesaunce become his thral / With good wille, body, hert, and al" (766–68), even before his heart was set on anyone. The liberal use of the same kind of language by Machaut, from whose *Behaingne* and *Fortune* Chaucer draws liberally for this second monologue, neither redeems these passages nor justifies Wilcockson's claim: "Even some of the most individualizing traits in the picture are paralleled in the French sources. Yet it is hard to believe that the passage does not contain a real portrayal of the Duchess of Lancaster" (*Riv Ch* note to lines 817–1040). This view overlooks the emerging importance of the craft of poetry as a subject in the *Duchess*, as important as the duchess herself.

Evidence that the man's sense of decorum is making a late arrival surfaces in his embarrassed afterthought that the word *lymmes* may bring attention to the lady's legs—her arms have already been much approved in 953–55—for he ends his canny appraisal of flesh and confirmation with the disclaimer "In as fer as I had knowynge" (960). A curious remark, that he had little knowledge of her limbs, from a man who many assume was her husband.[37] The man apparently wishes to place on record a denial that he had intimate knowledge of the lady, consistent with lines earlier in this monologue giving assurance that for her part she was not a readily available courtly lady. Whoever may have misread the beauty of eyes that "semed anoon she wolde / Have mercy" (866–67) was a gravely mistaken fool, for regarding those struck by her beauty and her look "she ne roughte of hem a stree!" (887). That the man in black was one of those thus smitten with her, whether she knew it or not, mattered little, for she was absolutely unavailable, as he avers for the third time:

> To gete her love no ner nas he
> That woned at hom than he in Ynde;
> The formest was alway behynde.
> But goode folk, over al other,
> She loved as man may do hys brother.
>
> (888–92)

The man in black has been praising his lady in lines appropriate for a transcendent apparition, when the dreamer's response to his long monologue, though witty, amounts to a condemnation.

> y trowe yow wel!
> Hardely, your love was wel beset;
> I not how ye myghte have do bet.
>
> (1042–44)

When the mourning lover takes offense at this failure to be as moved by the re-created lady as her admirer is, "Bet? Ne no wyght so wel" (1045), the dreamer attempts to repair the damage with words that offend even more gravely:

> I leve yow wel, that trewely
> Yow thoghte that she was the beste
> And to beholde the alderfayreste,
> Whoso had loked hir with your eyen.
>
> (1048–51)

This unkind cut robs the lady of all the beauty the man in black has been clumsily portraying, by implying that his eyes alone see her thus. By effectively alleging that the two long monologues he has heard thus far are pure fiction, the dreamer confirms what he must have assumed—or pretended to assume—when he heard the man's brief lament many lines earlier, that it was a fictional love lament from a typical troubadour working on a new item for his repertoire. To the man in black, his song alludes to the defining moment of his life; loss of the lady it celebrates has been devastating.

In his present state, oblivious to all but his lady, the man in black is unlikely to answer the dreamer's request, now some three hundred lines old, which would require him to replace his stylized expressions of beauty and virtue with the dreaded words "my lady is dead." Hence monologue 3 makes no attempt to provide an answer, yet contains more significant information in its sixty lines than the first two monologues disclose in more than four hundred. In a long list of classical figures about whom the man has obviously been reading, two names stand out: Penelope and Lucrece (1081–82) who have always been held as ideals of feminine virtue, especially the virtue of chastity. Penelope is celebrated for her wit in staving off male admirers during her husband Ulysses' absence, Lucrece for having been the only wife among several found at her spindle when their husbands returned unexpectedly and for committing suicide to restore her husband's honor after Tarquin ravished her. Though the lady whom the Black Knight has been admiring suffered no misfortune of the kind Lucrece had at the hands of Sextus Tarquinius, he insists she was as true as Lucrece. Surprisingly, these were married women, hardly suitable heroines for comparison with the honoree of the *Duchess*, imaged as the love object of a twenty-four-year-old man imitating the advances of a troubadour. Why, then, would Chaucer have chosen two ideals of marital virtue as standards against whom to compare an honored lady, if this lady were about to be courted by her future husband, as many believe?

If, however, the lady honored in the original version of the *Book of the Duchess* was Queen Philippa, as I have been suggesting throughout this chapter, Penelope and Lucrece would be eminently suitable comparisons, since Philippa had been married to Edward III for forty-one years when she died.[38] These particular words of admiration are most fitting for the middle-aged queen, though they would not be inappropriate for the much younger Blanche.

Penelope and Lucrece provide still another argument for the innocence of the relationship between the lady and the man in black. Having already hinted broadly at lines 887, 892, and 959–60 that his relationship with the lady was not the typical courtly kind that has intimacy—sublimated or real—as its objective, the man in black reinforces the claim, albeit obliquely, by noting two famous married women to whom such a relationship would have been abhorrent. The argument for sexual innocence between the lady and the man in black does not, of course, require that the queen be the poem's subject. Yet even if Blanche had always been its subject, as I suggest judicious rewriting made her in later years, it would have been equally important that the author of the poem establish *his* innocence, perhaps more so in view of the closeness of age between Chaucer and Blanche.

The second half of monologue 3 commands interest of a different kind, for it leaps suddenly to a level of poetic maturity quite above the man's other speeches. To be sure, such assessments depend more on a reader's subjective judgment than on objective analysis. Nevertheless, the contrast between the ending of the previous monologue (1015–41) and approximately the same number of lines ending the third monologue (1088–1111) reveals a preponderance of end-stopped lines (1020–21, 1027–28, 1031–32) in the earlier speech that limps its staccato way through one catalogue after another, against these later, more lively lines that flow easily through a number of logically related ideas:[39]

Whan my herte wolde yerne
To love, hyt was a gret empryse.
But as my wyt koude best suffise,
After my yonge childly wyt,
Withoute drede, I besette hyt
To love hir in my beste wyse,
To do hir worship and the servise
That I koude thoo

(1092–99)

Revisiting a previous account of the man's early dedication to love (759–804) and picking up where the first one left off, these lines make a close connection between a recognition of immaturity, a desire to learn, and a decision to love his lady. Earlier the man moved quickly through a number of these same subjects without suggesting a necessary connection among them, darting from his curiosity about love to his dedication to Love, then comparing himself to the art of painting, commenting on love as a craft, and finally recognizing that his life was then governed by idle aimlessness. In this second account he begins with his first sighting of the lady (1089), then suggests that he felt a "ful gret nede ... to lerne" (1091), implying that learning and maturing beyond his "yonge childly wyt" (1095) would assuage him "Whan [his] herte wolde yerne / To love" (1092–93). Since a modern romantic meaning for the word *love* would make little sense in this context, the specialized sense advanced by Sheila Delany (1972), Paula Neuss (1981), and others since then comes to mind. Delany speaks of a connection between "dream" and "creative act" in *House of Fame*:

> That the Narrator's position as dreamer and as poet is the same suggests that the dream is not only analogous to the composition but may be a metaphor for it—or, more accurately, for the poetic conception embodied in the work. The process of dreaming becomes nearly synonymous with the creative act. (44)

Where Delany conflates dream and poetic composition, it may be more accurate, as she says, to separate them, to see the dream as representing an initial conception and the retelling of this dream as the poem itself. Paula Neuss acknowledges this distinction by tracing Chaucer's highly original cluster of metaphors and symbols, including "make," "portreye," "peynte," and "craft," to show that when the man in black says in line 776 that he gave himself over to love "Or that myn herte was set owher," he evidently means he set himself to learning the craft of poetry:

> The "table blanche" of Machaut was waiting to be painted on: "peindre et pourtraire" are intended literally. Chaucer's *portreye or peynte*, however, feels metaphorical: the occurrence of *make* in the context suggests the meaning "represent or depict in words" or at least *portreye*, as does the introduction of a *wal* and its Biblical associations with writing. (396)

That the subject of this poetry draws upon the language of conventional love for its superficial subject, as do nearly all the secular models available to the late fourteenth century, does not alter the main drive that brings a poem into existence, which is almost never libidinous, always literary.

As a young man attached to a great household, yet eager to become an accomplished poet, Chaucer would inevitably have heard the love lyrics composed by others. His own attempts at the craft, therefore, would naturally have echoed the same genre, even if he had no literal lady to whom he wished to offer his verses as sincere expressions of his feelings. The senior lady of the household where he lived and served, the *dame lointaine* Philippa, as I have been suggesting, like the great ladies whom the troubadours of the Midi celebrated in their *langue d'oc* fictions, may even have encouraged Chaucer's early efforts, especially if the words used by the man in black affirming "She loved as man may do hys brother" (892) may be taken as the limit of the queen's solicitation.[40]

The dreamer's rejection of monologue 3, sharp to the man in black perhaps, though witty to a reader, comes in three quick strokes. First, by analogy with penance in a confessional he remarks—perhaps unfairly, for there has been no hint of wrongdoing—that the man apparently seeks forgiveness without admitting, regretting, and atoning for his wrongdoing in loving his lady (1112–14). The annoyed response fetched by this calculated goad promotes love for a lady to the extraordinary level of loyalty to King David, to Troy, and to Charlemagne. Next, the dreamer gently admonishes the man for having already twice covered the same history of meeting his lady and coming to love her, "Hyt ys no nede to rehearse it more" (1128). And finally, for the third time, "telleth me eke what ye have lore, / I herde yow telle herebefore"

(1135–36; cf. 555, 745–48), emphatically repeated three lines later, "What los ys that?" (1139).

It may be callous to infer increasing frustration from the dreamer's replies to the man in black, for criticism has nearly canonized him for his patient sensitivity and sophisticated talents as a grief counselor. As a critic of verbal expression, however, the dreamer has been patiently repeating himself in the margins of the man's lines, as it were, urging that he not tell a diffusely developed story, but speak more directly, or risk losing the dreamer's forbearance. Chaucer orchestrates these cross-purposes with great subtlety, letting the dreamer seem eager to learn facts from the man in black, while his deeper interest redirects the man to literary style. The Black Knight, by contrast, has been drawing out his story, making its length match the depth of his pain. From both viewpoints the objective is the story itself and how to tell it.

The failure of the man in black to advance poetically over a stretch of time, as witness the sameness of the first and last poems he wrote, suggests that monologue 4 would be as unappealing as monologue 3. Surprisingly the man displays some skill, at least in his willingness to answer the dreamer's most recent request for an account of "the manere / To hire which was your firste speche" (1130–31). Limiting himself to only a brief summary of what he has already given in detail, namely his habit of keeping from idleness by composing songs, the earliest of which he recites for his listener (1175–80), he then launches into the whole story of how he declared to his lady the feelings he had for her. His summary of this pitiable declaration culminates in yet another insistence that his relationship was confined to innocent affection. It is the fourth such protest, unless the oblique examples of Penelope and Lucrece make it the fifth. The lady flatly says "Nay" (1243). A year later he apparently gains the courage to explain that his intentions were always entirely proper:

> I ne wilned thyng but god,
> And worship, and to kepe hir name
> Over alle thynges, and drede hir shame,
> And was so besy hyr to serve,
> And pitee were I shulde sterve,
> Syth that I wilned noon harm, ywis.
>
> (1262–67)

At length the lady apparently permits him to serve her, "Savynge hir worship by al weyes—/ Dredles, I mene noon other weyes" (1271–72).

The platonic nature of the friendship between the man in black and his lady puts in proper perspective the next event in the poem: "And therwith she yaf me a ryng" (1273). Since a ring often signifies marriage and the woman giving the gift of this ring is obviously Blanche of Lancaster, critics find this line a compelling argument for identifying the man in black as Blanche's husband John of Gaunt. I disagree. Notice, first, the absence of reciprocation; this is not a double-ring ceremony, but a gesture of largesse. Then, consider the timing. The ring is given immediately after the man establishes his honorable intentions, long before romantic feelings could have developed, even in a lady who would eventually acquire such feelings. These several passages insisting that the lady and her admirer were not romantically involved preclude viewing them as husband and wife. Romantic feelings are out of the question. Every speech recollected by the man in black suggests the obsequious approach of a man who assumes—or actually holds—a rank lower than the lady's. Indeed, the poetic lines make the relationship sound exactly like what must have been the historical relationship between Chaucer in his early twenties and Queen Philippa in her midfifties.

Before leaving these monologues, we should not fail to notice an important structural and thematic detail. Similar to the way two of the grieving man's songs bracket his exchange with the dreamer, the conversation is also bracketed by two unrelated occurrences of the name Pythagoras. In what may seem a gratuitous display of book learning, the mournful lover first mentions this name during his lengthy allegory of chess, where he reveals his regret at not knowing

> the jeupardyes
> That kowde the Grek Pictagores!
> I shulde have pleyd the bet at ches
> And kept my fers the bet therby.
>
> (666–69)

Because Pythagoras normally brings to mind mathematics, not chess, an early version of probability theory may have partly prompted this reference; a chess player considers many possible moves before selecting the one he deems best and rejecting others.

A more interesting interpretation stems from the well-known connection between mathematical proportions and musical intervals, accounting for various myths of Pythagoras as the inventor of music to which the man in black later alludes (1167–70). Such a context could also have recommended "jeupardyes" (666). Despite OED evidence that the game of chess appropriated this word for its nearly exclusive use, a close cognate, *joc partit*, signified a well-represented genre among the troubadours of the twelfth century.[41] As a subgenre of the *tenson*, or *débat* among trouvères, the *joc partit*

> est constituée par une discussion entre deux ou plusieurs troubadours qui soutiennent respectivement des opinions opposées relatives à une même question.... [D]ans le ... joc partit (le *jeu-parti* des trouvères), c'est le questionneur lui-même qui pose à son interlocuteur le choix entre les deux hypothèses, se réservant automatiquement de défendre le parti inverse. On disait: *partir un joc*, d'où le nom de *joc partit*. (Bec 1966, 70–71)

The implied connection between mathematics and music, including the songs music accompanies, becomes explicit in the second occurrence of the name "Pictagoras" (1167). The *Book of the Duchess* has, then, two clear indications that the subjects of music/poetry and mathematics, in combination, surround the series of exchanges between the dreamer and the man in black, occurrences that might even satisfy Peterson's (1976) stringent requirements that a work have explicit warrant of an author's intention to justify studies of numerical design.[42] These exchanges, featuring monologues by the man in black and dialogues where the two men converse, closely echo the essence of the *joc partit*. The part taken by the man in black endorses the stylized lines of French love poetry. The other, "le parti inverse," is taken by the two men together enacting the quick exchanges that advance the natural, spontaneous language of men in actual conversation.

A double reference to song during the prolonged encounter of dreamer and man in black requires no extraordinary leap of logic. But calling upon Pythagoras to introduce this music does seem unusual. By introducing music through its mathematical dimension, however, Chaucer achieves the subtlest of grace notes. A clever mathematical encoding announces that in this ver-

Table 2.4. *BD* 514–1310 apportioned to dialogues and monologues

Type of text Dialogue | Monologue	Inclusive lines	Totals Dialogue | Monologue	
Dialogue A	514–557	44	
Monologue 1	558–709[a]		152
Dialogue B	714–758	45	
Monologue 2	759–1041		283
Dialogue C	1042–1051	10	
Monologue 3	1052–1111		60
Dialogue D	1112–1143	32	
Monologue 4	1144–1297		154
Dialogue E	1298–1310	13	
		144	649

Note: a. Careful readers will notice that the four lines immediately following the conclusion of monologue 1 and extending through the end of line 713 are not accounted for in table 2.4. These lines are neither "monologue" nor "dialogue." In an expanse of 797 lines, these lines alone step back from the unfolding scene to let the dreamer express to an imagined reader his emotional reaction to the first monologue by the man in black.

sion of *joc partit* natural spontaneity wins the prize over the mannered style of the man in black.

Table 2.4 displays the interleaved structure of these two very different modes of address. To facilitate comparison, the conversational exchanges are labeled dialogue A through E, while the lengthy remarks of the man in black are named monologue 1 through 4.[43]

The right-hand column of table 2.4 shows the line totals of each dialogue and each monologue, with grand totals in the lowest box. Nothing of Pythagorean significance emerges from any of the four monologues by the man in black or from all four of them together.[44] The total number of lines in the five dialogues, however, and the relation of the line totals in the first two dialogues to the line totals of the last three, are significant enough to catch the eye of anyone in the fourteenth century who had an understanding of the Pythagorean basis of a quadrivial education.[45] To the Middle Ages the number 144, the square of twelve, held great significance as the foundation of the duodecimal system. It also held special prominence as the tenth number in the series of squares, a series that began with the square of 3, or 9, since classical and medieval mathematics considered 1 and 2 to be principles rather than numbers (Heath 1921, 1: 71). This number was perhaps best known in medieval debating halls for its combination of convenience and conviction: convenient because low enough to be easily handled in computation; convincing because high enough to yield ratios acceptably close to the most famous proportion in all mathematics, "division into mean and extreme ratio," known popularly as the "divine proportion" until Kepler attached to it the felicitous epithet "golden."[46] Modern mathematicians now refer to it by the Greek letter *phi* (φ), after a suggestion by Mark Barr (Cook [1914] 1978, 420). Three magnitudes, *a*, *b*, and *c*, arranged in a series such that *b* is greater than *a* and *c* is greater than *b*, are said to be in the unique golden proportion if they satisfy two equations:

$$a + b = c$$
and
$$b \div a = c \div b$$

Although many ratios approach a golden proportion, at best they only approximate *phi*, for modern mathematicians consider a perfect golden ratio to be the irrational 1.61803 . . . : 1. Virgil uses the magnitudes 55, 89, and 144 to reveal this proportion in the sections of *Georgics I*.[47] See appendix B for a mathematical explanation of this irrational proportion, including a discussion of Virgil's poem.[48]

As table 2.4 reveals, Chaucer uses these same magnitudes for the dialogues between the man in black and the dreamer, a design that can hardly be explained by coincidence. I do not claim that *Georgics I* influenced Chaucer, for there is no evidence he knew the work, though he certainly knew Virgil's *Aeneid*. I do claim that the magnitudes 55, 89, and 144 were so well known among the learned as the most widely cited demonstration of the divine proportion that they were naturally available to Chaucer from other sources. The total number of lines in the first two dialogues of table 2.4 is 89. The final three dialogues total 55. Therefore the sum of all the dialogues together is 144.

As if all this aesthetic and mathematical appeal were not enough to draw Chaucer's attention to the divine proportion, still another of this proportion's features may have been the main reason for his incorporating it into

58 / Chapter 2

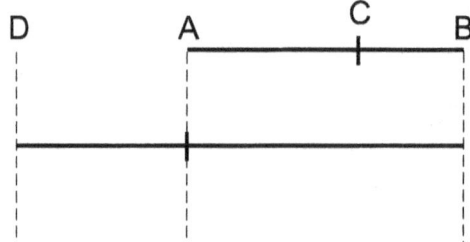

Figure 2.1. Golden proportion with its self-contained next step made explicit

the *Book of the Duchess*. *Phi* is the only proportion among Euclid's ten proportions listed by Nicomachus that, when stated, has the next step already present before the eye.

In the upper line of figure 2.1 the relation of the smaller extreme BC to the mean AC is the same as the relation of this mean AC to the larger extreme AB. In both instances the relation of the smaller line to the larger is approximately 1 : 1.61803. Thus the upper horizontal line of figure 2.1 has two demonstrations of *phi*, one that is already evident as AC, and another that must be imagined by mentally removing the segmentation at C to reveal a new segment AB as the mean in the next demonstration. By constructing an exact copy of this newly constructed demonstration in the lower horizontal line, making DA = AC and thus displaying what had been partly concealed, we can see this second demonstration of *phi*, DA : AB = AB : DB. By definition, the demonstration in the lower line is actually two demonstrations, one of which, again, requires mental construction. If AB is folded out from the lower line to the right (not shown), still another pair of equations satisfying *phi* automatically appears. And so on toward infinity.

Within Chaucer's elegy, infinity commences for the Duchess of Lancaster with the final line of the divine proportion at the end of line 1310. Leading to this finality, a change has occurred in who takes the role of frustrated interlocutor. Where the dreamer's impatience on a variety of subjects, but especially on the question of the lady's literal death, has grown during his time with the mourner, the Black Knight himself has grown impatient at the dreamer's persistence. At length harmony comes, as the bereft lover abandons hyperbole at the same time the dreamer drops the charade of incomprehension. The two men exchange the briefest of lines, which, despite their unpretentious words, grow to a harmonious duet, humble in its simplicity, yet profound in its temporal and eternal significance:

> "Sir," quod I, "where is she now?"
> "Now?" quod he, and stynte anoon.
> Therwith he wax as ded as stoon
> And seyde, "Allas, that I was bore!
> That was the los that here-before
> I tolde the that I hadde lorn.
> Bethenke how I seyde here-beforn,
> 'Thow wost ful lytel what thow menest;
> I have lost more than thow wenest.'
> God wot, allas! Ryght that was she!"
> "Allas, sir, how? What may that be?"
> "She ys ded!" "Nay!" "Yis, be my trouthe!"
> "Is that youre los? Be God, hyt ys routhe!"
>
> (1298–1310)

Two developments occur simultaneously. The man in black triumphs over sorrow by the very act of departing from his habitual mode of stylized expression, permitting direct communication free of metaphor and hyperbole. At the same time, the dreamer is freed from "ydel thoght" (4), from his own torpid lethargy, from an inability to distinguish "leef" from "looth" (8), capable now "be processe of tyme" of putting his "queynt . . . sweven" into "ryme" (1330–32). The phrase "be processe of tyme" does not refer to some future elapse of time, but to the fitting of words into metrical form. The "sweven" that recounts the dreamer's psychological recovery represents in compressed form Chaucer's eight-year progress from eager, inept imitator to promising poet now able to control meter and rhyme. To put all this another way, the man in black does not so much disappear at the end of line 1310 as complete the process of growing into the dreamer.

A variety of sustained themes enables Chaucer to reach a literal resolution to the debate at the same time he completes the divine proportion. This proportion's power to expand indefinitely, associated with infinite divine power, suits perfectly an elegy for a woman whose death, to all who knew her, would bring the lady herself to the expansion of heavenly bliss, as Ovid's charming tropes metamorphose his heroes and heroines into birds and trees forever to flourish in the air. As well, the contrast between the monologues of the man in black, reflecting the immature poetry of a twenty-four-year-old Chaucer, and the adroit expressions of the more poetically skillful thirty-two-year-old dreamer, provides a palpable tableau of the artistic expansion Chaucer accomplished in a short eight years. The lines produced by the twenty-four-year-old Chaucerian persona achieve little that deserves admiration. But the finished poem, combining multiple levels of meaning, time-schemes that take us from the past through the present and on to the world beyond, reflects the mathematics that underscores the central part of the poem. The divine proportion begins with the ordinariness of mere numbers, yet arranges itself into an ineffable relationship that approaches God. Let us add the poet himself, noticing in particular how appropriately the divine proportion anatomizes him. When first encountered, he strikes the least interesting pose in the poem, all sadness and self-involvement, as unremarkable as an arbitrary collection of numbers, of which he may be the least digit. With the help of the literature of the past and a distanced look at an image of himself, he rearranges his experience so as to expand the very ordinariness of mortality into the little sliver of eternity that the poem, Blanche, the suggestion of future favor, and his own immortal soul portend.

Chaucer saves for the final twenty-four lines of the *Book of the Duchess* an emphatic hint of the personal reason for which he gave his poem the form it now has. Professionally speaking, the great year in Chaucer's life was 1374, when his fortunes increased immeasurably, taking him from a condition of full dependence on largesse to terms approximating salaried employment as collector of customs, with a residence and wine ration to boot. These positions came to Chaucer, of course, from Edward III and were expected to be renewed by fiat of the king's heir apparent, the Black Prince, from whom Chaucer may have been given assurances of continued support. It must have been a shock, not only for Chaucer but for all who depended on the king's favor, when the Black Prince's premature death on June 8, 1376, from a gastrointestinal disease contracted in Spain, threw the matter of royal succession into uncertainty. Anyone who held a position by the grace of the king, whose health had long been failing by 1376, faced the task of ingratiating himself to the king's likely successor. When it became evident that the king's successor would be the Black Prince's ten-year-old son Richard, and that the Lancastrian John of Gaunt, acting as unofficial regent, would therefore be the most powerful man in England, a legion of princepleasers must have been tripping over each other as they sought access to John of Gaunt. To Gaunt's credit, he loyally supported his young nephew-king for many years.[49]

Geoffrey Chaucer was one of those who needed confirmation, in his post as collector of customs and for his and his wife's annuities. These grants were not likely to be denied, but they were never a certainty, especially in the angry times of the Good Parliament when acrimony was intense on all sides. Nothing can be taken from the fact that Chaucer's patronage was not renewed until Letters Patent were enrolled on March 23, 1378, and authorized by the Privy Seal on April 18 (*Ch L-R* 303–6), some ten months after Edward III died; bureaucracy moved equally slowly at every regal succession. Nevertheless, it is undeniable that during the months when the Black Prince was dying and the succession was set to pass to Richard, Chaucer had to have some way of calling specific attention to himself, to his long service to the royal family and, by implication, to Gaunt. This would have been between April 1376, when Gaunt returned from the Continent, and late spring of 1377, when everyone knew that Edward III's death was imminent. The strategy Chaucer settled on, I believe, was the brilliant idea of converting his clumsy elegy for Queen Philippa into an imagined meeting between his current self and his younger self. The poem relishes its artful strategy, superficially praising Blanche while also demonstrating that it took him eight years to learn how to write acceptable poetry.

With the line "al was doon, / For that tyme, the hert-huntyng" (1312–13), the poem shifts its attention from matters poetic to matters of patronage. The hunt began with a leader named Octovyen, a probable reference to Edward III, whom Chaucer served from 1367 to 1374, and ends with an obvious reference to Gaunt riding to his castle. The two references, then, identify Chaucer's patron at the beginning of the early period covered in the poem and end with an image of the man Chaucer undoubtedly hoped would be his patron in the future.

Some may argue that the questions discussed in this chapter—whether Chaucer always intended the *Book of the Duchess* to honor Blanche of Lancaster or began it as a tribute to Queen Philippa, and whether he designed the man in black to represent John of Gaunt or a twenty-four-year-old image of himself—matter to history but not to literature. I would argue otherwise. A thorough engagement of these questions, unlike the discovery of a deed or confirmation that a grant was received, forces scholars to confront the very essence of literature, perhaps freeing the poem for a critical consideration on its own terms. Not coincidentally, the lines of the *Duchess* and of poems discussed in following chapters address this same essence: the subjects and forms of literature, the relation between literature and life, literary construction, self-representation, and the important matter of royal favor, all questions that would concern Chaucer throughout his career.

3

Parliament of Fowls

All modern editions of Chaucer's work print his poems in the chronological order in which he is assumed to have composed them, and therefore follow the *Book of the Duchess* with the *House of Fame*.[1] I prefer to turn next to the *Parliament of Fowls*. By doing so, I do not insist that *Fowls* was composed before *Fame*, though it is an opinion Helen Cooper shares and Alastair Minnis is beginning to consider, even extending *Fame*'s date until after *Troilus and Criseyde* was completed.[2] The wit and dialogue in *Fame* easily suggest the poetry of Chaucer's most mature years, while thematically it nearly echoes *Troilus and Criseyde*. *Fowls*, of course, has very little to do with that beautiful poem about love and sorrow in Troy, despite sharing its metrical form. Actually, no convincing evidence supports the prevailing opinion that *Fame* preceded *Fowls*. Most of the arguments advanced—apart from the powerful influence of tradition—depend on our assuming that three technically incorrect statements in *Fame* reflect Chaucer's limited knowledge of Cicero's *Somnium* and Macrobius's *Commentary*, a limitation he is thought to have corrected before writing *Fowls*.[3] Rather, I choose to treat *Fowls* before *Fame* for two other reasons. First, the thematic echoes just noted between *Fame* and *Troilus* suggest that these two poems belong to the same period, implying that the relationship between them may be the same as that between *Troilus* and the *Legend of Good Women* including its prologues. Logic suggests, therefore, that Chaucer may have composed *Fame* under the same circumstances that produced the *Legend* and its prologues—that is, very shortly after he received what many assume was a disparaging critical response to *Troilus and Criseyde*. Second, I shall argue in chapters 4 and 5 that the *House of Fame*, though written after *Troilus*, was nonetheless intended to serve as Chaucer's authenticating prologue to his extended poem about love. Both of these theories argue for a discussion of *Fowls* here and of *Fame* just before *Troilus*.

Spatial Construction

The previous chapter argues that Chaucer's altered purposes in creating the *Book of the Duchess* over an eight-year period, abetted by the misleading gloss of an early commentator, make the central point of his first sustained work difficult to grasp. Authorial revision and critical misdirection, in other words, have had more influence on interpretative tradition of the *Duchess* than have the very lines of its text. The present chapter advances a rather different argument, as iconoclastic in its way as the previous chapter's discussion of the *Duchess*. Not only is the *Parliament of Fowls* one of the finest of medieval dream visions; it follows, I propose, a rich compositional strategy that began to fall out of fashion in the Renaissance and is now almost entirely unavailable to modern criticism. To make this authorial strategy more accessible, I shall begin by looking at a famous seventeenth-century poem, where this now-lost tradition may be seen in a simpler form than in the *Parliament*, and then proceed to Chaucer's poem, a philosophical meditation that leaps into a jeu d'esprit, as clearly as the Renaissance poem itself does in a less ambitious way.

To introduce one of the most delightful collections of poetry in English literature, Robert Herrick offers a kind of overture, a demonstration of what the entire volume achieves in its subtle movements. Blandly titled "The Argument of His Book," the poem identifies two activities, singing and writing (shown below in boldface), that, while seemingly antithetical, are inspired by the same secular delights:

> I **sing** of brooks, of blossoms, birds, and bowers,
> Of April, May, of June, and Júly flowers.
> I **sing** of Maypoles, hock carts, wassails, wakes,   3
> Of bridegrooms, brides, and of their bridal cakes.
> I **write** of youth, of love, and have access
> By these to **sing** of cleanly wantonness.   6
> I **sing** of dews, of rains, and, piece by piece,
> Of balm, of oil, of spice, and ambergris.
> I **sing** of times trans-shifting, and I **write**   9
> How roses first came red and lilies white.
> I **write** of groves, of twilights, and I **sing**
> The court of Mab and of the fairy king.   12

> I **write** of hell; I **sing** (and ever shall)
> Of heaven, and hope to have it after all.

We may be excused for wondering why editions of Herrick neglect to include the word *sonnet* in this fourteen-line poem's title, despite its traditional quatrains and its dramatic shift of subject in the final couplet, all typical marks of a sonnet's form. To contradict Herrick's apparent wish not to name it a sonnet, however, would miss the point of the poem and of the whole volume: the subtle expansions that create movement in a reader's mind. For it is *we* who are to notice its form and to elevate its status, despite its appearance as a simple effusion taking pleasure from the scenes and subjects it touches. A gentle shift from earthen and animate nature in the poem's first two lines reaches human activity in the third and the culminating delight of a wedding in the fourth. The fundamental impulse that leads to a wedding, and is certainly shared by the birds of line 1, begins the second quatrain, yet takes the poem to a fleeting oxymoron rising to a paradox, "cleanly wantonness" (6). A similar refinement occurs when mere condensed water in "dews" and "rains" (7) yields to the rarefied liquids and aromatic substances of line 8, balm, oil, spice, and ambergris. That this ascent occurs "piece by piece" (7) can hardly be other than a reference to the poem-by-poem progress of the collection that will follow. The poem's final six lines—not a sestet really, though it helps to think of them thus—commence their crescendo silently: "times trans-shifting" (9) imparts a subconscious notion of eternal permanence, while the contradictory references to passion and purity in the colors "red" and "white" (10) soften into distant theological allusions to Christ's Passion and the Virgin. Finally, the imaginary, intoxicating court of "Mab and of the fairy king" (12) leads inexorably, if unexpectedly, to the realm of "heaven" (14)—no elevated fairy kingdom now, but a reality Herrick hopes to have "after all" (14).

While moving from natural charms to more complicated delights, the poem conveys its most profound truth spatially, in the shifting placement of the two main verbs, "sing" and "write." These are almost the only verbs in the entire poem, "sing" occurring seven times and "write" four times. The only other verbs, "have" (5), "came" (10) and "hope to have" (14), merely expand the temporal context to include past and future, or eternity. These main verbs gravitate to each other as the poem progresses. "Sing" alone governs the first quatrain, repeated twice, as if the subjects themselves compel the poet to break into song. These subjects differ little from those in the second quatrain, which begins with a different verb, "write," tentatively introduced but quickly driven away by two more appearances of "sing." Not until lines 9 through 12 does "write" earn leave to stay, though remaining at a discreet distance. Its claim to appear in the poem gains strength, not only by appearing in the same line as "sing" (9), but also by changing places with "sing" in line 11, as if masculine "write" and feminine "sing" had already understood the complicated minuet they would dance. The crowning resolution of this courtship occurs in the thirteenth line, where the mutual attraction of the two verbs juxtaposes them so closely they almost wed. Though writing and singing call for different kinds of effort, as they address the same subjects, together they produce an ineffable expansion. The rigor and discipline of writing impose themselves on the light, joyful airs of the season and its activities, until writing and singing are partners, almost independent of the poem. Passion inspires reason. Reason strengthens passion. The two faculties unite in one sublime effusion, song.

I have taken time with Herrick's poem to show that a visual strategy, almost a geometric progress, can contribute a profound, though unspoken, dimension to the poem's surface. In the present chapter I suggest that, while advancing the exciting themes of a typical epithalamion, the *Parliament of Fowls* also employs a mathematical strategy similar to, though far more complicated than, the visual strategy of Herrick's *Argument*.

Thematics of the *Parliament of Fowls*

Couched in the delightful fiction of a narrator who experiences a dream, the *Parliament of Fowls* has always been understood to have three parts—referenced here as parts I, II, and III, though unmarked in the poem—one devoted to the dreamer before he sleeps (1–119) and two others to his dream, which very noticeably shifts its tone, feel, and subject when it turns its attention from the sterile protests of three tercels to the lively activity of lesser birds.[4] The first half of this dream (120–490) presents in the static fashion of Old French allegory every imaginable feeling, impulse, thought, and action associated with love. The latter half (491–692), covering the same subjects, represents them in dynamic scenes where birds struggle to achieve the harmony of nature.[5]

Scholars have never doubted the charm and poetic beauty of the *Parliament*'s three separate parts, although no consensus has emerged regarding the aesthetic conception that moved Chaucer to assemble them in one poem. Charles Muscatine notes: "The chief critical problem has been to explain the apparent discordances among its successive parts: the dour summary of the *Somnium Scipionis* suggests allegiance to 'common profit' and to transcendental values; the temple of Venus and Nature's comic assembly of birds suggest different and conflicting sublunary and private values" (*Riv Ch* 994). Leicester, too, captures well the apparent inconsistency many have seen between the poem's various literary and philosophical topoi, all of which had benefited from a rich rhetorical tradition by the time Chaucer was writing, and the contradictions that arise from what he calls the "thought-marked" attempts to embrace these traditions as God-given, yet capable somehow of being grasped by an inadequate human understanding: "It began to become apparent that the sense of unity [in medieval culture as well as in the *Parliament*] could only be safely maintained as long as it remained *latent*, as long as nobody tried to spell it out too thoroughly" (1974, 19). Leicester repeats a point made by others, that in the poem's opening stanzas "the poet is seeking and exploring" (Clemen 1964, 122) but not finding (Howard 1987, 317), an unsuccessful quest shared by modern scholars and critics still searching for the poem's organizing principle.

True enough. But a distinction must be made between a search for something concerning romantic love and a quest for something more fundamental and wider-reaching. Chaucer calls his subject "Love" (4, 8), a word that easily evokes the courtship and romance that "Loves servaunt[s]" (159) rhyme about endlessly. But the word can also convey what Boethius means in explaining that the elements, the movements of the planets, the alternations of night and day, indeed "al this accordaunce [and] ordenaunce of thynges is bounde with love, that governeth erthe and see, and hath also comandement to the hevene" (*Boece* II.m.8, 13–16).[6] This chapter suggests that Chaucer the poet (a term normally found with reference to the *Canterbury Tales*, but equally apt here to distinguish between the poet and the narrator of the poem) had in mind this wider-reaching understanding when he wrote "Al this mene I by Love" (4).

Contrary to a long-standing fashion to think of Chaucer as uncontaminated by university learning—the poet of felt life, master of dialogue and pregnant detail, rather than "thought-marked" Scholasticism—the assumption that the intellectually curious Chaucer would not have pursued the deepest currents of his day cannot long stand. For the love celebrated in the *Parliament* as the harmony of the nine spheres, the mating of birds, and the roundel sung at the end of the poem is the same power that Plato credits in his *Timaeus* (31b–32c) with holding the universe together, and the same force that Theseus calls "love" in the *Knight's Tale*:[7]

> For with that faire cheyne of love he bond
> The fyr, the eyr, the water, and the lond
> In certeyn boundes, that they may nat flee.
>
> (*CT* I.2991–93)

Yet it is also fair to assume that Chaucer had only a gifted layman's interest in the science of his day, enough to satisfy his general curiosity and support his belletristic conceptions but not enough—nor any need, for his literary purposes—to study the depths of Plotinus, Porphyry, Iamblichus, or Proclus. In this sense, Macrobius, from whom Chaucer probably learned of Cicero's *Somnium*, was an ideal source. Not only was he, after Chalcidius, "the most important source of Platonism in the Latin West in the Middle Ages" (Stahl 1952, 10), he was also writing for the general reader, not the scientist. "As an exposition of Neoplatonism [Macrobius's *Commentary*] has been praised for its succinctness and lucidity. The frequent references throughout the Middle Ages to Macrobius as an authority on Neoplatonism testify to his ability to make the system intelligible to his readers" (10). Macrobius earns praise as a transmitter of ancient, mostly Greek philosophy, not as a student of dream lore or treatises on romantic love. Chaucer undoubtedly began his *Parliament* with a précis of Cicero's *Somnium* for the same reason Macrobius edited the same text in its entirety to introduce the science he intended to explore. The two books, Macrobius's *Commentary* and Chaucer's *Parliament*, are two versions of one philosophy. As well as referring to Cicero's *Somnium*, the "olde feldes" (22) that Chaucer says produce "newe corn" (23) each year probably also refer to the Neoplatonism that occupies most of Macrobius's *Commentary*, perhaps especially its mathematics that he may have in mind as "al this newe science that men lere" (25).

Let us defer a discussion of whether a unifying principle governs the *Parliament*, and, if so, what this principle may be, until we understand its thematic design, or rather, discover the poem's own quest for the unity that Leicester fears may "slit so yerne" (3) from our grasp if we try to spell it out.

Chaucer certainly knew that the majority of his audience, on hearing the word *Love*, would think only of activity that would energize a Pandarus. He may have imagined his own narrator of the *Parliament* as one of those who hopes to understand the elusive nature of romance, perhaps the "certeyn thing to lerne" (20) that would recover his taste for love (160). The distinction between the romantic understanding of "love" as a force that brings two people together and the philosophic understanding of the force that binds together the whole of the universe and everything in it may well explain the narrator's cryptic comment after reading Scipio's dream:

For bothe I hadde thyng which that I nolde,
And ek I ne hadde that thyng that I wolde.

(90–91)

Reminiscent of the pre-dreaming sequence in the *Book of the Duchess* where an Ovidian story points to an important motif in the dream to follow, the opening movement of the *Parliament* presents a number of paths the poem might pursue. The nature and cause of dreams, for example, may occur to some readers as the organizing principle of the poem, for this subject has a suitable introduction in the Latin title of the book the narrator will read, *Somnium Scipionis* (*The Dream of Scipio*), and in the unanswerable logic that brings this reading to a close at stanza 15 (lines 99–105). Others may find the governing motif in "commune profyt," mentioned twice by Affrican the Elder (47, 75), for this ideal seems pertinent to the unruly bird-parliament occupying the last two-thirds of the poem. Pure philosophy, too, could survive the final cut, for Cicero's thoughts in the *Somnium* accord well with those of Macrobius, Boethius, Martianus Capella, and especially Plato, all revered authorities whom we would call pure philosophers.[8] Nor can we overlook the "love" minimized above, which appears as the poem's main subject to most readers, including Donaldson, who limits himself to only one word pointing to the direction proposed here: "The *Parliament of Fowls* is a poem about love that is both lyric and philosophical" (1975, 1119).

However much the poem enriches these and a variety of other subjects, its diction points to still another, loftier principle that subsumes all these others. For his actual subject might better be called "harmony"—social, musical, celestial, theological, literary, and as wide a variety of other harmonies as one can imagine—of which human love is only one manifestation.[9] No fewer than fourteen explicit references to forms of "harmony" occur by line 84, where the narrator completes his summary of Cicero's treatise, among them the two literal appearances of the word *Love*. If we also include the five images of disharmony in these lines, offered as fearful contrast to harmony's quiet appeal, there are nineteen occurrences in 84 lines.[10]

Though images of accord are unmentioned in the transitional scenes that take the narrator to his sleep, to his dream, and within that dream to the garden of Venus, references to harmony and disharmony appear explicitly as inscriptions over the gate to this garden in stanzas 18 and 19 (127–40). As with any inscription over a gate, especially Dante's gate to hell to which this scene is indebted,[11] these seem to announce what one will find within. But by contradicting each other, and by shifting from abstractions for humanity to nature's concrete images associated with these abstractions—one moving from "blysful place" (127) and "hertes hele" (128) to "grene and lusty May" (130), the other noting "Disdayn and Daunger" (136) that lead to locales "Ther nevere tre shal fruyt ne leves bere" (137)—these inscriptions seem to embrace a larger subject than either human activity or the natural world by themselves.

After "Affrican" (120) disappears from the poem, symbols of what the enticing golden inscription promises begin to appear in a group of six stanzas, 25 through 30 (169–210), describing the vegetative world and the little creatures living in it. Every type of tree is associated with a specific contribution arising from its particular nature, not only the strength of oak and ash for building, the pliability of fir to withstand strong winds, and the suitability of boxwood for musical instruments, but also the mournful, peaceful, victorious, or knowing thoughts various woods inspire. Above all, the active collaboration between types of trees and human needs and faculties governs the whole of stanza 26 (176–82). The garden, too, in stanza 27 (183–89) teems with active life, but a life that proves beneficial to others by offering its beautiful flowers, its cool streams and nourishing fish. Shifting to aural harmony, stanza 28 remarks the angelic voices of birds singing "in here armonye" (191) on every bough. The word *acord* (197) in the opening line of the next stanza describes the music of stringed instruments, while a gentle breeze stirs in green leaves "a noyse softe / Acordaunt to the foules song alofte" (202–3). All seven lines in stanza 30 (204–10) identify individual states of perfect appeal: of air, greenery, health, joy, and light. These first six stanzas following the narrator's entry through the gates agree perfectly with what the golden inscription promises.

At this point an abrupt shift takes the poem to a well where "Cupide" (212) forges and files arrows, while his daughter, "Wille" (214), tempers their heads and arranges them according to the work they will do, slaying, wounding, and carving. In the dozen stanzas containing this shift, 31 through 42 (211–94), an extraordinary thing occurs. Harmony vanishes. Not a single image of it appears in the descriptions outside Venus's "temple of bras" (231) nor within the temple itself. This is not to say disharmony reigns, only that no reference is made to what obviously caught the narrator's eye in the earlier lines. Instead, nearly fifty figures of myth, allegory, and ancient literature represent the emotions associated with literary accounts of unhappy love, for we are now in the fearful realm announced by the black letters above the gate, the disharmony to which Disdayn and Daunger lead the dreamer. This long stretch of twelve stanzas—twice the size of his description of the lively, vital scenes he saw when his guide first pushed him through a set of gates—creates an unrelieved sense of static display, entirely lacking in movement of any kind save the narrator's slow walk through its successive scenes, like a visitor to a dated museum wandering among silent, motionless, and forbidding cycloramas.

The harmony to which the narrator so often responds while summarizing Scipio's dream returns in stages, as if he reawakens to it timidly, while regaining "the place / . . . that was so sote and grene" (295–96). From stanza 43 through stanza 54 (295–378), a twelve-stanza cluster seems to reply to the twelve stanzas that describe the sterile, lifeless area before and inside Venus's temple. This garden, very different from the one visited in lines 211–45, appeals to the narrator for its solace and for the beauty of Nature herself, a queen who exceeds every other creature's beauty as the light of the sun surpasses that of every star. Images of harmony do not immediately dominate the scene over which Nature presides, as they did earlier, but the "halles" and "boures" (304) where harmony will prevail are obviously in place. Nature's locales are "Iwrought after here cast and here mesure" (305). Every bird on earth obeys her order to attend the annual parliament each "Valentynes day" (309), to give her their attention and to accept her judgment. A brief mention of Alanus de Insulis's "Pleynt of Kynde" (316) reminds an audience of that book's main point, that same-sex intercourse violates nature's laws. A specific relation is noted between each species of bird and the wider world: the royal eagle whose eyes, it is believed, can look at the sun; the falcon who teams with the king at sport; the dove whose meek eyes suggest human emotion; the swan known for its song before death; the peacock with feathers bright as an angel's; and the long list of birds that are both predators and prey (330–64).

Harmony begins to reestablish its preeminence when the attending birds, ordered by the goddess to take their places, arrange themselves according to a natural hierarchy, a probable instance of social satire when birds that prey on flesh are set highest:

> the foules of ravyne
> Weere hyest set, and thanne the foules smale
> That eten, as hem Nature wolde enclyne,
> As worm or thyng of which I telle no tale;
> And water-foul sat lowest in the dale;
> But foul that lyveth by sed sat on the grene,
> And that so fele that wonder was to sene.
>
> (323–29)

The long catalogue of birds in stanzas 48 through 52 (330–64), like the catalogue of trees in stanza 26 (176–82), implies a subtle orderliness, for Nature has given every species a peculiar ability or characteristic behavior that all its members exercise without demur. Each species obeys Nature's law because it owes its very existence to her. That some avian behavior implies the death of other creatures should not be taken as evidence of disharmony and therefore a violation of Nature's dictate. No waning of anything in nature contradicts Nature's laws, but rather occurs by Nature's design, as Theseus, paraphrasing Lady Philosophy, articulates well in the *Knight's Tale*:

> nature hath nat taken his bigynnyng
> Of no partie or cantel of a thyng,
> But of a thyng that parfit is and stable,
> Descendynge so til it be corrumpable.
> And therfore, of his wise purveiaunce,
> He hath so wel biset his ordinaunce

That speces of thynges and progressiouns
Shullen enduren by successiouns

(*CT* I.3007–14; cf. *Boece* II.m.8)

The *Parliament*'s explicit allusions to the Creation at 305, 312, and 380–81, discussed below, draw attention to the parallel between the elevation of primordial matter into created form and the elevation of a confusing assemblage of birds into a triumph of harmony at the end of the poem. This progress begins when Nature arrives with all her powers to explain the key to the harmony she intends to promote, the "acord" (371) of each bird's chosen mate. Unless "she agre to his eleccioun, / Whoso he be that shulde be hire feere" (409–10), no match will occur. Not even royalty can claim exemption from Nature's ruling that accord must prevail, as the goddess's careful wording makes explicit, "Whoso he be" (410). What a telling irony, then, that among all the birds attending the parliament only the royal birds ignore this single requirement of Lady Nature. Flouting Nature's law, they rest their arguments on the formel's obligation, rather than her free choice, to select the one who loves her most, or longest, or truest. Their elaborate petitions amount to another absence of harmony, like its disappearance from lines 211 to 294. Yet harmony only partly vanishes here, for the orderliness with which these royal eagles make their pleas still governs, while the docile attendance of the lesser birds still prevails. But the speeches themselves militate against what Nature ordered.

In addition to the unwitting humor of broadly ironic speeches that satirize the sugared offerings of many a troubadour (the narrator would disagree with this assessment of course; cf. lines 484–88), the three tercels' speeches afford insight into the royal eagles' allegorical meaning. Despite a strong tendency to assume these eagles represent the first estate, while all the other species of bird represent the commons, these royal birds alone ignore the necessity of securing the formel's agreement, while all the other birds apparently obey her rule, else they could not fly away with newly chosen mates at the end of the poem. It is more likely, then, that the tercels' fatuous proposals mark them as representatives of humanity, the only species whose members have a level of intelligence and the free will enabling them, whether rightly or wrongly, to place their private desires above the laws of Nature. Since the lesser birds seem to obey Nature without reserve, they apparently represent all nonhuman creatures, including birds.

Notwithstanding the royal birds' implied refusal to honor Nature's insistence on mutual accord, the concept of harmony gains a foothold by degrees, as the lesser birds wait patiently for the eagles to conclude their "cursede pletynge" (495), while only the goose, cuckoo, and duck burst out in brief mayhem near the end of the day. Realizing that some order should govern the still unresolved parliament, the goose and cuckoo appoint themselves spokesmen, respectively, for waterfowl and worm fowl, to the disgust of the turtledove who reminds the assemblage that, though a member may have leave to speak, he might better keep his mouth shut (510–11). Still advancing the notion of mutual accord, albeit futilely, and urging the gathering to "Hold youre tonges there!" (521), Nature overrules self-appointment in favor of election, to which the birds surprisingly assent. The truce, only temporary, again disintegrates into name-calling and insult—brilliantly if one considers that poetry produces the scene, sadly when one reckons that the scene typifies more parliaments than one would care to admit.[12]

To cut off debate at long last, Nature sharply commands "pes" (617), this time to lasting effect. Never mind spokesmen. The formel herself will make her choice, Nature orders, as she has unambiguously insisted from the beginning. With an artifice that is hardly expected, the formel softens her response to all three suitors by requesting a postponement until the following year. In fact, her requested postponement rejects the tercels, since she must return for next year's parliament in either case. When no one objects to the formel's request—not Nature nor especially any of the three royal suitors—another level of irony enters the poem. Each tercel's tiresome speech, though failing to impress the formel despite declaiming the virtues of the speaker, clearly conveys the highest wish of all three eagles. None of these suitors wishes to win the formel's love, or even to gain a mate—for these achievements would end their game. Their sole objective is to return annually, to preen, to protest undying love, and to emote forever on the subject that holds their deepest interest—themselves.[13]

After mates are chosen, the assembled birds have one final ritual to perform, to sing a roundel in celebration of the season and to rejoice in the purpose for which they came. Not only does the exuberance of this roundel reflect the very essence of Nature's parliament in the exhilaration of the birds who sing it, but the song also brings Chaucer's *Parliament* to its clearest demonstration of harmony.¹⁴ We know little of the song Chaucer had in mind to conclude his poem: "None of the MSS of *PF* indicate how the refrains should go, and only one (Gg) gives a full text (but in a later hand)" (*Riv Ch* 394, note to line 675). In other words, we cannot even be certain that "Now welcome, somor" (680) was Chaucer's intention;¹⁵ it may have been suggested by an early editor because the name "Saynt Valentyn" (683) occurs in one of its verses, in keeping with the earlier announcement that the parliament met on "Seynt Valentynes day" (309).

We do feel certain about several facts, however, all of which point to the logic of concluding the poem with the kind of song Chaucer seems to have wanted, whatever that song was. The author himself tells us the birds sang a "roundel" (675). Guillaume de Machaut (ca. 1300–1377), whom Chaucer knew and whose poems, or parts of them, he adapted to Middle English, was one of the most active composers of rondeaux throughout his life in music. Most significant of all, the rondeau and the motet were favorites of Machaut for adaptation to the *ars nova*, a polyphonic, isorhythmic innovation which Machaut himself pioneered on mathematical proportions even more than on melody.¹⁶ Indeed, Machaut is often accused for this reason of appealing only to intellectuals and the clergy. All of these facts suggest that a roundel, as Machaut would have composed it, was a perfect miniaturization of Chaucer's conception of the *Parliament of Fowls*.

Although the mathematics of the poem will be discussed presently, we might note here that Chaucer succeeds in fitting the roundel, a two-rhyme form not easily amenable to rhyme royal, into the space allotted to exactly two rhyme-royal stanzas, thus "by evene noumbres of acord" (381) mathematically satisfying the demands of both genres.

From the thematic discussion that has been holding our attention, let us now shift our critical approach to the poem's underlying design, concealed like the minuet danced by feminine "sing" and masculine "write" in Herrick's "Argument." For Chaucer gave his poem a hidden code that makes in a rigorous mathematical way the same point about harmony that the poem's literal language achieves with elegance and charm.

Chaucer's Design for the *Parliament of Fowls*

The *Parliament of Fowls* echoes Macrobius's *Commentary* in a way that reveals the different sensibilities of the scholar and the poet. Brilliant as both works are, neither offers a connection to Cicero's text as explicitly as a critic might do when discussing a work's literary unity. Macrobius presents the *Somnium* in its entirety in order to explain basic doctrines of Neoplatonism, quoting "passages from *Scipio's Dream* as pretexts for entering upon lengthy excursuses which, in some cases, might be called digressions" (Stahl, 13). Very often these so-called digressions give detailed explanations of Pythagorean mathematics, or what the modern world calls number theory, and the relationship of this discipline to the structure of the universe. Chaucer, too, begins his poem with Cicero's *Somnium*, though summarized and compressed rather than quoted in its entirety, then presents his own dream as a sequence of scenes implicitly related to the central tenets of Neoplatonism. To both Macrobius and Chaucer, then, the matter they present after Cicero's *Somnium* is more important than the *Somnium* itself, which apparently serves only as an entrée, or a gloss, to the material each author considers more important.

If Macrobius believes the *Somnium* unavoidably implies mathematics, and if Chaucer commits himself to representing in his *Parliament* the essence of Cicero's *Somnium*, as he seems to suggest—

> Of which Macrobye roughte nat a lyte,
> That sumdel of thy labour wolde I quyte
>
> (*PF* 111–12)

—then a modern critic faces two difficult questions: Does Chaucer believe mathematics is equally important to his *Parliament*? And, if so, is mathematics somehow present in his poem, partly discharging his promise "That sumdel of thy labour wolde I quyte"?

To the first question I must say "yes," for I believe mathematics makes a very important contribution, not only to the *Parliament*, but to more of his poetry as well. The preceding chapter suggests he may have been experimenting with mathematics in the *Book of the Duchess*, for the divine proportion seems more than a simple coincidence in the distribution of lines during the conversations between the dreamer and the man in black. And in the *Canterbury Tales* he still seems to play with mathematics from time to time, though not as fully as in his earlier years, unless something has escaped our notice. For example, the *Tale of Sir Thopas* halves the number of stanzas as it proceeds through three fitts, 18 in the first, 9 in the second, and 4½ in the third (Burrow 1971). Its approach to nothingness comments on the absence of poetry—an opinion shared by the Host, who limits its teller's next tale to prose. A similar technique occurs in Fragment I, where moral and social levels progressively deteriorate through four tales until the fragment terminates on the most degrading line in the whole poem. Chaucer may have encoded this decline mathematically, at least by making these tales progressively shorter, 2,256 lines (*Knight's Tale*), 668 (*Miller's Tale*), 404 (*Reeve's Tale*), and 58 (*Cook's Tale*), and then by precisely measuring the four fitts in the *Knight's Tale* to announce his numerical organization with a curious apportionment of lines: 502,[17] 526, 602, and 626. This technique is called "ring structure," where the sum of the medials equals the sum of the ends: 526 + 602 = 1,128 and 502 + 626 = 1,128. Moreover, Chaucer apportions to the remaining tales of Fragment I a total number of lines almost exactly one-half what he gives to the *Knight's Tale*, 2,256 for the first tale, 1,130 for the remaining three tales.

As for the occurrence of numerical design in the *Parliament of Fowls*, earlier we noted the halls and bowers fashioned after Nature's "cast" and "mesure" (305). These are mathematical terms, the former glossed in *The Riverside Chaucer* as "design," the latter from Solomon's persona who in a famous line refers to the mathematical ordering of creation, "Sed omnia in mensura, et numero, et pondere disposuisti" (*Wisdom* 11: 21) [Douay version: But thou hast ordered all things in measure, and number, and weight].

This explicit reference notwithstanding, the current laudatory opinion of the *Parliament of Fowls*, said to be the most highly "finished" of Chaucer's major poems, rests mainly on thematic considerations and the elegance of Chaucer's own invention, the rhyme-royal stanza.[18] Yet one cannot read the poem without suspecting that measurement, or number in general, has some role in Chaucer's design, beyond acknowledging its presence at the Creation. Its one hundred stanzas, for example, look very much like an author's numerical intention. The same is true of the seven-line stanza, now known as rhyme royal, for the number seven is the most extensively discussed number in all of Pythagorean mathematics.[19] There are subtler hints of number as well. Reference to Macrobius and selection of his *Commentary on the Somnium Scipionis*, which gives Macrobius occasion to discuss mathematics more than any other subject, cannot be called arbitrary. Subtler still, Chaucer allots a specific number of stanzas to thematic points. Venus and the nearly inert literary figures associated with her temple receive twelve stanzas, 31 through

42 (211–94), alluding mainly to unhappy strife. An equal number of stanzas, 43 through 54 (295–378), answers this disharmony by describing the assemblage of birds full of eager vitality. The speeches of the tercel eagles may also contribute to the mathematical character of the poem's design. The tercel eagles are not given an equal number of stanzas, as one may expect, but four stanzas to the first eagle, two to the second, and three to the third. The competition among these eagles for the formel naturally implies a series of comparisons. Thus, when compared, these numbers not only signify a simple arithmetic progression, 2, 3, 4, but also allude to the three most favored intervals in music—the fourth, indicated by musicologists as the ratio 4 : 3; the fifth, 3 : 2; and the octave, 4 : 2, the same as a musicologist's 2 : 1.[20] Let us note, however, that the harmony to which the poem faintly alludes here lies beyond the capacity of these eagles.

Closer to the poem's thematic dimension, the concept of number emerges more clearly from two prominent allusions to Creation which bracket Nature's first appearance, from the ordering of the assembled birds to her presentation of the formel eagle on her arm. The first image seems to refer casually to the temporary resting places of the birds—

> Of every kynde that men thynke may,
> And that so huge a noyse gan they make
> That erthe, and eyr, and tre, and every lake
> So ful was that unethe was there space
> For me to stonde
>
> (311–15)

—but with "tre" implying the wood that fuels fire and "every lake" denoting water, these lines actually name the four elements from which all created things are made: earth, air, fire, and water—the "omnia" harmonized at the Creation, to which the *Book of Wisdom* refers above.[21] After nine full stanzas, the second image explicitly names the three pairs of antitheses that attended Creation and the mathematical method that gives Nature her most significant power:

> "Nature, the vicaire of the almyghty Lord,
> That hot, cold, hevy, lyght, moyst, and dreye
> Hath knyt by evene noumbres of acord
>
> (379–81)

While "acord" apparently names the objective for which this knitting process is employed, the precise meaning of "evene noumbres of acord" (*Riv Ch* gloss: "equal, matching proportions") remains uncertain. The unmistakable mathematics lying at the heart of the phrase refers to Macrobius's explanation of the method by which Nature, God's vicar, bound together the four primary elements, harmonizing them with three pairs of opposites into each and every created thing (I.6.25).[22] He amplifies with words of much significance for Chaucer's poem: "The demarcation between water and air is called *Harmony*, that is, a *compatible and harmonious* union: for this is the interval which unites the lower with the upper, reconciling incongruent factors" (Stahl, 107, emphasis added).[23] By degrees the appropriateness of the *Somnium Scipionis* becomes obvious—not Cicero's *Somnium Scipionis*, but Macrobius's *Commentary* on Cicero's work—for in his *Commentary* Macrobius turns again and again to mathematics, the only availing method for human intelligence to understand the Creation and its divine harmony. Let us note as well that Dante, whose *Commedia* Chaucer knew well, makes abundant use of mathematics of both the numerological and the structural kind, as John J. Guzzardo (1987) has persuasively shown.[24]

The allusions in lines 305 and 381 to the mathematics of the Creation suggest Chaucer may have wanted a mathematical enrichment in his own act of creation. Suspecting that these one hundred stanzas and Chaucer's seven-line invention have more significance than a professional nod directed to Dante and Macrobius, we are naturally curious to know if Chaucer had a mind to advance further his controlling theme of harmony by also giving his poem and its three parts a Neoplatonic numerical harmony to match the literal instances of harmony in the *Somnium*, in Nature's garden, in the birds' act of choosing their mates, and in the celebratory roundel sung at the end of the poem. Such curiosity is abundantly rewarded if we focus on stanzas rather than lines.

Careful examination reveals that he did indeed insinuate into his poem an unannounced mathematical design, a rigorous, measured way of making the same point about harmony that his literal language achieves with elegance and charm. By apportioning a given number of stanzas to each of the three major parts of the poem, and to the subsections within each part, Chaucer enriches his poem with the four major proportions of mathematics: the geometric, the arithmetic, the harmonic, and the "divine proportion," as the golden section was called in the fourteenth century. An ill-advised emendation in the publication history of *Parliament of Fowls* has perhaps concealed this design from earlier analysis. All modern editions print the poem with one hundred stanzas, equaling the number of cantos in Dante's *Commedia*, but with 699 lines. Most modern editions follow Skeat's reconstruction of the roundel (680–92) sung near the end of the poem, which dropped one of the lines of the refrain to make the first seven lines of the roundel match Chaucer's seven-line rhyme royal stanzas. This distortion leaves the *Parliament* with 699 lines. Only Donaldson's edition reflects the form that Chaucer probably intended, 700 lines in 100 stanzas.[25]

The number seven can never be considered arbitrary in a medieval context. As mentioned earlier, the longest chapter in Macrobius's *Commentary*, I.vi, covering numbers, devotes most of its discussion to the number seven (Stahl, 99–117), the undoubted influence on Chaucer's invention of the seven-line rhyme royal. Among other things, Macrobius notes that "no other number has such a fruitful variety of powers" (Stahl, 100). Of particular pertinence for the musical harmony of the roundel with which Chaucer's poem concludes, the seven intervals within the eight notes of an octave comprised the "music of the spheres." Another observation by Macrobius confirms the importance that attached to the number seven as a harmonizing value:

> [A] plane cannot be firmly bound together except by the number three, nor a solid except by four. Hence the number seven possesses a dual power of binding, for both parts of it have inherited the primary links, three with one mean and four with two means. That is why Cicero, in another passage in *Scipio's Dream*, says concerning the number seven, *It is, one might almost say, the key to the universe.*[26]

The number ten was also considered highly significant, since it achieves a state of perfection by being the sum of all the numbers in the *tetractys*, the sacred tetrad, embracing 1, 2, 3, and 4, that "vied with the pentagon for veneration in Pythagorean number theory" (Boyer 1989, 54).

The poem's mathematics is not absolutely perfect; poetry is not, after all, made by God but by flawed humanity. In fact, to accommodate the perfection of the universe, Chaucer must make two minor concessions to the inadequacy of a whole-number system.[27] Nevertheless, the various narrative breaks in the poem are so clear, and so obviously grouped to fit almost to perfection the four most prominent proportions of mathematics, that to dismiss as unproven a prior mathematical design would impose a greater burden than to accept it. As the remainder of this discussion demonstrates, Chaucer chose mathematics as a leitmotif in harmony with his literal subject to produce a poem more exactingly designed and more rigorously executed than anything else he ever wrote.[28]

Numerical Design of the Whole

With the opening narrative well under way, and reader interest increased by Scipio Affrican's sudden appearance before the narrator himself, albeit in a dream, the poem surprisingly halts its progress for what seems to be a misplaced invocation to Venus Cytherea. Invocations normally occur at the beginning of a literary work, not at the seventeenth stanza, 113 lines into a work. Stranger still, the direction of the poem is broken when the narrator's interest abruptly shifts from the substance of his dream to the skills of a poet, as stanza 17 asks Venus, not for clear recollection lest he omit important details of the marvelous dream she sent him, but for the "myght to ryme, and endyte!" (119). In a similar way, later in the poem, stanza 70 (484–90) shifts suddenly from the narrator's dream to his reaction upon hearing the pleas of three tercel eagles for the affection of a formel on Nature's hand. Neither he nor anyone else, the narrator claims (484–86), has ever heard so gentle a pleading in love. Upon this declaration closure settles on the scene as "dounward went the sonne wonder faste" (490). Nothing intrinsic to the progress of the poem can be found in either stanza 17 or 70. A third stanza, equally remote from the poem's apparent subject, calls the same kind of attention to itself. Stanza 100 insists that we bring the dreamer/narrator back into our thoughts by noting that, after the birds finish singing their roundel, the noise they make at their departing awakens him, permitting him to resume his long-standing habit of reading books. That he reads avidly we learned in the second stanza and saw for ourselves in stanzas 4 through 13. The point scarcely needs restatement. Nor do we doubt he will continue to read voraciously. In addition, the ordinariness of this final stanza, like small talk exchanged with acquaintances, quite unlike the important information in the final fourteen lines of *Book of the Duchess*, coupled with the invocation to Venus at stanza 17 and the narrator's admiration for the royal eagles' pleas at the end of the day in stanza 70, makes us suspect that, if these stanzas contribute little to the poem's progress, they perhaps have something to do with its structural design.

Like the *Pearl* manuscript's decorated initial letters, whose placement

82 / Chapter 3

says nothing about the surface meaning of its individual poems but reveals a wonderfully complicated mathematical design crucial to the overall meaning of the whole manuscript,[29] these three stanzas in the *Parliament* may be devices to separate from each other the poem's major parts. The allotment of stanzas to these three parts, seems to disclose a geometric proportion, mathematics' most important proportion for the harmony of sublunar creation. As Donald W. Rowe explains, the Pythagorean theory that "four points are necessary to define a solid" is fully discussed in Plato: "It is not the number four but four numbers in geometrical progression which are necessary to create the world. The four elements must be united in the proper proportions" (1976, 34).[30]

The three parts of the poem, exclusive of its stanza markers at 17, 70, and 100, comprise respectively the sixteen stanzas from 1 through 16 (1–112), the fifty-two stanzas from 18 through 69 (120–483), and the twenty-nine stanzas from 71 through 99 (491–692). In addition to dividing the poem into parts by using stanzas as markers, Chaucer also gives each part a discrete subject almost with a heading of its own, as it were. Part I, "The Given," describes the God-given harmony of the created universe; part II, "The Challenge," of which Scipio Affrican speaks so movingly, concerns the difficult task human beings face to resist a wide variety of competing interests to reach their desired harmonious state; and part III, "The Achievement," presents an instance when this harmony is actually reached, though through a glass darkly, in the mating of the birds and the annual singing of a song. To compare the stanza count of these three parts, rearranged in ascending order, is to disclose an almost perfect geometric proportion, 16 : 29 : 52 (see figure 3.1).[31]

The ratio of the first two numbers, 16 ÷ 29, is 0.55172, while the ratio of the second two, 29 ÷ 52, is 0.55769. Though not identical, as in a perfect geometric proportion, these two ratios are extremely close, a scant .006 apart. To be sure, English mathematics in the fourteenth century did not yet possess Indian decimals, having at its disposal only the far more cumbersome unit fraction,[32] so Chaucer could not have worked to the exacting standards of modern mathematics. He may have begun by choosing a specific magnitude he wished to include—perhaps the 52 stanzas that now comprise part II, reflecting the weeks of a year as Rothschild (1984) suggests. Then, to illustrate in whole numbers the *phi* proportion he wanted for part III (discussed below), he may have sought a ratio that would produce a number less than

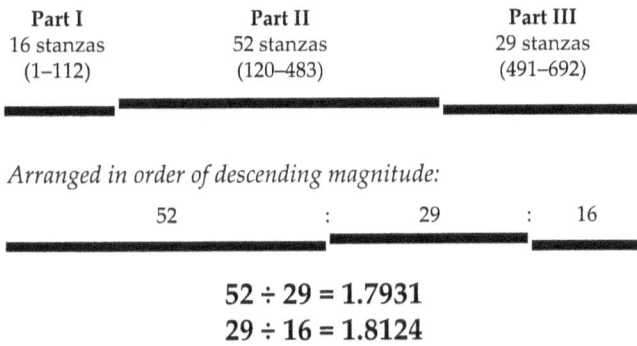

Figure 3.1. *PF* complete with parts 1–3 in geometric harmony

52. The ratio he would have chosen, if this speculation is accurate, was 5/9, producing a rounded 29 stanzas for part III. Applying this same ratio again yields a rounded 16. He would now have a geometric series of three magnitudes, 16, 29, and 52, totaling 97, which would leave him 3 stanzas to use as marks of separation or buffer stanzas to serve whatever need might arise. Unlike the 52 stanzas he needed for part II to give attention to the weeks of a year and to subdivide into a geometric proportion, and unlike the number of stanzas he needed to demonstrate the divine proportion in part III, he could have accepted any number of stanzas for part I, as long as they totaled 100 or fewer.

Chaucer's progression of three movements in his poem as "The Given," "The Challenge," and "The Achievement" reflects a logical assignment of ideas to parts. The scientific truths of his day, essentially those summarized in the *Somnium Scipionis* and the *Commentary* of Macrobius, could be given the sixteen-stanza smallest part of the poem, for they were already well known and widely accepted. Assembling the manifold challenges humanity faces daily would require the fifty-two-stanza largest part, as no single formula has yet been discovered for surviving these challenges. And a demonstration of achievement, while wholly imaginative and a culmination in any case, would naturally suit the twenty-nine stanzas of the remaining third part. Thus it is that the three parts of the *Parliament* are arranged as 16, 52, and 29, a geometric series in an aesthetically pleasing display, with two different mathematical demonstrations flanking the immediacy of the human condition, like bronze and silver on either side of the gold.

84 / Chapter 3

Numerical Design of the Parts

The ease with which the three parts of the poem snugly fit a geometric proportion encourages us to look further at the poem's individual parts—and to do so in the same mathematically proportionate way, for everyday mathematics in the fourteenth century, as today, had four well-known proportions. That the three parts of the *Parliament* plus its whole offer four magnitudes for a mathematically curious poet to think about should not go unnoticed. If the three parts of the whole poem, taken together, satisfy one of these proportions, the **geometric**, it is worth testing the parts individually to discover whether they too have not perhaps been designed to demonstrate the three remaining major proportions, the **arithmetic**, the **harmonic**, and the **golden proportion**.

Working through these parts, with only the mathematical tools available to the fourteenth century, not only reveals the mathematical design we suspected might be present, it nearly transports one to a peak in Darien. A simple arithmetic progression governs part I. The more complicated harmonic proportion governs part II. And the most highly revered proportion in all mathematics, the "divine proportion" or "golden section"—pertinent for the earthly world as well as the metaphysical realms that approach infinity and eternity—crowns part III where the poem reaches its highest achievement, the harmony of birds selecting mates who agree with their selection, and their singing a roundel. The figures illustrating these proportions in the remainder of this chapter show the first stanza at the top, last stanza at the bottom, stanza numbers to the left, followed by a few words to identify each stanza, and the section sizes marked off to the right. Note, however, that stanza 17 is included in part I, as shown in figure 3.2, to let this part achieve an arithmetic series.[33]

Assuming the inclusion of stanza 17, part I has three sections thematically set off from each other, the most obvious being the "Chapitres sevene" (32), the seven-stanza précis from 6 through 12 (36–84), that the narrator says he found in the *Somnium Scipionis*. Cicero actually wrote nine chapters, not seven. That Chaucer calls Cicero's nine chapters "Chapitres sevene" tends to confirm a mathematical plan that calls attention to the number seven. This clearly differentiated group of seven rests within a larger, equally distinct group of twelve stanzas describing the whole reading session that occupied the narrator, he says, on a particular evening. Stanzas 5 through 16 (29–112)

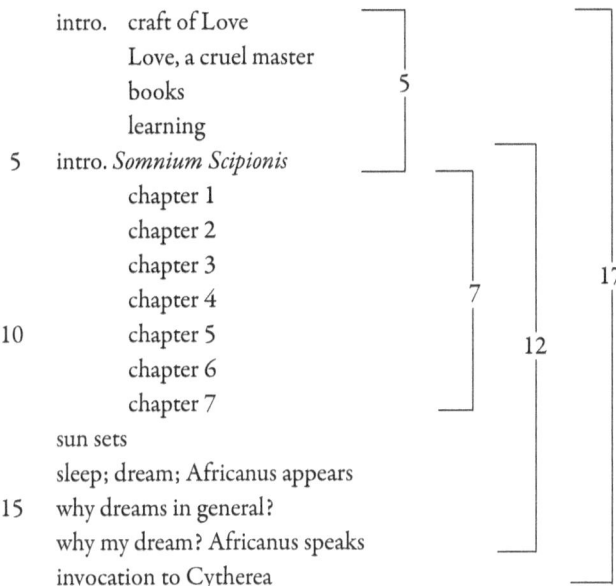

7 + 5 = 12; 12 + 5 = 17

Figure 3.2. *PF* part 1 in arithmetic harmony

include the single stanza announcing the book's title, the seven-stanza précis, and the four stanzas giving the narrator's reaction to his reading. In turn, this group of twelve stanzas nestles within the seventeen initial stanzas (1–119) that precede the narrator's uninterrupted retelling of the dream he experienced.

The stanza counts of the sections shown in figure 3.2, arranged in ascending order, reveal an arithmetic progression in part I. The smallest group of five stanzas announces the constant increment by which the group of seven expands to twelve and this twelve to seventeen. In the simple arithmetic series 7 : 12 : 17, each magnitude exceeds its predecessor by this fixed amount of five stanzas.[34] The arrangement of part I's three sections, where the narrator's twelve-stanza rumination on the *Somnium* embraces the seven-stanza summary of Cicero's *Somnium*, while the seventeen stanzas of the narrator's entire pre-dreaming episode envelop the other two sections, effects a kind of simultaneity that does not appear again in the sequential arrangement of sections in parts II and III.

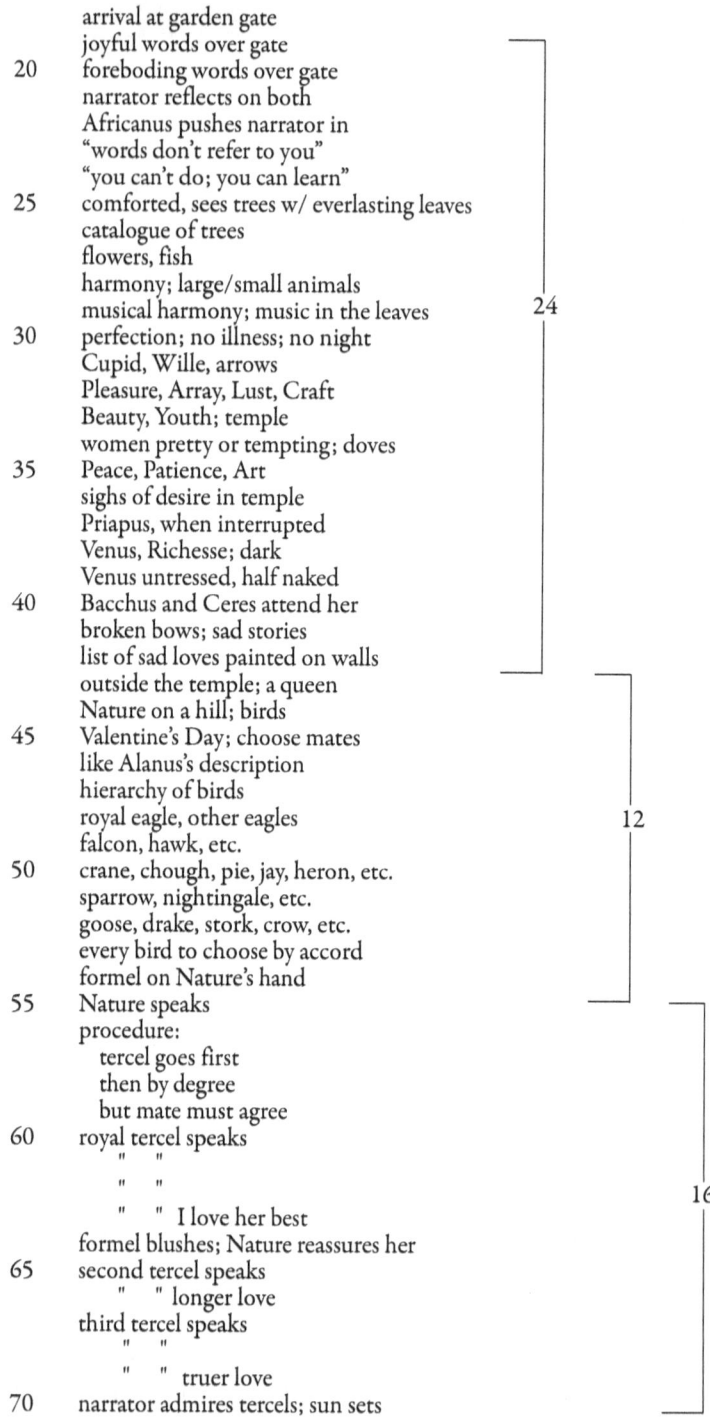

```
          arrival at garden gate
          joyful words over gate                    ⎤
   20     foreboding words over gate                |
          narrator reflects on both                  |
          Africanus pushes narrator in               |
          "words don't refer to you"                 |
          "you can't do; you can learn"              |
   25     comforted, sees trees w/ everlasting leaves|
          catalogue of trees                         |
          flowers, fish                              |
          harmony; large/small animals               |
          musical harmony; music in the leaves   24  |
   30     perfection; no illness; no night           |
          Cupid, Wille, arrows                       |
          Pleasure, Array, Lust, Craft               |
          Beauty, Youth; temple                      |
          women pretty or tempting; doves            |
   35     Peace, Patience, Art                       |
          sighs of desire in temple                  |
          Priapus, when interrupted                  |
          Venus, Richesse; dark                      |
          Venus untressed, half naked                |
   40     Bacchus and Ceres attend her               |
          broken bows; sad stories                   |
          list of sad loves painted on walls        ⎦
          outside the temple; a queen               ⎤
          Nature on a hill; birds                    |
   45     Valentine's Day; choose mates              |
          like Alanus's description                  |
          hierarchy of birds                         |
          royal eagle, other eagles              12  |
          falcon, hawk, etc.                         |
   50     crane, chough, pie, jay, heron, etc.       |
          sparrow, nightingale, etc.                 |
          goose, drake, stork, crow, etc.            |
          every bird to choose by accord             |
          formel on Nature's hand                   ⎦
   55     Nature speaks                             ⎤
          procedure:                                 |
             tercel goes first                       |
             then by degree                          |
             but mate must agree                     |
   60     royal tercel speaks                        |
             "    "                                  |
             "    "                              16  |
             "    "  I love her best                 |
          formel blushes; Nature reassures her       |
   65     second tercel speaks                       |
             "    "  longer love                     |
          third tercel speaks                        |
             "    "                                  |
             "    "  truer love                      |
   70     narrator admires tercels; sun sets        ⎦
```

Figure 3.3. *PF* part 2 in harmonic proportion

The fifty-two-stanza part II of the poem, from 19 through 70 (127–490), is displayed in figure 3.3 to show the thematic divisions that begin as soon as "Affrican" brings the dreamer to the outside of a garden where significant activity will begin.

This middle part of the poem has a very complicated design that might better be understood by first looking at its two clearest sections—the twelve stanzas 43 through 54 that greet the narrator when he emerges from Venus's allegorical temple, and the sixteen stanzas 55 through 70 that commence the business of the parliament. The twelve-stanza section sets the stage: Nature, a queen in all her beauty, though temporarily inactive, obviously presides. The attending birds are catalogued by species, concluding with a lone "formel egle" (373) perched on the hand of Nature, as the annual selection of mates is about to begin. The final sixteen stanzas of part II are taken up entirely by Nature's announcement of rules—these are her first words in the poem—and the proposals crafted by three royal tercels eager to win the formel as a mate. As there can be no doubt that the poem clearly sets these two sections apart from other matters, it remains to discover Chaucer's rationale for the opening lines of part II.

The preclusive alternatives announced by the garden gate in stanzas 19 and 20 (127–40) certainly govern in some way what will follow, yet it is difficult to see what parts of these following lines flow from which inscription. The narrator may be exempted from this dilemma, of course, for Scipio Africanus recognizes an observer/reporter of Love's games when he sees one, as stanza 24 (162–68) acknowledges. The eighteen stanzas that follow, however, present a puzzle. The six stanzas 25 through 30, despite a note of artificiality, seem to offer an ideal of harmony, perhaps related to the "blysful place" mentioned twice by Africanus (48, 83) and the "welle of grace" where "grene and lusty May shal evere endure" (129–30) noted in gold on the garden gate. But the next twelve, 31 through 42 (211–94), defy categorizing. Some of the lines seem to invite condemnation, but only because we are accustomed to reading medieval authors who condemn the activity Venus's presence implies. Her description, for example, implying nothing sordid, affirms a sensual inclination as much a part of "grene and lusty May" as anything else in the entire poem:

> Hyre gilte heres with a golden thred
> Ibounden were, untressed as she lay,
> And naked from the brest unto the hed

Men myghte hire sen; and, sothly for to say,
The remenaunt was wel kevered to my pay,
Ryght with a subtyl coverchef of Valence —
Ther was no thikkere cloth of no defense.

(267–73)

The dream's allegorical garden occupies the whole of stanzas 19 through 69 (127–483), where the astonishing variety of human love stretches before us. "Men" are literally noted in both the golden and the black inscriptions above the gate (127, 134). Scipio places the narrator, too, in the context of human love, though guessing he has "lost [his] tast" for that irresistible activity (155–66). Each species of tree within the garden supplies a human need (176–82), while flowers, birdsong, and musical instruments enhance human life (183–203). If these stanzas answer the golden inscription above the gate, those immediately following allude to the artistic depictions of the opposite, the sorrowful stories foretold by the gate's dark inscription (211–94).

At the beginning of part II, the twenty-four stanzas 19 through 42 (127–294) divide neatly into two twelve-stanza halves. Stanzas 19 through 30 get the narrator into the garden (127–70) and describe the beauty and energy that come from the many manifestations of natural harmony (171–210). Pleasant details imply vitality, as in lines 173–203, suggesting a natural harmony present through all time, like the harmony of birdsong (190–91) and the accord of musical instruments (197–203). For the most part, artificiality appears to rule: temperatures do not fluctuate (204–5); no one becomes ill or grows old (207); and the joy that reigns everywhere is simply a gift given, part of the harmony of Creation.

The next twelve stanzas, 31 through 42 (211–94), note at first the unpleasantness that harmony's opposite produces, the disharmony that human activity too often reaps. Despite allusions to activity, static display characterizes these stanzas, not unlike the artificial wood where the dreamer meets the man in black in the *Book of the Duchess*. Cupide may forge and file his arrows, while his daughter Wille tempers their heads, but their allegorical names alone take all vitality from the scene. Following the opening stanza of this second section of part II, an allegorical parade passes by. Yet figures like Plesaunce, Aray, Lust, Craft, and Foolhardynesse, hinting of unrelieved hedonism, are not the only figures the narrator sees. They alternate with figures like Curteysie and Gentilesse. The stanzas, too, seem to alternate hedonism with activity that, if not entirely innocent, shows only the normal inclinations of natural creatures:

> Aboute the temple daunsedyn alwey
> Women inowe, of whiche some ther weere
> Fayre of hemself, and some of hem were gay;
> In kertels, al dishevele, wente they there:
> That was here offyce alwey, yer by yeere.
> And on the temple, of dowves white and fayre
> Saw I syttynge many an hundred peyre.
>
> (232–38)

Whereas the first eighteen stanzas of part II present in an abstract way potential harmony as well as the frivolous, vain and hurtful acts that suggest its opposite, the subsequent six stanzas 37 through 42 (253–94) give these abstractions a palpable reality. An embarrassed Priapus, a seductive Venus, and a dozen others from actual stories of antiquity give immediacy to the choices humans must make as they live their natural lives. In one respect they represent humanity's moral dilemmas, foreshadowed by the narrator's simile of himself as "betwixen adamauntes two" (148), and in another they concretize the alternatives announced over the gate at the entrance to the garden.

The second section of part II, stanzas 43 through 54 (295–378), a dramatic departure from the first, begins unmistakably when the narrator "was come ayeyn unto the place / That I of spak, that was so sote and grene" (295–96). He leaves the temple of Venus for the garden he visited earlier, where now the bustle of nature crowds the scene with the sounds and acts of living. Whereas the "goddesse Nature" (303) had scarcely been noticed earlier, now she occupies the place of prominence: "For this was on Seynt Valentynes day, / Whan every foul cometh there to chese his make" (309–10). As many species of bird as were named earlier congregate in Nature's garden, but now energy courses through this group of lively creatures, urging them to get on with what their nature enjoins them to do. Unlike the statuesque displays in and around the temple of Venus, here the assembled birds are under the rule of Nature, willing "To take hire dom and yeve hire audyence" (308).

When the scene makes another dramatic shift to introduce Nature's first speech at stanza 55, it signals the beginning of the third section of part II. This all-powerful queen, the "vicaire of the almyghty Lord" (379), explains

90 / Chapter 3

the day's procedures within the terms of her immutable laws of generation (380–81). The orderliness for which Lady Nature may have hoped, when she explained the single most important rule governing the day, that the mate chosen must agree to be selected (409; cf. 371), is not yet to be. The royal tercels, being "above [all others] in degre" (394), begin the process of selection, yet offer proposals that contradict the entire purpose of the parliament. Far from being conventional proposals of marriage, these speeches flatly state the merit of the proposer, each tercel protesting his greater entitlement to the formel than his two rivals. At the conclusion of these speeches, the narrator avers that neither he in his entire lifetime nor any other man at any time has ever before heard such "gentil" (485) pleas. Obviously incapable of distinguishing the claims of merit from merit itself, as he expresses his deep admiration for the eagles who have just fallen silent, the narrator might have added "lengthy" to "gentil," for these speeches have lasted the entire day. Upon completion of their unctuous presentations and the narrator's declaration of awe, part II comes to a close as the sun sets at the end of the long day (490).

With part II having begun thematically at stanza 19 with the first of two inscriptions above the gate and concluded at the end of stanza 70 with the setting of the sun (490), the two strong thematic shifts, between stanzas 42 and 43 where the narrator emerges from Venus's temple and again between stanzas 54 and 55 where Lady Nature takes charge, reveal three clearly defined sections: the twenty-four stanzas from 19 through 42, the twelve stanzas from 43 through 54 and the sixteen stanzas from 55 through 70. These magnitudes, arranged as before in ascending order, disclose a perfect harmonic proportion, 12 : 16 : 24.

A brief explanation of harmonic proportion may be helpful for those unfamiliar with it. Though often involving a series of more than three members, a harmonic string is usually represented by three numbers, a, b, and c, of ascending magnitude. A harmonic proportion is satisfied, to paraphrase Porphyry, if the percentage of a by which b exceeds a is the same as the percentage of c by which c exceeds b (Heath 1921, 1: 85). Euclid has a different and more accessible way of expressing this proportion. Among the ten proportions scattered through his *Elements* and conveniently brought together in one place by Nicomachus of Gerasa, who was likewise well known in the fourteenth century, a harmonic proportion appears third and satisfies the following equation, where $c > b$ and $b > a$:

$$\frac{b-a}{c-b} = \frac{a}{c}$$

Two simple examples of the harmonic proportion $a : b : c$ are 3 : 4 : 6 and 2 : 3 : 6, easily proved by testing them against Euclid's equation. These proportions also satisfy Porphyry's definition. In the first example, the middle term 4 exceeds the first term 3 by one-third of 3, while the third term 6 exceeds the middle term 4 by the same one-third of 6. Similarly in the second example, 3 exceeds 2 by one-half of 2, while 6 exceeds 3 by one-half of 6.

The three sections of part II in Chaucer's *Parliament* satisfy a harmonic proportion according to Porphyry's formulation—16 exceeds 12 by one-third of 12, and 24 exceeds 16 by one-third of 24—and according to Euclid's. In addition, as the harmonic string 12 : 16 : 24 is a multiple of 3 : 4 : 6, it also expresses the three most satisfying musical intervals, a fourth (indicated as the ratio 4 : 3, a reduction of 16 : 12), a fifth (indicated as 3 : 2, a reduction of 24 : 16), and an octave (indicated as 2 : 1, a reduction of 24 : 12), more precisely an inner fourth, an inner fifth, and an outer octave (Heath 1921, 1: 75–76).

Stanza 71 (491–97) obviously marks the beginning of an entirely different part of the poem. At the end of stanza 69 (483), three tercels of royal rank conclude their overly elegant speeches, each alleging that his claim upon the formel *must* be accepted, followed by the narrator's verbal applause in stanza 70. At this precise moment, at line 491, the lesser birds burst out in universal complaint, "Have don, . . . Com of! . . . Whan shal youre cursede pletynge have an ende?" (492–95). Part III of the *Parliament* now begins (see figure 3.4).

This final major division of the *Parliament*, stanzas 71 through 99 (491–692), though covering almost a third of the poem, occupies little time in the parliament itself. Echoing the many confrontations between nature and her contradictions, seen earlier in the poem's first two stanzas, in the inscriptions above the garden gate, and in the positive and negative responses to harmony's invitation in the garden and temple, this part too has its preclusive actions. The lesser birds lose their composure at the interminable pleadings of the tercel eagles and threaten a mêlée of epithet and vilification, a crescendo of increasing impatience leading to what could easily become a brawl.[35] Only Nature's assertion of authority prevents disaster: "Now pes . . . I comaunde

92 / Chapter 3

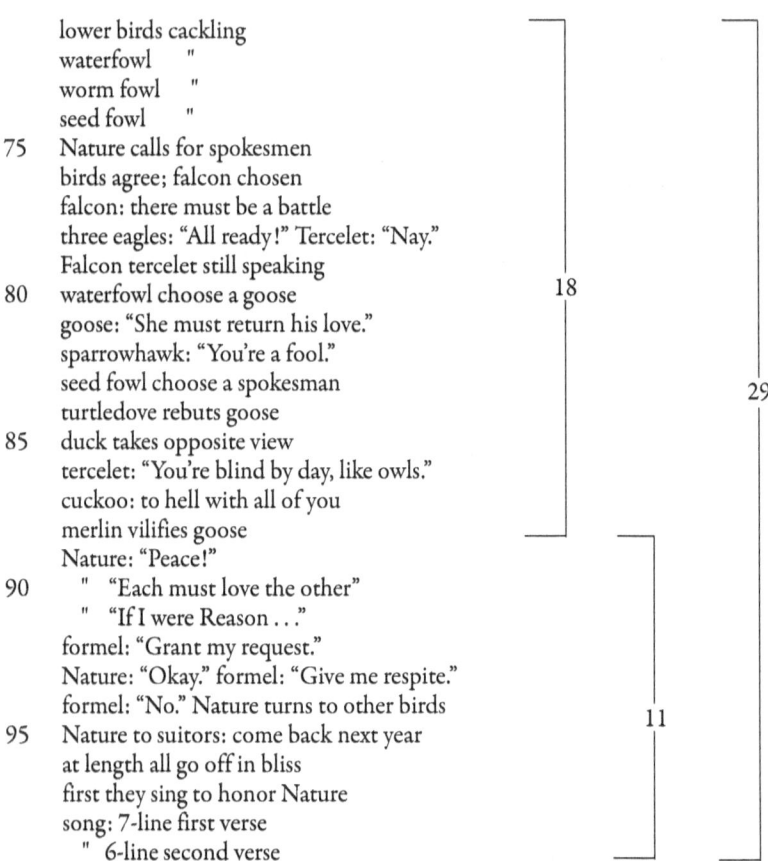

```
            lower birds cackling
            waterfowl      "
            worm fowl      "
            seed fowl      "
     75     Nature calls for spokesmen
            birds agree; falcon chosen
            falcon: there must be a battle
            three eagles: "All ready!" Tercelet: "Nay."
            Falcon tercelet still speaking
     80     waterfowl choose a goose
            goose: "She must return his love."
            sparrowhawk: "You're a fool."
            seed fowl choose a spokesman
            turtledove rebuts goose
     85     duck takes opposite view
            tercelet: "You're blind by day, like owls."
            cuckoo: to hell with all of you
            merlin vilifies goose
            Nature: "Peace!"
     90       "  "Each must love the other"
              "  "If I were Reason . . ."
            formel: "Grant my request."
            Nature: "Okay." formel: "Give me respite."
            formel: "No." Nature turns to other birds
     95     Nature to suitors: come back next year
            at length all go off in bliss
            first they sing to honor Nature
            song: 7-line first verse
              "  6-line second verse
```

Figure 3.4. *PF* part 3 in the golden proportion

heer!" (617). The point at which Nature imposes order on the increasing cacophony and approaching violence is well chosen. For the break between stanzas 88 and 89 is the golden cut of this twenty-nine-stanza part III of the poem, the division that produces the most celebrated of the four major proportions of ancient, medieval, and Renaissance mathematics, the divine proportion. Abundant evidence testifies to a full understanding of this proportion from the ancients to the present day, although we must rely on the mathematicians who wrote at least a century after Chaucer for a critical discussion of the golden proportion's significance.[36]

The divine proportion was given its name and accorded preeminence because, as Luca Pacioli explained in his 1509 dissertation (for which Leonardo da Vinci contributed sketches and the preface), it shares with God four principal attributes: it is a unity, it is a trinity, it is inexpressible ("occult and secret"), and it is omnipresent and unchangeable.[37] Named *phi* by mathematicians in the early twentieth century and known popularly as "the golden section" after Kepler, the divine proportion was described in another passage by Kepler which expands Pacioli's four attributes and explains the proportion's enormous appeal:

> I believe that this [divine] proportion served as idea to the Creator when He introduced the creation of likeness out of likeness, which also continues indefinitely. I see the number five [from which the divine proportion is derived] in almost all blossoms which lead the way for a fruit, that is, for creation, and which exist, not for their own sake, but for that of the fruit to follow.[38]

This proportion convinced ancient mathematicians of the harmony among all parts of the created universe. Indeed, the modern era is becoming increasingly aware of the countless places where the divine proportion appears in a variety of botanical, biological, and natural forms—in leaves on plants, the shell growths of several crustaceans, the five points of a starfish, the flight paths of diving eagles, the swirls surrounding hurricanes and galaxies, the work of numerous artists as varied as Leonardo da Vinci and Salvador Dalí, and in the Fifth Platonic Solid, the dodecahedron, which the ancients revered as the symbol of the universe.[39] It can be readily seen that an understanding of the principle that *phi* represents offers enormous appeal to a poet who wishes symbolically to convey harmony with increasingly greater and more complex parts of the universe, even to the threshold of infinity.

Having begun with an outburst of birds (491) who object to the interminable boasts of three royal eagles, part III extends until the completion of the roundel sung at the end of the bird parliament (692). It cannot be coincidental that the break between the end of stanza 88, where the name-calling and the charges of gluttony and murder threaten bloodshed (616), and the beginning of stanza 89, when Lady Nature silences the near riot (617), is almost precisely the golden cut of part III. The two segments into which part III is divided have 18 and 11 stanzas, the larger extending from stanza 71 through stanza 88 (491–616), the shorter from 89 through 99 (617–92). The whole of part III, with 29 stanzas broken into segments of 18 and 11, of-

94 / Chapter 3

fers the proportion 11 : 18 : 29, which comes strikingly close to satisfying the equation $a : b = b : c$, confirming this nearly perfect divine proportion. The ratio on the left falls short of *phi* (1.61803 . . .) by just 0.00692, while the one on the right exceeds *phi* by 0.01833:

$$29 : 18 \cong 18 : 11$$
$$\text{or}$$
$$1.61111 \cong 1.63636$$

These figures are generated from stanza totals. Their ratios would not be the same if one were to calculate with the number of lines, for most modern editions follow Skeat's nineteenth-century lead and drop a line from stanza 98, leaving the poem with a total of 699 lines, not 700 as Chaucer probably intended. Chaucer's design, then, may have been closer to *phi* than the figures produced from the actual line totals of most modern editions. Had we used line totals instead of stanzas, the preceding proportion would have looked like this:

$$202 : 126 \cong 126 : 76$$
$$\text{or}$$
$$1.60317 \cong 1.65789$$

Here both ratios are now farther from *phi* than they were when calculated with stanzas. As we can see, a single dropped line makes a great difference—as mathematicians understand "great." Finding in Chaucer a lesser mathematical error than in modern editions of his work may not persuade us that he wanted the roundel to appear as we have suggested, or that the whole poem should have 700 lines, thereby coming as close to *phi* as possible, but it certainly points in this direction.

Conclusion

Order is restored to Lady Nature's parliament, the formel gracefully declines to make a choice among her three suitors, and, as was ordered much earlier, "To every foul Nature yaf his make / By evene acord" (667–68). A picked group of choristers sings a roundel, and both the meeting of birds and the *Parliament of Fowls* come to a harmonious close.

With the completion of his stunning *Parliament of Fowls*, Chaucer places himself among the ancients. If the subject he explores in *Troilus and Criseyde*, a poem composed at about the same time as the *Parliament*, admits him to a literary pantheon with "Ovide, Omer, Lucan, and Stace" (*T&C*

V.1792), the numerical methodology he follows in the *Parliament* earns for him a place at Virgil's and Dante's table. His purpose differs somewhat from that of Plato and Cicero, who were eager to argue for the immortality of the soul, a debate unnecessary in Chaucer's fourteenth-century England when few doubted the Christian belief in an afterlife. Yet it is not accurate to say he has no interest in representing the immortality of the soul, a topos he subtly insinuates in a variety of ways in the *Book of the Duchess*. By using an Ovidian story that makes explicit Ceyx's and Alcione's life after death as seabirds; by actually showing Ceyx apparently alive after a death the pseudo-Ceyx claims he has just experienced; by tolling bells at the end of that poem—by these and a number of other details, Chaucer very much introduces into his poem the matter of immortality. His *Troilus*, too, spirits Troilus to the eighth sphere, certainly a foreshadowing of the Christian heaven. Chaucer's immediate purpose in the *Parliament*, while not negating an afterlife, seems rather to recapture an ancient method of construction that emphasizes the coherence and harmony of the created universe, a method that had slipped from the collective memory of all but the very learned in the Middle Ages. Thus he designs the *Parliament* as if he were a Virgil composing *Georgics I*, or a Dante planning certain sections of the *Commedia*.[40]

Virgil places *Georgics I* in the context of a calendar. So too Spenser in creating his *Epithalamion*, a tribute to Chaucer written almost two hundred years after Chaucer's death.[41] But Chaucer's *Parliament* itself can likewise be called a marriage poem, if we accept that its dream progresses toward a kind of marriage in the choosing of mates, and if the birds who choose them, or at least some of them, represent human beings.[42] Thus we may speculate that *epithalamia* and calendars were traditionally linked in Chaucer's day. If the *Parliament* is considered such a calendar poem, not as an alternative to the mathematical arguments presented here but in addition to them, its design astonishes us yet further. No adjustment whatever is needed to accommodate a calendar to the findings advanced above. The twelve months and fifty-two weeks of a year, the seven days of a week, the twenty-four hours of a day, are all prominently in place.[43] In view of the remarkable numerical design advanced here, it seems more than likely that Chaucer's *Parliament of Fowls* was designed from the beginning to be both a spatial and a temporal representation of the wondrous harmony of the created world.[44]

4

House of Fame

The *House of Fame* may be the earliest and best example in English of a poem that went from the hand of the author directly into the hands of critics, almost completely bypassing its audience. A few decades after its completion, in a critical comment remarkable for both its insight and its misdirection, Lydgate would refer to the poem as "Dante in ynglissh."[1] We do not know if Lydgate's remark was generally accepted, or if he enjoyed no greater success in persuading his contemporaries than modern critics have in persuading theirs, but one of the earliest modern students of the poem challenged this judgment with a confident assertion of permanence that his own words ironically undercut. "The realization that the *Hous of Fame* was influenced by the *Divine Comedy*," wrote Bronson in 1934, "and was developed out of the attempt to make the former the complete counterpart of the latter . . . is now . . . permanently discredited" (173). This noble defense of the poem deals its own blow to critical permanence by implying a break in the hermeneutic circle of artistic integrity and organic unity:

> we owe it to Chaucer to respect the artistic integrity of his poem. . . . any acceptable interpretation must adhere to those probabilities which arise immediately from the presumption of [*Fame*'s] organic unity. . . . There is something . . . highly suspicious about the poem's breaking off just at the crucial point of the narrative. (178, 190)

As these quotations from earlier eras make clear, a researcher examining the literature on the *House of Fame* discovers a fascinating variety of critical attitudes—not regarding the poem, but regarding each other. If Bronson seems indecisive, Clemen is positively obsequious, yet he unwittingly indicts this most modern of the medievals:

> if we were to require organic unity from a literary work of art and to demand that all its constituent parts shall be directed towards one central subject, we would be thinking along the lines of a modern conception

of poetry; and we are not entitled to do this without question in the case of a medieval poem. (1964, 72)

These opposing attitudes, by no means unique, in fact characterize most of the discussions of what have come to be the two points critics worry over the most, unity and topicality. While critical arguments asserting the poem's aesthetic or philosophical unity are as numerous as those denying it,[2] one trusts that this long and, to date, unresolved debate will one day settle on a satisfactory interpretation. The question of the poem's topicality poses other problems. Since the poem calls attention in its last line to "A man of gret auctorite" (2158) in a corner of the House of Rumor where "men of love-tydynges tolde" (2143), yet breaks off before this unnamed man recites his contribution to these tidings, numerous critics have speculated about what the poem's "missing tidings" might have been. Each of these discussions hypothesizes about the occasion that prompted Chaucer to write the poem. Others insist that, with the historical occasion lost forever, we should use what we do have as a means of inferring the *poetic* nature of the missing conclusion.

One is not so much struck by the overwhelming implausibility of these theories, all mutually exclusive, as by their overwhelming plausibility. That the poem might have been (among other things) a veiled rebuke to John of Gaunt for appearing in public with his mistress Katherine Swynford in the summer of 1378, as F. C. Riedel proposed back in 1928, makes eminently good sense. The missing conclusion could certainly have been this choice bit of gossip. Of course, it seems just as reasonable to accept Larry Benson's 1986 suggestion that the poem was originally prepared to celebrate the announcement of betrothal between Richard II and Caterina Visconti, but had to be shortened to the point in the poem just before these tidings are announced because a man named Nicolò, nuncio to Cardinal Pileo, arrived in England from Ravenna a day or two before December 10, bringing the sad news that the marriage would not take place. On the other hand, the poem could well have been intended as a longish introduction for a cycle of tales like the *Legend of Good Women*, or the *Canterbury Tales*, or some other group now lost or never written.[3] The poem cannot be all of these things, though sheer critical ingenuity partly persuades one that it is. Not all attempts are equally successful. The argument that the poem alludes to events in the year 1372 because that was a year heavy with births in the Gaunt ménage, and "the corseynt Leonard" (117) was thought to help pregnant women through confinement (Williams 1965, 120), has not had many takers. Unless new historical evidence is uncovered, and perhaps even in light of such evidence, all these theories about the poem's topicality remain irrelevant to literary criticism.

The present chapter—yet another attempt to find unity in the *House of Fame*—differs from the theories noted above by remaining within the lines of Chaucer's poetry, obtaining leads for interpretation from other works in his canon and from what has already been advanced in earlier chapters of this book. This comparative approach lets us see *House of Fame* as a highly unified poem, occupying a clear position in Chaucer's developing attitudes toward poetry, and pointing to an authority's tidings that are not "missing" but standing preeminently where they have always been—elsewhere in the Chaucerian canon, under the title *Troilus and Criseyde*.

Let us note initially the many general similarities between the *House of Fame* and the two poems already studied. All three poems are dream visions, containing a somewhat detailed account of the narrator before sleep, and a much more thorough account of the dream he experiences during sleep. Like the *Book of the Duchess* and the *Parliament of Fowls*, the *House of Fame* seems very much involved with the question of love: book I mainly emphasizes the Dido-Aeneas story (239–382), in particular the sorrow love can cause; book II, where a golden eagle carries the narrator away from a desert surrounding the glass temple of Venus, covers the purpose of the journey, to give the narrator tidings of love's folk (612–99); and book III, having shown Fame granting fine reputations to some of the supplicants eager to be known as great lovers, concludes with a rush toward a corner of the House of Rumor where love tidings are being exchanged. The *House of Fame* even uses a metaphor that appears in the *Parliament of Fowls*, the thought that Love repays people for their employment (*PF* 9; *HF* 619, 670). Finally, the narrators in all three poems follow parallel paths. Each narrator, though initially a passive observer, occupies a central position at the beginning of his story, vaguely referring to an important problem or question he has been pondering. Then he retreats to near obscurity, even before the dream begins in the *Duchess* and *Fowls* and soon after it begins in *Fame*. At length he returns, if not to his prominence in the opening lines, at least to an active presence as a participant rather than an observer. (These parallels may be seen in schematic form in appendix A.)

Taking guidance from this pattern of parallels in the three narrators' presence enables us to focus on more significant parallels among the poems and not be misled by merely superficial similarities. For example, the long account of Dido and Aeneas in the *House of Fame* may wrongly encourage readers to limit this Virgilian episode's correspondence to only the Ceyx-Alcione story in the *Duchess* and to the *Dream of Scipio* in the *Parliament*. All three are, after all, drawn from the literature with which Chaucer was familiar and seem to offer some kind of starting point for the rest of the narrative. But if the narrator's participation in the events of the poem is kept in mind, the Dido-Aeneas episode corresponds not only to the Ceyx-Alcione episode of the *Duchess* but also to that poem's scene in the sleeping chamber where the narrator remains in a passive state. For the *Parliament*, however, the same principle shows the Dido-Aeneas episode corresponding only to the account of the narrator's reading of Macrobius, for he participates actively in the transition to Venus's garden. The point has more significance than may first appear, for it enables us to see structural correspondences among these poems at virtually every scene. Thus the entire book II of *Fame* performs the same function as the guidance of Affrican in the *Parliament*, as well as the hunting call of Octovyen and the chase after a little whelp in the *Duchess*. Similarly, the division between the Houses of Fame and Rumor corresponds to the *Duchess*'s division between the man in black and the dreamer, and to the *Parliament*'s division between the temple of Venus with its museumlike surroundings and the annual gathering of the birds.

More important than a similarity of structure, *Duchess*, *Fowls* and *Fame* have the same "categories of matter," a phrase used here to distinguish a level of meaning from the specific meaning each individual level may yield. The most noticeable of these is a practical or personal stance assumed by a narrator who reflects the poet himself, but has been softened to a comic, self-effacing presence. Lightly concealed behind this façade, a speculative or, perhaps more accurately, a philosophic concern shapes each poem's progress, though little may be inferred from this orientation, for no aperçu rises in sharply chiseled lines. Rather, a sustained series of thoughts, different from one poem to the next, intrudes upon the narrator to worry his poem. Finally, at what may be considered each poem's most profound level, Chaucer addresses the art of poetry. Again, no systematic *ars* emerges, though consistent beliefs appear again and again.

The immediate personal concern of the *Book of the Duchess* begins with the description of a man who suffers from a sleeplessness he eventually overcomes with the delightful experience of an eventful dream. As we saw in chapter 2, all of this thinly veils in metaphor the poet-narrator's struggle to create a eulogy on the death of his hoped-for patron's wife, Blanche of Lancaster. As a philosophic speculation, the poem presents love as a source of inspiration for the poet and, when unavailable, the cause of his melancholia, while the painful attempt to describe these feelings enables the grieving survivor to live through his suffering. As well, the poem's promise of eternal life provides the most effective anodyne. Addressing its artistic meaning—that is, representing the narrator as one who makes things beautiful through language—the *Duchess* uses dream as a surrogate for poem, as this narrator seeks inspiration. It also represents two contrasting kinds of poetic beauty, a stylized form in the manner of a number of the poem's sources, and a form that creates the natural behavior of believable people.

The *Parliament of Fowls*, developing its meaning in almost exactly the same way, records the felt life of its narrator's thinking, reading, and dreaming. It may also allude to the political moves surrounding a particular Valentine's Day, although present scholarship has yet to propose a compelling scenario.[4] Considered philosophically, the poem is both a theoretical discussion of harmony and disharmony in nature, supported by a mathematical demonstration of harmony, and a vivid representation of this harmony from the macrocosmic perspective of the heavens and the microcosmic view of an annual gathering of birds. The poem's discussion of art includes much that we saw in the *Duchess*: an inspirational dream, or metaphor actually, for the creation of poetry, while the retelling of this dream is the poem itself, presenting in part a debate between two antithetical styles, the artificial and the natural.

The same categories of matter we see in *Duchess* and *Fowls* appear as well in *Fame*. If among its three levels of meaning the *Book of the Duchess* develops most fully the practical circumstances of a poet's life in a climate of patronage, while the *Parliament* avers universal harmony as endless "mater of to wryte"—if only its narrator had the "connyng for t'endite" (*PF* 167–68)—*Fame* has these or closely related focal points as well. In addition, *Fame* plays out a sustained debate on the relation between poetry and truth, in particular challenging Dante's belief that poets reveal truth, a challenge with which Helen Cooper agrees, though she finds *Fame* the only "poem of Chaucer's that sets out his own poetic theory" (1999, 52), in contrast to much that is argued here. The narrator in *Fame*, well foreshadowed in both struggling poets of the *Duchess*, argues charmingly for some of the most fundamental truths of literary art, including an author's "refus[al] to defer authority beyond the imagination of the individual writer" (Cooper, 55). This third dream vision, though simultaneously more direct and more profound than the earlier two, gives its most concentrated attention to literary art, for which the narrator's symbolic flight in the talons of a golden eagle has a central function. As a practical matter, this flight accounts for the source of the material intended for the poem's "missing" tidings, while also alleging that caprice has as much (or more) to do with creating fame as history itself does. Amidst this whimsy, the poem carries "Geffrey" the narrator (729) to a realm that represents the professional activity to which Geoffrey the author was entirely dedicated, the creation of poetry. The discussion of fame, showing both deserved and undeserved reputations, whether favorable or not, and utterly capricious in either case, demonstrates that poetry depends neither on historical truth nor on the inspiration of a lady or a deity, but on the internal integrity of the story the poet chooses to tell.[5] Poetry has its own truth. Chaucer's poem thus symbolically flees the traditional view of poetry as the transmission of "historical" material, which may be more faithful to an earlier fiction than to truth, to arrive at a new environment, not of facts variously reported but of feelings sensitively realized. Symbolic flight brings Geffrey to the only legitimate workshop ever known to practicing poets—the constantly active mind of the creative artist, realized later as the House of Rumor, and filled with imaginative observations of an infinite number of people and ideas.

The keys to the *House of Fame*, therefore, are to be sought on three levels. Dido noted in a different context that a man serves three mistresses:

of oon he wolde have fame
In magnyfyinge of hys name;
Another for frendshippe, seyth he;
And yet ther shal the thridde be

That shal be take for delyt,
Loo, or for synguler profit.

(305–10)

Dido's insight perhaps applies as well to poets, first chasing their craft for the "fame" poetry can bring, next for the "frendshippe" of speculative thought, and finally for the "delyt" of total immersion in a world of creative art.[6]

Book I

For a poem explicitly addressing love and fame, a theoretical inquiry into the causes and categories of dreams would seem a most unusual way to begin. Not only does the *House of Fame* begin thus, it also dismisses the subject with an anti-intellectual flick of the hand (13 ff., 53–58). The poem's narrator apparently dismisses only the scholarly inquiry into dreams, not the fact of their existence or their substance. "[T]he miraculous world of love is almost coterminous with the world of dream," says J.A.W. Bennett (1968, 2) explaining the connection, for "dream and poetry are as closely 'intermeddled' as the winged tidings that are to appear at the very end of *Fame* (2118)" (3). If one takes this suggestion a small step further, as previous chapters suggest, dream and poetry are not just "intermeddled"; the "process of dreaming becomes nearly synonymous with the creative act" (S. Delany 1972, 44), and its retelling must be nearly synonymous with a completed poem. Is not every poem—or every piece of writing, for that matter—the fixed, visible form of conscious thinking, of someone's daydreaming? That the Middle Ages had no "theory to describe and justify the fictions which were stimulated by the facts of visionary experience" (Minnis 1995, 43), perhaps testifies to the self-evident ubiquity and necessity of literary fiction, in no need of philosophical description. At least one commentator, however, Evrart de Conty writing in the 1390s, acknowledged the existence of fiction as a valid human phenomenon, and devised a way to fit it into the existing categories of dream. I quote Minnis's summary (45) of Evrart:

> For the poet wished to imagine (*presendre*) that this vision of Nature and the things which later followed from it were neither a dream—presumably he means a real dream that the poet had actually experienced—nor a vision as real as those corporeal sights which are to be taken at face value. Thus, his vision was an 'imagined thing,' a fiction.

Imaginary vision, then, has moved from being a divine gift of significant imagery... to something made up, quite voluntary, within human control... an act of deliberate literary creation.⁷

Although we have no reason to suspect Chaucer was aware of this passage, *Fame* nonetheless captures in its opening line the wistful thought that fictional writings result from a kind of dream, or at least from the elusive boundaries where well-recognized categories of dream meet or overlap. "God turne us every drem to goode!" (*HF* 1; cf. 58, 83–84) expresses the hope that all our imaginings will reach final poetic fruition.

The invocation of Morpheus, identified only as "the god of slep" (69), slightly complicates this straightforward meaning. We recall that the narrator of the *Book of the Duchess*, reconstructing the events that led to his dream, seeks the help of Morpheus that he might be sent sleep, implying as well his eagerness to receive the dream that sleep will bring. In *Fame*, however, a subtle division of labor between inspiration and execution implies the narrator has already had his dream, though he has not yet turned it into poetry:

> And to this god that I of rede
> Prey I that he wol me spede
> My sweven for to telle aryght,
> Yf every drem stonde in his myght.
>
> (*HF* 77–80)

Despite crediting Morpheus with power over every dream, the narrator implies that the images, scenes, and sequences of his dream are already clearly imprinted in his imagination. Hence, he needs only to ask the god of sleep for help "My sweven for to telle aryght"—that is, for help converting this mental activity into intelligible, appealing words.

The narrator's dismissal of theoretical inquiry qualifies his invocation in still another way. After electing to begin his poem by implying that a discussion of dreams is actually a discussion of the poetic imagination, Chaucer has his surrogate narrator suggest strongly that none of this material should be taken seriously. Clemen, referring to lines 2–58, summarizes (1964, 75):

> Chaucer pretends that all these theories about dreams and the discussion of them is no affair of his, and yet he brings his whole knowledge—and he proves more 'learned' than most of his contemporaries—to bear on

the matter. At the same time he reduces all this learning to a farce; for the conjectures and suggestions crowded into small compass (indeed into a single sentence!) cancel one another out, at least in their effect on the reader. Meantime, throughout these contrivances the poet himself affects innocence and astonishment, extricating himself adroitly by shifting responsibility for the questions asked, on to the 'grete clerkys' (53) and declaring himself to be 'of noon opinion' (55).

Nor does the narrator spare the god of sleep. Echoing the light treatment he gives Morpheus in the beginning of the *Book of the Duchess*, Chaucer's nearly epic invocation to the god in *Fame* concludes, first, with the skeptical conditional clause at line 80 quoted above and, second, with a fervent appeal to the God "that mover ys of al, / That is and was and ever shal" (81–82), an appeal to the triune God that obviously supersedes the prayer to Morpheus.

This separate appeal made to the God of Christianity, like a similar aside in *Book of the Duchess*, "For I ne knew never god but oon" (*BD* 237), fleetingly counters the narrator's playful attitude to Morpheus. Both allusions let audiences know that the gods of the poets, including Morpheus, are never more than useful fictions. Yet even this appeal to the Christian God, never only a "useful fiction" in Chaucer, serves comic purposes. Here the narrator does not ask for help with either his poetic conception or its literal composition, but begs God to favor those who find his dream pleasing and punish those who do not, as he himself would do if only he had divine power. The invocation is thus a complicated *reductio* on the one hand and on the other a gentle reminder of the God in whom he does believe. The point is comic exaggeration, as witty in its own way as the whole of book II will be in a quite different way.

The strategy driving this exaggeration, though never explicitly stated, begins to emerge in another claim that has a tendency to go unnoticed because it seems formulaic:

> For never sith that I was born,
> Ne no man elles me beforn,
> Mette, I trowe stedfastly,
> So wonderful a drem as I
> The tenthe day now of Decembre,

The which, as I kan now remembre,
I wol yow tellen everydel.

(59–65)

These lines leave little doubt what the narrator thinks of the singular wonder of his dream, or more specifically, if "recounted dream" metaphorically signifies "completed poem," the brilliance of one of his poems.[8] As so often in Chaucer, the humor stems from an ironic disparity between the narrator's evaluation of himself and the opinion others have of him. He has asserted, as if it were a fact not open to dispute, that on December 10 he had the greatest dream ever experienced. That others may think differently—a necessity for comedy's success—will be possible only if, at the moment he makes this exorbitant claim, the audience has already heard the dream and knows it falls well short of the narrator's high opinion. Those who may not have heard the recitation will easily fall in step by doubting the narrator has the ability to create as wonderful a dream as he claims. Otherwise, there seems no point in calling so much attention to his experience, twice giving the precise date on which it occurred (63, 111).[9] The effect is to call attention to both extremes of his little joke: the naïveté with which he inflates the quality of his dream, calling on the Lord to bless those who agree with him; and the anger he directs at the incompetence of those who disagree, again imploring God (as every poet has done in every age) to punish those who misjudge his work "thorgh presumpcion, / Or hate, or skorn, or thorgh envye, / Dispit, or jape, or vilanye" (94–96).

By the end of the invocation to book I, any listener aware of Chaucer's poetic avocation would recall the events leading up to the recitation of some other poem the audience very likely has already heard. The point would not be to deliver *Fame* as a formal prologue and then recite the earlier poem a second time, but merely to lay before this audience a fictional account, no matter how implausible, of the legitimacy—the "historicity"—of the material he recited on December 10, as do the prologues of his other dream visions. It all came from a dream, he would be able to say, a dream that occurred logically from what he was doing before falling asleep. At the same time his version of the Dido and Aeneas story would establish his compassion for women and present certain truths about belletristic literature, both of which would make earlier complaints about the "dream" he had on December 10, as referenced in the prologues to the *Legend of Good Women* (F 308–40; G 234–316), seem foolish in retrospect.

The complicated process of disposing a narrator for sleep, getting him to drop off, and finally having him dream, proceeds more straightforwardly in *Fame* than in *Duchess* or *Fowls*. Very different from the insomniac of the former and the curious scholar of the latter, the narrator of *Fame*, fatigued from a two-mile journey, falls asleep without difficulty. The first locale he sees in his dream, however, recalls the beginning of the dream in *Duchess*. He finds himself in a glass temple surrounded by painted images from literature. Instead of the *Roman de la rose* and the Troy legend that decorate the windows and walls of the sleeping chamber in the *Duchess*, this narrator sees a translation of the opening lines of Virgil's *Aeneid*, which the fourteenth century understood as a sequel to the Troy legend. Except to point out these unusual inscriptions and paintings, the narrator almost fades into obscurity as he begins to retell the story of Aeneas. Though Chaucer summarizes the *Aeneid* in bare outline (he compresses Virgil's last six books into fifteen lines), the account of Aeneas's relationship with Dido catches his deepest interest. What we saw of Chaucer's strategy in *Duchess* and *Parliament* leads a reader to assume that this episode, a love story less fascinating than a dozen others, was selected because it foreshadows some material appearing later in the poem. In other words, his allusion to Virgil promotes the organic unity (*pace* Clemen) of the whole poem.

Chaucer elects not to give a full account of the Dido-Aeneas episode, available in the chief sources for the passage, Virgil's *Aeneid* book IV and Ovid's *Heroides* vii, preferring to emphasize only two matters: Aeneas's betrayal of Dido, and Dido's lament for her reputation at the hands of "wikke Fame" (349). He has his narrator unquestionably take Dido's point of view, making her a more fully developed character, and a far more sympathetic woman, than her counterpart in Virgil. But he also seems eager to announce that it is his own point of view, for he introduces Dido's long lament (315–60) with explicit words alleging that he alone dreamed her words, "Non other auctour alegge I" (314). These words are not about pride of authorship, as if he were insisting that praise should come to him for the excellence of the composition. They set out, instead, a manifesto of authorship: a poet's lines do not come from history or from some prior *auctour*, but from his own creative imagination.¹⁰

Whereas the *Aeneid* follows its hero to Italy, Chaucer's poem drops Aeneas. Once, when the narrator says he will speak of him—

> But let us speke of Eneas,
> How he betrayed hir, allas,
> And lefte hir ful unkyndely
>
> (293–95)

—he still returns to Dido's concerns:

> So when she saw al utterly
> That he wolde hir of trouthe fayle,
> And wende fro hir to Itayle,
> She gan to wringe hir hondes two.
>
> (296–99)

As a result, we tend to ignore Aeneas's motives, almost completely overlooking that he has no control over his "betrayal":

> But to excusen Eneas
> Fullyche of al his grete trespas,
> The book seyth Mercurie, sauns fayle,
> Bad hym goo into Itayle,
> And leve Auffrikes regioun,
> And Dido and hir faire toun.
>
> (427–32)

Had Chaucer distributed his attention evenly to the two principals in this episode and the impulses that motivate them, the result might have been effective Hegelian tragedy, where the tension arises from the conflict of two equally valid points of view. If he had—though to do so would not have served his purposes—the word *betrayal* still would not have been inappropriate. Whatever the reason, or however justified the motive, Aeneas does leave Dido. Apparently Chaucer does not want a competing motif to mitigate Aeneas's cruel treatment of Dido or lessen the pain it brings her.

The sincerity of Dido's love for Aeneas and her desire to have him remain with her are eclipsed by her fear of a more certain threat than her lover's inevitable departure:

> O wel-awey that I was born!
> For thorgh yow is my name lorn,
> And alle myn actes red and songe
> Over al thys lond, on every tonge.
>
> (345–48)

Nothing can suppress the report that Aeneas's abandonment shames Dido, especially its implication that he must not have valued her highly, much less loved her. His betrayal thus exposes her to a future in which other unflattering rumors will continue to circulate:

> And that I shal thus juged be:
> "Loo, ryght as she hath don, now she
> Wol doo eft-sones, hardely"—
> Thus seyth the peple prively.
>
> (357–60)

Though she cannot alter the implications of Aeneas's betrayal, she can at least prevent the rumor that her part in the affair was as trivial and fleeting as her lover's. In addition to putting an end to her pain, the suicide she resolves upon will prove that her love for Aeneas cannot become, either in fact or in repute, the first in a long series of wanton intimacies, as she imagines "the peple prively" (360) suppose. Dido's anxiety about Fame, followed almost immediately by her suicide (373–74), implies her understanding that fame eclipses historical fact; that reputation, rather than truth, is the immutable condition from which her entire future will flow.

We must look far ahead—even to the "love-tydynges" (2143) the narrator eagerly awaits yet does not hear—to appreciate why Chaucer not only emphasizes Dido's innocence by recasting Virgil's account but, indeed, takes it even further than did Ovid. The importance of these missing tidings cannot be doubted, for they emanate from a busy, noisy corner of the structure where the narrator has been wandering about eager to learn what he can, especially from some faraway country he chooses not to name—other "Folk kan synge hit bet than I" (2138). A great crowd rush toward this corner, some climbing over others to get a better view and to hear what will be exchanged there. At just this point "A man of gret auctorite" (2158) is announced and the poem ends. Everything up to this line, it is not unreasonable to assume, has been structural preparation for the story about to be divulged by this man of authority. Since the story is not shared, to many the poem has seemed incomplete. If, then, we are to speculate about the poem's missing tiding, hints of its substance and form are probably to be found among the extant scenes and motifs that have been leading to it. We shall postpone to the next chapter, however, the compelling arguments pointing to the tiding *Fame* leads its readers to expect, while we return to the philosophical and artistic implications of the *House of Fame*.

A discussion of the creative process begins in earnest after the narrator leaves the painted scenes on the interior walls of the glass temple of Venus and wanders outside to see the temple for what it is, a glass structure bereft of all vitality, located in a desert barren as far as the eye can see (480–91). Chaucer unmistakably implies that the traditional association of poetry with Venus, or of poetry in the service of Venus, provides a sterile vantage from which to stimulate his own creative imagination. Prompted as much by the desert he beholds as by the temple he left, the narrator utters an impassioned prayer whose words, referring unambiguously to the imagination, plead for a different kind of artistic inspiration:

"O Crist," thoughte I, "that art in blysse,
Fro fantome and illusion
Me save!"

(492–94)

To answer his prayer, a messenger in the form of a golden eagle arrives as promptly as Pandarus responds to a similar prayer in a parallel situation (*T&C* I.519–53). Both scenes have marked implications for philosophy as well as art. Startled by this golden emissary are a narrator mired in a sterile environment, yet teeming with fresh thoughts of a love story from the Troy legend, and an audience eager to learn how these disparate thoughts and images will coalesce, if at all.

Book II

Caxton, not Chaucer, divided the *House of Fame* into books, but it was certainly Chaucer who intended the poem to have some kind of break to separate book I from book II, as an invocation placed here indicates. Lest this invocation cause us to forget the scene that has been so carefully laid, introductory lines (512–17) return the poem to its dreaming context, claiming that even the great figures associated with famous dreams of the past had never dreamed "So sely an avisyon" (513) as the narrator is about to relate. Revealing wonder rather than braggadocio, the claim recalls a similar remark in the *Book of the Duchess* (*BD* 276–89), where the complexity of a dream was alleged to confound even the most celebrated interpreters. An equally complex dream is apparently promised in *Fame*, virtually challenging an audience to interpret its meaning.

Before book II resumes its narrative, learned members of the audience will have made a few important associations, for not every day does a huge golden eagle as bright as the sun descend from heaven. The precursors of such an eagle include: the well-known symbol of St. John the Evangelist, who represents, among other things, love and mysticism; the eagle that descends in Dante's *Purgatorio* (ix.19–33) unmistakably symbolizing poetic inspiration; and the eagle in Boethius's *Consolation* (IV.met.1) signifying philosophy. Even more, as thought by many to be the only creature able to stare at the sun, the eagle carries the reputation of a seer or visionary.[11]

While Chaucer's more widely-read listeners may have understood the implications of this particular messenger of Jove, the triple invocation to Venus, the muses, and Thought (518–28) makes them explicit. The eagle's association with two of those invoked—muses and philosophy—is readily apparent, but the appeal to Venus may seem misconceived, as her temple has been set within a wasteland. Though an appropriate deity to invoke when so much discussion of lovers will shortly follow, and when a great authority will shortly disclose tidings of love, Venus surfaces here for an even subtler reason. If the eagle speaks correctly to the narrator that "thou haddest never part" (628) in love's deeds, and if the eagle conveys a mystic symbol, then the appeal to Venus may suggest that the act of poetic creation captures for Chaucer the essence of love more precisely than do the physical acts of love.

The spheres of influence suggested by the triple invocation to book II also foreshadow the lively scene between the eagle and his burden en route to the

House of Fame. In his first long speech the eagle explains why he has swooped down to pick up Geffrey and carry him aloft:

> thou so longe trewely
> Hast served so ententyfly
> [Jupiter's] blynde nevew Cupido,
> And faire Venus also,
> Withoute guerdon ever yit, . . .
> To make bookys, songes, dytees
>
> (615–22)

Since the poet whom Geffrey represents often has his surrogate claim only poetic service to Love, a listener would be inclined to assume these lines refer to his far-from-distinguished career as a conventional lover. Yet this thought is prevented by what immediately follows. For his diligence Jupiter intends to reward Geffrey the narrator, now merged with Geoffrey the poet, not by granting him success as a conventional lover, but by making available to him more "tydynges / Of Loves folk . . . Then ever cornes were in graunges" (644–98).[12]

Here an important inference must be drawn from the distinction between deserving a reward and the reward itself. Though earned by long and faithful service, the reward itself is shaped by the narrator's failure to achieve success, already identified as his poetic failure. In Jove's opinion, the reward will correct the deficiency. Geoffrey has been unsuccessful, his tutor explains, because he has been mistaking remote lovers buried in books made by ancient authors (655–58) for believable lovers made by God (646), lovers whose thoughts and actions would more readily elicit pathos. Not that the eagle disparages these literary lovers for their remoteness in time, but because they share none of the universal characteristics of lovers in every age, from every land.

> thou hast no tydynges
> Of Loves folk yf they be glade,
> Ne of noght elles that God made;
> And noght oonly fro fer contree
> That ther no tydynge cometh to thee,
> But of thy verray neyghebores,
> That duellen almost at thy dores
>
> (644–50)

The eagle is taking Geffrey *to* the House of Fame, and especially the House of Rumor, where news of these realistic folk may be heard, and *from* the temple of Venus where only gods and goddesses are likely to be met, like those he has found in Virgil, Statius, Homer, and others—figures whom he will celebrate (or has already celebrated) in the *Legend of Good Women*. As both a statement of poetic theory and the reason for his invocation to the muses, Geffrey's flight in the talons of an eagle symbolically rejects one poetic environment to embrace another.

In a more practical realm, where Houses of Fame and Rumor do not float at will, nor are eagles available to answer a prayer, Geffrey can only improve his record of serving Cupid and Venus, "Withoute guerdon ever yit" (619), by lifting his face up from books (652–58) about famous lovers and observing the widest possible range of lovers—recipients of God's love—plain people whose lives reflect the litany of joys and sorrows in lines 672–98. For every poem, those that celebrate successful consummations as well as chronicles of failure, is a love poem that must be true to the poet's own conception, not imagined from other poets' poems.

The invocation to Thought anticipates a subject foreshadowed by the eagle's association with philosophy, a discipline by which the fourteenth century understood abstract thought as well as what we today call the natural sciences. Geoffrey doubts he can be shown all the subjects promised:

> For hyt
> Were impossible, to my wit,
> Though that Fame had alle the pies
> In al a realme, and alle the spies,
> How that yet she shulde here al this,
> Or they espie hyt.
>
> (701–6)

In view of the personality the eagle has already revealed, he cannot pass up this chance to display his grasp of scientific truth or his talent for making it all seem transparently simple. These six skeptical lines just quoted from the narrator touch off a spate of rhetoric that will not stop for another 165 lines.

The ensuing comic dialogue is one of the finest in all of Chaucer, the only part of *Fame* that Donaldson includes in his anthology, remarking that its humor "enables it to stand alone" (1975, 1118). Its brilliance rests less, perhaps, on the eagle's classic representation of prolixity than on the professor's inspired explanation of valid theories in support of a consummately absurd idea.[13] While we enjoy the humor of book II, let us not overlook its practical function in the poem. Assuming the exchange between the narrator and his transporting eagle alludes to a philosophic debate, one thinks of Boethius, Martianus Capella, and Alanus de Insulis writing on the distinction between accepting as truth what one reads and "seeing and believing what one reads" (Ferster 1985, 18), especially in light of the narrator's remark, "I leve ... Hem that write of this matere" (1012–13). Rather, these words, spoken directly to the eagle, attempt to discourage further lecturing. Indeed, the narrator reveals his actual belief more clearly some twenty-five lines earlier, in meditative words spoken to himself:

> And than thoughte y on Marcian,
> And eke on Anteclaudian,
> That sooth was her descripsion
> Of alle the hevenes region,
> As fer as that y sey the preve;
> Therfore y kan hem now beleve.
>
> (985–90)

He had read Martianus, he implies, presumably his *Marriage of Mercury and Philology*, and Alanus's *Anticlaudianus*. Apparently he did not then accept their works as literal truth. Only now, when his own experience enables him to judge for himself, does he believe that "sooth was her descripsion." Even so, he limits this belief to his own experience, "As fer as that y sey the preve." Instead of referring to deep philosophical matters, this part of book II seems to dismiss the bookish learning then current. As with material transmitted by his earlier reading in the *Roman de la rose*, Machaut, and others—even Statius and Virgil—he prefers to let them be, and to produce work that he creates or, as he puts it metaphorically, work that "me mette ... / Non other auctour allege I" (313–14).

This gentle indifference to whether the works of earlier authors convey truth, or something altogether remote from truth, reveals an area where Chaucer might well disagree with a current strain of modern criticism. Many a reader of Chaucer assumes that differing accounts of some well-known story naturally raise the question of which one reflects historical truth.[14] For Chaucer, in contrast, the historical truth or falsehood of a particular story holds less interest than whether or not any particular version rings true poetically. That Nicholas in the *Miller's Tale* cannot possibly overhear the thoughts of Absolon, who leaves the shot-window bewildered and then angry, matters to scholarly inquiries into verisimilitude, not to the poetic brilliance that demands he overhear why Absolon "thoughte it was amys . . . A berd! A berd!" (*CT* I.3736–42). So, too, in the *House of Fame* where the narrator views the subject of Martianus's and Boethius's writings from aloft, he now understands these authors reveal reality, a truth he will leave for clerks and others. The immediate demands of the poem require the more important poetic truth—never mind its scientific falsehood—of undiminished sound circulating forever through the House of Rumor.

Book II's implication for literary art agrees in some ways with this notion of poetic truth, and differs in others. Wherever artistic endeavors are to be found, as distinct from, say, the beauties of nature, uninitiated audiences often insist that the artifact operate within *their* terms of reference. Though no one would inquire, on looking at a noble stand of redwoods, for example, or at an exquisitely subtle sunset, "What is its point?," artifacts do not escape this scrutiny. Instead of "point," one often hears "What is its moral?" Or, "What does the artist mean?" Or, with an implicit challenge, "How could the author possibly know this?" Anticipating this last response, and hoping to preempt it, authors often preface their works with an explanation that passes for history, however implausible the explanation and doubtful the history. Hawthorne creates an old manse and a neglected manuscript in its attic to lend credibility to the story of Hester Prynne and Pearl. Shakespeare guarantees for his sonnets an audience in perpetuity by titillating readers with a suggestion of a personal bisexual history (very likely a fiction, though irrelevant in any case) that still energizes critics every few years to identify the "man right fair" and the "woman coloured ill" (*Sonnets* 144).[15]

When Chaucer began writing, he used a long-tested formula to ingratiate his work—the product, after all, of a humble former page—claiming beforehand that the poem is actually a still-unexplained dream he experienced. Historical truth and plausibility are of no concern. Nothing more than a dream fantasy was ever claimed for the *Book of the Duchess* or the *Parliament of Fowls*. Chaucer abandoned this practice when creating *Troilus and Criseyde*, perhaps tiring of the overused convention, or following the practice of ancient authors who seem not to have needed this transparent ruse. When the critical response to his brilliant Troy poem was disastrous, as we can infer from the prologue to the *Legend of Good Women* (F 308–40; G 234–316), he apparently resolved never again to trust an audience to appreciate the difference between historical fact and literary fiction. He returned to an authenticating frame for *House of Fame*, the whole of which would provide the frame for another of his poems. For the *Canterbury Tales* he created a prologue that adequately alleges its "historicity," as does that poem's narrator with a sly explanation in the prologue to the *Miller's Tale* that he must tell this bawdy tale as he heard it, or else falsify his material (*CT* I.3171–75).

The narrator "Geffrey" explains very nicely how *House of Fame* came into existence. Another dream, alleged by the proud narrator to be the finest he has ever had, occurred during the night of December 10. So remarkable was this dream that he shares with his audience a meditation on the nature of dreams before describing the dream itself. Except for stopping short of its tidings at the end, the poem closely parallels the structure of his two previous dream visions, *Duchess* and *Fowls*. My present purpose, however, has not been to focus on this structure in order to explicate the *House of Fame*, but to emphasize how effectively *Fame* accounts for the source of whatever material he made public on December 10 and how persuasively it should silence critics who may have already questioned its historicity.

For all the ingenuity of the eagle's theory of sound, and for all the promise that lay in his threat to talk about the stars, Geffrey remains indifferent to this science. He does not refute it but merely claims it is not for him. When the eagle asks what his listener thinks of his theory, the answer first assesses the method of argument and then diminishes the theory by granting only its likelihood:

"But telle me this, now praye y the,
How thinketh the my conclusyon?"
[Quod he]. "A good persuasion,"
Quod I, "hyt is, and lyk to be
Ryght so as thou hast preved me."

(870–74)

The eagle seems a bit piqued by this faint praise, for he immediately insists that before evening Geffrey will be given a demonstration of everything that has been said; "what wilt thou more?" (883). By the time the eagle turns to a proposed lecture on the stars, Geffrey is firm in his desire not to have anything to do with such matter:

> With that this egle gan to crye,
> "Lat be," quod he, "thy fantasye!
> Wilt thou lere of sterres aught?"
> "Nay, certeynly," quod y, "ryght naught."
> "And why?" "For y am now to old."
> "Elles I wolde the have told,"
> Quod he, "the sterres names, lo,
> And al the hevenes sygnes therto,
> And which they ben." "No fors," quod y.
>
> (991–99)

Both of these dismissals of science echo Geffrey's opinion of the cause of dreams at the beginning of the poem. It is really out of his line:

> But why the cause is, noght wot I.
> Wel worthe of this thyng grete clerkys
> That trete of this and other werkes.
>
> (52–54)

Through this entire second book, tension has been developing between poetry and science. Not only does Geffrey imply as much with his rejection of respected scientific knowledge, but he also disparages the soaring attempts of Icarus and Phaeton to transcend natural limitations with scientific invention (919–23, 941–56). At the same time, he enthusiastically endorses the ability of pure thought, or the imagination, to transcend those same limits:

> "O God," quod y, "that made Adam,
> Moche ys thy myght and thy noblesse!"
> And thoo thoughte y upon Boece,
> That writ, "A thought may flee so hye
> Wyth fetheres of Philosophye,
> To passen everych element,
> And whan he hath so fer ywent,
> Than may be seen behynde hys bak
> Cloude"—
>
> (970–78)

Geffrey's admiration for writers like Martianus Capella and Alanus de Insulis, who wrote in detail of subjects treated cursorily in *Fame*, suggests that book II wholeheartedly endorses creative writing, while it treats with playful skepticism the fanciful mythology that former writers chose to celebrate. The insightful observation of Robert J. Allen has been hard to improve:

> The contrast between the literary artist's approach to experience and the scholar's approach could hardly be more dramatically stated, and it is noteworthy that most of the intellectual comedy in the poem arises from the presentation of these contrasting temperaments.
>
> The position here taken by Geffrey—that belief in what one reads in a poem does not depend on its factual accuracy, that artistic "truth" is not necessarily demonstrable—approximates the famous statement near the beginning of the prologue to *The Legend of Good Women*:
>
> Than mote we to bokes that we fynde,
> Thurgh whiche that olde thinges ben in mynde,
> And to the doctrine of these olde wyse,
> Yeve credence, in every skylful wise,
> That tellen of these olde appreved stories
> Of holynesse, of regnes, of victories,
> Of love, of hate, of other sondry thynges,
> Of whiche I may not maken rehersynges.
> And yf that olde bokes were aweye,
> Yloren were of remembraunce the keye.
> Wel ought us thanne honouren and beleve
> These bokes, there we han noon other preve.
>
> Two kinds of knowledge are being considered, and Chaucer is protesting his devotion to the same kind in the prologue to the *Legend* and in *The House of Fame*. The eagle's kind of truth is not Geffrey's kind.
>
> (Allen 1956, 400)[16]

Book II echoes book I in how it addresses the poem's three levels of meaning. Literally, it takes Geffrey away from his passive literary environment and drops him off in a locale that will eventually be alive with active people. Philosophically, it broaches the question of two kinds of fame—historical accuracy and the reputation that accrues from the reports of others. And artistically it justifies omniscient narration with a humorous fiction, while more seriously insisting that poetry has a right to independent existence. The invocation that began book II has steadily narrowed. The eagle rejects Venus while endorsing Poetry and Thought; Geffrey rejects Thought, leaving only those remaining "that on Parnaso duelle" (521), the muses who represent literary expression.

Book III

Through books I and II the *House of Fame* has been moving inexorably toward literary art as its main concern. To make the rhymes and verses agreeable, the narrator appropriately invokes only Apollo:

> O God of science and of lyght,
> Appollo, thurgh thy grete myght,
> This lytel laste bok thou gye!
>
> (1091–93)

A literal claim that he does "no diligence / To shewe craft, but o sentence" (1099–1100) should not be taken as disregard for poetic form, but as an apology for having spent so much time working out what "in myn hed ymarked ys" (1103). He now need only entrust expression to Apollo. This, and also to forestall criticism that his rhyming metrics exhibit little skill; to admit a failing beforehand often silences detractors.

After the eagle drops Geffrey off at the "Hous of Fame" (1105), the recent arrival first notices the giant mound of ice on which the palace sits. In addition to suggesting the goddess Fame's cold, indifferent nature, this same ice also accounts for the unequal durability of the names engraved on it, some almost completely melted by the sun, others still fresh in protective shade. An apt metaphor confirms that a name's ability to endure has nothing to do with itself or with the kind of fame it deserves. Both preservation and disappearance depend exclusively on outside agencies—the medium in which they are engraved and their exposure. Nothing can be done to preserve the names Fame intends to melt, or to obliterate others she has chosen to preserve. The goddess Fama is as chilly as the material in which she engraves every name. Even more telling, the still-legible names, "conserved with the shade / Of a castel that stood on high" (1160–61), faintly suggest the power of noble patronage to protect what would otherwise melt from view.

The palace itself, quite a different matter, has beauty and craft in abundance (1165–80). It could have been named the Palace of Art. Its principal material, beryl stone, echoes the three addressees of book II's invocation (518–28). Identified with truth (Thought) and possessing qualities supposed to increase love (Venus), beryl was also associated with poetry (the muses).[17] In ways difficult to overlook, the outside appearance of Fame's house reminds a reader of the temple of Venus in book I, made entirely of glass. Nor do the values these structures represent greatly differ. Whereas the *House of Fame* as a whole associates the temple of Venus with a particular poetic work, linking Virgil's *Aeneid* with a given theory of poetic inspiration, Fame's House amounts to a kind of museum of artistic creation, especially the creation of literary art. It embraces as well the three groups of agents responsible for shaping fame's existence, those whom literary art enshrines, Lady Fame herself, and the authors whose works initiate individual reputations.

The kinds of activity found outside the house confirm this meaning. Harpers, pipers, and several kinds of musicians; magicians, jugglers, and a variety of sorceresses; a number of legendary people associated with activities of this kind—all share an ability to create a complete range of images. Musicians, of course, create moods in others, not unrelated to the themes of which poets sing. The others create genuine illusions. These image makers are held in less esteem than the third group of agents assembled on pedestals within the house (1429–1511), literary artists, a category loosely including anyone who writes. But first, Geffrey catches sight of a scene much favored by medieval authors, an allegory of the entire process of fame making. Three groups of fame seekers busily attend Lady Fame, who is in fact the second agent in this triangle, a creature constantly in motion:

> For alther-first, soth for to seye,
> Me thoughte that she was so lyte
> That the lengthe of a cubite
> Was lengere than she semed be.
> But thus sone in a whyle she
> Hir tho so wonderliche streighte
> That with hir fet she erthe reighte,
> And with hir hed she touched hevene,
> Ther as shynen sterres sevene.
>
> (1368–76)

Lastly, as if in regal tableau, a motionless assemblage of writers whose subject was the matter of antiquity is attended by the nine muses. Only "Englyssh Gaufride" (1470), traditionally assumed to represent Geoffrey of Monmouth, is an exception. Welsh rather than English, Geoffrey of Monmouth celebrated the matter of Britain (that is, Arthur and the Round Table) instead of the matter of antiquity. He is nevertheless said to qualify for inclusion because the earliest mythical kings of Britain were thought to be Trojans. One wonders, however, if this Geoffrey could not perhaps refer to Chaucer himself, another instance of the self-referential characteristic that spans the author's lifetime, from his earliest extended poem, the *Book of the Duchess*, where (I argue in chapter 2) he appears as both the man in black and the dreamer, to the latest, the *Retraction* of the *Canterbury Tales*, where he speaks in his own historical persona. He certainly belongs in *Fame*'s largest single cluster of authors (1464–70), all of whom were "besy for to bere up Troye" (1472).[18]

Neither seeking fame, like the first group, nor alternately diminishing and growing in stature, as Lady Fame does, the authors who comprise this third group apparently have a self-sufficiency that confers on them an eminent position in Fame's house. They seem to be the only residents of the house who represent an absolute, immutable value. Indeed, it is authors who initially create a particular fame for their subjects. Depending upon treatment and sympathies that are perhaps unconscious, a writer's subjects receive good, bad, or indifferent fame from the writers themselves. We have already seen an instance of the relationship between author and subject in the Dido-Aeneas story, where two different poets, Virgil and Ovid (Chaucer will eventually be a third), create different reputations for Aeneas and Dido. Fame, too, takes her initial existence from authors. As their accounts spread, she grows; when their work no longer circulates, she can become "the lengthe of a cubite" (1370). This fine instance of the medieval fondness for allegory presents the whole largely capricious process of fame's generation, growth, and circulation as if it were a giant woven tapestry, or a carpet page in a manuscript, like the famous frontispiece of Corpus Christi College Cambridge MS 61 that shows Chaucer reading *Troilus and Criseyde* to a noble audience; the three apexes of literature are arrayed in one place, at one time—the poet, the audience, and the story Chaucer came to tell.

If Fame's house reveals the matter and result of this art, fame itself astonishingly bears no necessary relation to historical truth. Geffrey's quick, forceful reaction to this new revelation recalls the symbolic scene outside Venus's temple in the beginning of the poem. The wasteland in which the narrator then found himself expresses spatially what Geffrey now says literally. Speaking as both a supplicant seeking fame and as a poet who affects the fame of others, he replies somewhat angrily to a questioner:

>   "Frend, what is thy name?
> Artow come hider to han fame?"
> "Nay, for sothe, frend," quod y;
> "I cam noght hyder, graunt mercy,
> For no such cause, by my hed!
> Sufficeth me, as I were ded,
> That no wight have my name in honde."
>
>   (1871–77)

Not content merely to state that he does not want to be a subject in someone else's literary output, he amplifies his remark in an interesting way:

> "I wot myself best how y stonde;
> For what I drye, or what I thynke,
> I wil myselven al hyt drynke,
> Certeyn, for the more part,
> As fer forth as I kan myn art."
>
>   (1878–82)

Curious reasoning lies behind the qualification in line 1882. First, Geffrey assumes people become subjects in literature because they (or future writers) want to share with others the joys, sufferings, and thoughts of these subjects. Insisting he does not want to be the subject of literature, he answers his neighbor emphatically: he will endure his own sorrows as long as he knows his art. This declaration, that the poems he creates assuage his most sensitively felt experiences, recalls a prominent theme running through the whole *Book of the Duchess*. As to his presence as an author in Fame's house, here again he unambiguously rejects what he sees as assuredly as the desert in book I symbolizes a rejection of prior literature: "these be no suche tydynges / As I mene of" (1894–95). The experience would have been satisfactory, he explains, had he been interested in the activities, location, and description of Fame herself, but such is not what he was seeking. Geffrey's nonce acquaintance, an agreeable sort able to infer the narrator's real desire, therefore takes him close to the House of Rumor (1912–15).

In its description, in the characteristic activity one finds there, and in Geffrey's reaction to it, the House of Rumor differs markedly from what Geffrey leaves behind. If artifice is the essence of Fame's house, noise and activity distinguish the House of Rumor—indeed it is continually in motion (1925), suggesting something makeshift or workaday. The objects to which it is likened for the purpose of making the description precise are straw baskets and wicker cages—objects designed for use rather than adornment. By far its most noticeable feature is noise, the sounds of every conceivable kind of activity.[19] Here then is the logical destination of the sound waves about which the eagle lectured so well in book II, as well as the reward the golden eagle had in mind when he promised to show Geffrey new subjects to write about (661–710). Appropriately, the eagle appears again—it is a kind of curtain call—to carry Geffrey into the house, to the accompaniment of one final attack of logorrhea (2000–2026).

Within this second house a bustle of activity gives Rumor an atmosphere very different from Fame's house. Here no groups of people seek one kind of fame or another; no static displays show authors who have contributed to the fame of the past; nor does a goddess arbitrarily dispense reputations. Rather, the House of Rumor is the still-living record of everything that has happened and is happening in the world and of all the human reactions to these events. Consequently, truth and falsehood exist together, since they are no more than different reactions to one event. In this respect, the House of Rumor is right at the center of human activity, whereas the House of Fame is several steps removed. Rumor represents the direct observations of people; Fame presents their settled accounts. Rumor embraces all the conflicting reports and opinions of an event; Fame offers a single reaction, after selective reporting and the arbitrary decisions of Lady Fame adulterate the event. Rumor is the new source of poetic material for a new theory of poetry; Fame is the old storehouse of Geffrey's literary inheritance, symbolically the old books in which his face has long been buried.

Geffrey's revealing reactions in the House of Rumor are in striking contrast to his behavior in the House of Fame. Earlier he rejected any thought of imagining himself a subject of song, and refused to accept Fame's house as a source of new poetic themes. In Rumor's house, by contrast, he is so intrigued and enthusiastic that he goes about learning what he can:

And as I alther-fastest wente
About, and dide al myn entente
Me for to pleyen and for to lere,
And eke a tydynge for to here

   (2131–34)

A commonplace of criticism holds that Chaucer's progress as a poet gained momentum when he increasingly replaced books as a source of inspiration with experience and direct observation of the world. If the *House of Fame*, as a theoretical discussion of the art of poetry, embodies symbolically Geffrey's literary inheritance in Fame's house, it follows that the House of Rumor symbolically represents Chaucer in the act of observing the world around him.[20] Some lines in book II offer evidence that the House of Rumor may be something more.

O Thought, that wrot al that I mette,
And in the tresorye hyt shette
Of my brayn, now shal men se
Yf any vertu in the be
To tellen al my drem aryght.
Now kythe thy engyn and myght!

   (523–28)

Interest first attaches to the apparent contradiction in these lines, that Thought, a conscious activity, can have been the cause of a dream which the narrator experiences in his sleep. Moreover, Thought is not credited as the sender of his dream, but as its maker—the word *wrot*, obviously meaning more than simple scribal activity, suggests a careful shaping, fashioning, in order to make something conform to a preexisting idea. The word *dream*, then, obviously means the whole of this poem. We are left now with a more serious contradiction. The eagle's suggestion was for Geffrey to get out and observe people, to make poems from his observations. The House of Rumor would logically be a representation of this idea. But the House of Rumor itself is part of a poem, and here in the narrator's own words we have testimony that he made this poem not from observation and experience but by Thought enclosed in the treasury of his brain—that is, not as a visual image but as a mental image. On the other hand, we cannot ignore that the House of Rumor seems to be filled with much human activity, the kind of thing that would come from observation. The contradiction seems to be whether the House of Rumor represents pure imagination (Thought) as the source of poetry, or the technique of copying nature, "as craft countrefeteth kynde" (1213), as the proper source. What the House of Rumor must represent, then, is neither the technique of going directly from poetic conception to expression nor the technique of going directly from observation to expression. Rather it seems to represent both observation and imagination in perfect concert. The "mirror" and the "lamp" are no longer distinguishable.[21] Both have become the "onlie begetter" of an art wholly imaginative in conception, perfectly realistic in execution.

When the narrator notices one who "semed for to be / A man of gret auctorite" (2157–58), his poem abruptly stops, rather than ends. Its last words recall lines from the *Book of the Duchess*, "I was war of a man in blak ... A wonder wel-farynge knyght—/ By the maner me thoghte so—/ Of good mochel" (445, 452–54). The same lack of a precise identity; the same favorable response to the man, although "wel-farynge knyght" and "Of good mochel" in *Duchess* convey reasons for admiration different from "auctorite" in *Fame*; and the same care to admit these as inferences, not certainties. A final similarity, though requiring a leap of imagination, the "man of gret auctorite" in *Fame* is as much an image of the mature Chaucer as the "man in blak" in *Duchess* captures the same authorial self-image at the age of twenty-four. But a significant difference surprises the reader. Whereas the *Duchess* needs another thousand lines to complete its meaning, the mere presence of this particular "auctorite" in *Fame* completes a three-part design running through the whole poem. The poem literally takes us to a place of omniscience, where we can hear the intimate details of a love story told by one who was not a witness. Philosophically, the poem shows the coldly impersonal and capricious nature of Fame, implicitly calling into question the "historical truth" of all past literature. Finally, as a comment on literary art, the poem insists on a new theory of poetic inspiration in which the poet's limitless imagination combines with his ability to make that imagination suggest reality and replaces the traditional theory in which inspiration was said to come in dreams influenced by the Goddess of Love. Here the mind of the poet—or, in a phrase from Keats suggesting the visual image of Rumor's house, "the wreathed trellis of a working brain"[22]—creates a new kind of truth: poetic truth.

5

The Missing Tidings of the *House of Fame*

Critics generally assume that Chaucer had a plan in mind for the missing tidings of *House of Fame* but neglected to put his plan into verse. This chapter advances a very different suggestion, that Chaucer never planned for *House of Fame* anything beyond what is now extant. Compared with other Chaucerian poems that are obviously unfinished, *Fame* displays none of their marks of incompleteness. In *Anelida and Arcite*, to take an the clearest example, after an elaborate complaint (211–350) by the title lady, the poem returns to the seven-line stanza with which it began. Although this is the last stanza in the poem, it promises to describe a temple "That shapen was as ye shal after here" (357). Chaucer undoubtedly had more in mind for this poem. Similarly, the *Legend of Good Women* breaks off in the middle of a sentence announcing more to follow: "This tale is seyd for this conclusioun–" (2723). The *Canterbury Tales*, replete with evidence of its unfinished state, leaves the connections between some tales unwritten or unclear. It uses feminine pronouns to refer to its male narrator in the prologue to the *Shipman's Tale*, perhaps because the tale was originally intended for the Wife of Bath. And it assigns no tale at all to a Yeoman, a Plowman, two Priests, and five guildsmen, though all the pilgrims agreed to tell two tales on the journey to Canterbury and two tales returning.[1]

By contrast, the *House of Fame* leaves no unfulfilled promises. True, the narrator describes with enthusiasm a man who seems to be a great authority; true also that this man stands

> In a corner of the halle,
> Ther men of love-tydynges tolde.
>
> (2142–43)

But these words do not claim the man in question will recite one of these love tidings as "ye shal after here." Nor does the poem taken as a whole leave any loose ends, since every theme introduced comes to its own logical conclusion. If the great authority had been given some slight thing to do or say—

> Wrothe he quod, "To youre bokes y sey,
> Er Fame lyte wol rede of Geffrey."

—the completeness of the poem would never have been doubted.

The poem, nevertheless, gives a strange feeling of incompleteness—not, perhaps, the kind of incompleteness *The Riverside Chaucer* suggests by appending the rubric "[unfinished]." Rather, one has the strong impression the author had finished working on the poem and intentionally left it as we now have it. Several suspicions, hints, and logical inferences contribute to this impression, rather than any single compelling argument. Take for example Chaucer's own reference to the poem "the book . . . of Fame" (*CT* X.1086). This does not seem to be the wording Chaucer would have chosen if he were describing this poem according to the principles that led to his other references. Or, to rephrase the point, if in listing his other poems he had followed the procedure used here, we should not now have the familiar names by which we know these poems. To match "the book . . . of Fame" we should now have the *Book of Melancholy*, the *Book of Nature*, and the *Book of Alceste*. Chaucer apparently chose "the book of the XXV. Ladies; the book of the Duchesse; [and] the book of Seint Valentynes day of the Parlement of Briddes" (*CT* X.1086) because they pointed to the most important part of each poem, the last part, for which everything else had been preparing. If *Fame* had been named thus, we should at least have had the *House of Rumor*, certainly not a place twice rejected by the narrator.[2] Or, if not the *House of Rumor*, then perhaps the *Book of Tidings*. Almost anything would seem more apt than "the book . . . of Fame." This title does, however, adequately identify the poem, provided we understand that Chaucer's usual method of referring to one of his poems was not available because the most important activity to take place in the House of Rumor would not be included.

The last few lines of the poem have a familiar ring that suggests a parallel with what we have already seen in two previous dream visions. During the generalized account of the persons and activities of the House of Rumor, no warning is given of a particularized commotion in one corner of the structure, a rush toward a man of authority announced by the narrator:

> Atte laste y saugh a man,
> Which that y [nevene] nat ne kan;

> But he semed for to be
> A man of gret auctorite ...
>
> (2155–58)

The suddenness of the change from leisurely description to something specially singled out has occurred before. In the *Book of the Duchess*, immediately following a forty-five-line description of an enchanting forest crowded with marvelous details, none of which commands our attention more than any other, the narrator abruptly announces "a man in blak" (445):

> But forth they romed ryght wonder faste
> Doun the woode; so at the laste
> I was war of a man in blak,
> That sat and had yturned his bak
> To an ook, an huge tree.
>
> (*BD* 443–47)

In the *Parliament of Fowls* we meet Lady Nature in a similar way, after a long, even account of the temple of Venus and a description of extensive paintings or texts on its walls:

> Whan I was come ayeyn into the place
> That I of spak, that was so sote and grene,
> Forth welk I tho myselven to solace.
> Tho was I war wher that ther sat a queene
> That, as of lyght the somer sonne shene
> Passeth the sterre, right so over mesure
> She fayrer was than any creature.
>
> (*PF* 295–301)

Now in both of these other instances, *Duchess* and *Fowls*, the figures introduced occupy central roles in the remainder of these poems and contribute substantially to their most important parts. If one considers the possibility of similar construction in all three poems—it seems impossible not to—the man of authority introduced at the end of *Fame* must have been intended as a central figure in some following material toward which books I, II, and

III were tending. Whereas *Duchess* reveals a grieving poet of twenty-four years, and the *Parliament* introduces a goddess about to convene an annual meeting of birds, the unnamed man at the end of *Fame* is called only a great authority.

Latin *auctoritas*, an abstract noun derived from *auctor*, normally spelled *auctour* in the fourteenth century, conveys the identical meaning that its transliterated "author" renders in modern English. Thus, of the three personages who appear during the course of the three dream allegories we have been discussing, a man in black, Lady Nature, and a man of great authority, two of these are specifically shown or identified as conventional authors of written texts, while the third has authored, in a sense, every living creature, tree, and plant in the poem.

Most important, the implicit discussion of literary styles in *Duchess* and *Fowls*—shown in both poems as a confrontation between the stilted expressions of Chaucer's literary forebears and an unadorned representation of how people actually speak and act, followed by an endorsement of this new mode of realistic expression before these poems come to an end—suggests that *Fame* too may have been designed to follow such a compositional strategy. The contrast in *Fame* between the allegory of a beryl palace atop a mountain of ice and the busy activity in the House of Rumor certainly echoes the contrast in *Fowls* between Venus's sterile temple and the fertile garden surrounding it, repeated in the contrast between the stilted speeches of three tercels and the vitality of the parliament. This sharp contrast in *Fame* also reflects the confrontation in *Duchess* between the dated expressions of the man in black, when shaping his brief poems and formal monologues, and the accessible, unadorned speech of the narrator/dreamer, especially when conversing with the man in black. Since this juxtaposition of contrasting styles appears in all three dream visions, it is reasonable to expect that the resolutions to these contrasts would also be similar in all three dream visions. But *Fame* has no counterpart to the resolutions that bring *Duchess* and *Fowls* to a conclusion. In particular, *Fame* has no endorsement of a new literary style, similar to the conversion of the black knight's hyperbolic speech in *Duchess* to his later unambiguous "She ys ded!" (1309), nor to the surrender of an allegorical temple and formulaic speech in *Fowls* to the joy of newly matched birds and the harmony of a roundel.

If the tidings that are now missing from *Fame* would have been the evidence of that poem's endorsement of a new theory of poetic composition and style, the specific subject and shape of this center of interest remain a mystery. We may, nevertheless, speculate about what news the man of great authority might have shared, if Chaucer had intended the *House of Fame* to be its preamble or, if not a formal preamble, then at least an explanation of how these tidings came into existence.

In the previous chapter we noted several general characteristics such tidings would have had: love and betrayal in a foreign land; a questionable reflection of history; and concern for reputation. We might consider, however, the strategies we have already seen in *Duchess* and *Fowls* as potential models for a similar strategy governing the relation of *Fame* to the missing tiding we are trying to imagine. Of greatest significance, the Dido-Aeneas episode in the *House of Fame* may have been intended as a thematic overture to *Fame*'s center of interest, its missing tidings, in the same way the Ceyx-Alcione episode in *Duchess* prepares its audience for the most important part of that poem, the conversation about death and consolation that occupies the narrator and the man in black. In a similar way, Cicero's *Somnium Scipionis* orients the audience of the *Parliament of Fowls* to the dual representation of Love in that poem—first the static display in Venus's surroundings, and then its practical demonstration in the bird parliament. This hypothesis leads to several logical inferences about the tidings for which *Fame* has been preparing its audience.

To borrow a word from the Squire (*CT* V.401, 407), the "knotte" for which *Fame* was designed—undoubtedly the material the man of authority was preparing to deliver—would probably have been a poem featuring love and betrayal in a land remote from the betrayer's home, perhaps too a betrayal over which the principals have little control, and in which at least one character is developed to an extremely high degree. It would also have been a story that makes us reflect upon its historical accuracy, and on the social consequences of its love affair—how observers remote in time rewrite the lovers' reputations, whether false or true. Moreover, it would have been a story that lacks its own "authenticating frame." That is, the tiding we are trying to imagine would not have had material analogous to the introductory frames in *Duchess* and *Parliament* that account for the genesis of the stories those poems tell. Thus it would not have been the *Legend of Good Women*, which has two prologues of its own, nor the *Canterbury Tales*, whose *General Prologue* adequately accounts for its composition.

There is no need to wonder further about *Fame*'s center of interest. To our knowledge, Chaucer created only one poem that meets all these criteria: *Troilus and Criseyde*, a long narrative poem featuring love and its betrayal in a land remote from the alleged betrayer's Troy; a poem whose main characters have little control over their separation and the betrayal by one of them; a poem drawn from history, yet telling its own story; a poem that lacks its own authenticating frame.

Let us add another curious detail, not a similarity but a complementarity. Both *Duchess* and *Fowls* conclude with a clear identification of their preceding lines as complete and their narrators as the ones responsible for completing them:

> Thoghte I, "Thys ys so queynt a sweven
> That I wol, be processe of tyme,
> Fonde to put this sweven in ryme
> As I kan best, and that anoon."
> This was my sweven; now hit ys doon.
>
> (*BD* 1330–34)

> And with the shoutyng, whan the song was do
> That foules maden at here flyght awey,
> I wok, and othere bokes tok me to,
> To reede upon, and yit I rede alwey.
> I hope, ywis, to rede so som day
> That I shal mete som thyng for to fare
> The bet, and thus to rede I nyl nat spare.
>
> (*PF* 693–99)

Other of Chaucer's major works end on similar notes. Both prologues to the *Legend of Good Women* identify the narrator and the narrative: "And with that word my bokes gan I take, / And ryght thus on my Legende gan I make" (F 578–79; cf. G 544–45). The *Retraction*, too, brings to an explicit close both the *Canterbury Tales* and the life of its author as he lists his full bibliography for his readers. Only the *House of Fame* among Chaucer's major works has no corresponding lines signaling its conclusion. Further, it seems more than coincidence that *Troilus and Criseyde* is Chaucer's only major poem lacking its own prologue, and *House of Fame* his only major poem lacking an obvious leave-taking. If these two works are joined, with *Fame* preceding *Troilus*, both anomalies disappear.

House of Fame serves brilliantly and completely as a fictive account of how Chaucer happened to experience, perhaps on a December 10, the dream now known as *Troilus and Criseyde*. As well, the final twelve stanzas of his great Trojan love poem take such poignant leave of its story as to suggest they close more than the "litel bok ... litel myn tragedye" (V.1786) he has been composing. These stanzas preserve weeping verses by an author who commends himself to "Virgile, Ovide, Omer, Lucan, and Stace" (V.1792). But for one significant omission, these same authors are mentioned by name in *House of Fame* (*HF* 1460–99). "Englyssh Gaufride" (1470), occurring last in *Fame*'s list of those "besy for to bere up Troye" (1472), but omitted from the list of those to whom Chaucer commends himself at the end of *Troilus and Criseyde*, tends to support the suggestion that in *Fame* "Englyssh Gaufride" does not refer to Geoffrey of Monmouth, as most critics assume,[3] but to Chaucer himself. If the name were a reference to Geoffrey of Monmouth, a Welshman, there would have been no authority for calling him "Englyssh Gaufride." Nor would there have been a reason not to commend himself to this Geoffrey at the end of *Troilus and Criseyde*. The adjective "Englyssh" appears in *Fame*, I suggest, in order to prevent a reader from taking a reference to the Englishman Geoffrey Chaucer as a reference to the Welsh Geoffrey of Monmouth. If this suggestion is true, it implies that at the time Chaucer composed *Fame* he was already known as one who "Was besy for to bere up Troye" (1472), perhaps the most recent to do so, as his last-mentioned position among such authors implies. Chaucer's name does not appear at the end of *Troilus and Criseyde* because it would have been ludicrous for Chaucer to commend himself to Chaucer.

Readers familiar with either Virgil's account of how Aeneas, a man, abandons Dido, the woman he professes to love, or Chaucer's retelling of the sad affair in *Fame*, will be quick to note that this episode does not correspond to the love affair in *Troilus and Criseyde*, where a woman is widely decried as the betrayer of a man. Though correct, this unmatching of genders and roles by no means deals a fatal blow to the thought that the lovers in Virgil's story, especially as Chaucer depicts them, foreshadow thematically the tidings that could have completed *Fame*. The parallel between the affairs of

Dido-Aeneas and Criseyde-Troilus contains the same reversed genders as in *Book of the Duchess*, where the prologue recounts the Ovidian tale of a wife mourning the loss of her husband, whereas later in that poem a man in black grieves over the loss of a lady. If Chaucer chose the Ceyx-Alcione story to foreshadow the main material in the *Duchess*, as all critics believe, then Virgil's story of Dido and Aeneas anticipates equally well some of the important details in the relationship of Criseyde and Troilus.

We might still hesitate over the contradictory implications to which this train of thought leads. How can it be argued that the *House of Fame* fittingly foreshadows *Troilus and Criseyde*, when it was suggested in the previous chapter that, by alluding to events with which the audience is already familiar, *Fame* must postdate *Troilus*? How can *Fame* be both prologue and epilogue? Though apparently preclusive, these views do not in fact contradict each other. To appreciate this paradox necessitates a brief look at the *Legend of Good Women*, in particular its F and G prologues.

Critics apparently agree that *Troilus and Criseyde* separates chronologically the *House of Fame* from the *Legend of Good Women*, the former assumed to have been written before *Troilus*,[4] the latter shortly after *Troilus*.[5] According to the accepted critical view, then, the periods in which *Fame* and the *Legend* were written are separated from each other by however long it took Chaucer to create the more than eight thousand lines of *Troilus*, perhaps most of the decade of the 1380s.[6] Despite this elapsed time, critics find it nearly impossible to discuss either *Fame* or the *Legend* without referring to the other in the same sentence. This tendency to find similarities between the two poems arises not only from the prominence of the Dido-Aeneas episode in both poems but from the occurrence of other subjects as well.[7] All of this brings to mind a sound principle in geometry: two things similar to the same thing are similar to each other. For example, in his influential discussion of Chaucer's reliance on Ovid, John M. Fyler says that the ten Saints of Love in the *Legend* echo *Fame*'s catalogue of eight women betrayed by their men (1979, 98–99, citing *HF* 388–432). If *Fame* and the *Legend* are similar, as Fyler is right to point out, would not his further suggestion, that the *Legend* "is a palinode for *Troilus*" (96), potentially apply to *Fame* as well, making it too a palinode for *Troilus*? *Fame* formally retracts nothing, of course. Yet the total meaning of the poem may have the same effect of separating the author from the charge of misogyny.

Still other evidence leads Fyler to a parallel suggestion, now expanded to embrace *Troilus and Criseyde*. "Chaucer is again concerned," he says when speaking of the Legend of Phyllis, "with one of the central issues in the *House of Fame* and in *Troilus*: the poet's responsibility to keep the past in memory and revivify the fame of the dead; and his difficulty in finding the truth, and representing it accurately" (110). This observation grows naturally from an earlier claim that lines V.1772–85 of *Troilus and Criseyde* provide "an ironic preamble to the *Legend of Good Women*" (96). "Ironic" presumably because these lines, sounding more like the plea of a poet than the hope of a narrator asking women not to be angry with him for the story he has told, nevertheless acknowledge that "Criseyde was untrewe" (V.1774). The *Legend*, by ironic contrast, celebrates women of unshakable faith. By the same logic, *Troilus and Criseyde*'s lines V.1772–85 could also serve as an ironic preamble for the *House of Fame*. They show a narrator apologizing for, and distancing himself from, an unfaithful woman, whereas *Fame* admires the steadfast love of Dido and a score of other women wronged by men.

My point is not at all to challenge Fyler's interpretations, for I believe his instincts are sound. Rather, I wish to suggest that all three poems, *Troilus*, the *Legend*, and *Fame*, are almost of one piece. They grapple with the same themes, reveal indecision in the same ways, and leave readers with a profound sense of the insolubility of the human condition.

Strangely, critics do not ask whether the composition of *Fame* could not perhaps have followed as close upon the completion of *Troilus* as the *Legend* obviously does, instead of the 1379–80 date most readers accept.[8] Accounting for this silence, *Fame*'s octosyllabic meter, its alleged disunity, and its "unfinished" state have led to a critical commonplace, that *Fame* shows Chaucer not yet at the height of his poetic power and must therefore have an early date of composition.

None of these arguments is compelling. That Chaucer had once written in octosyllabics, but had thereafter immersed himself in the more exacting rhyme royal of *Fowls* and *Troilus*, hardly proves he could not have returned to the less demanding octosyllabics for a given work, especially if he wanted to complete *Fame* quickly. Would we assign "An ABC" to Chaucer's later years on account of its decasyllabics? Moreover, to assign *Fame* a date close to the *Duchess* on account of its verse form ignores the poem's more important thematic concerns, as we shall see. As to *Fame*'s alleged disunity, the charge remains debatable. Consider, for example, the motive that makes Aeneas abandon Dido. Though Virgil almost entirely exempts Anchises' son from wrongdoing, in view of his destiny in Latium, Chaucer adopts Ovid's harsher view, while also acknowledging briefly Mercury's order that Aeneas "goo into Itayle, / And leve Auffrikes regioun, / And Dido and hir faire toun" (430–32). To select only one detail from several on which her persuasive thesis rests, Sheila Delany rejects the notion that these apparently inconsistent interpretations demonstrate the poem's disunity. Both explanations are needed, she argues, to create the strong feel of ambivalence that precisely captures the essence of fame, more often a mixture of both truth and falsehood than an exclusive representation of one or the other (1972, 54–57). As for the "unfinished" state of *Fame*, the present chapter argues that *House of Fame* is both complete and finished as the prologue to *Troilus and Criseyde*, though it was probably written later. Finally, the claim that *Fame*'s disunity points to its author's poetic immaturity may simply attempt to shift blame from a critic's lack of imagination to the poem's lack of unity. As John Leyerle describes well, *House of Fame* is "a masterpiece of descriptive clarity . . . a clear and illuminating . . . statement of the dominant themes of Chaucer's mature poetry" (256, 261). And Alastair Minnis, lavishly praising *Fame*'s poetic style, remarks that "Chaucer can move from one register to another within the space of a few lines . . . with a dexterity and grace which is breathtaking" (1995, 180).

Nothing, save critical tradition, precludes our considering *Fame* as a product of the same time that produced the *Legend of Good Women*, and designed to achieve the same ends. If the *Legend* alludes to the displeasure that *Troilus* arouses (*LGW* F 320–40; G 246–316) and calls for Chaucer's atonement (F 479–91; G 469–81), *Fame* too remarks at length the inadequacy of Chaucer's works in the service of Love (*HF* 612–58) and orders him taken to higher realms where he might learn how to perform such service with greater skill (*HF* 661–98). Even more, as a fictional recollection of the events immediately preceding his creative effort in *Troilus and Criseyde*, as is proposed here, the *House of Fame* attempts an ambitious task that the *Legend of Good Women* leaves untouched. It charms to nothingness the charges leveled against Chaucer. First, to answer the explicit—and erroneous—notion that the author of *Troilus* belongs to the Theophrastan tradition, *Fame* establishes Chaucer's profeminist position by adapting the Ovidian tale of Dido, pointedly shaping the story to emphasize the innocence of a woman cruelly wronged by a man. And second, *Fame* counters the implicit charge that Chaucer's poem transmits unsupported facts whose authority he has not bothered to explain, and probably couldn't (except for the faintly angry line 314),[9] by offering an unanswerable, albeit fantastical, explanation of the immortality of sound, coincidentally defending authorial omniscience. Were he to offer a Schoolman's dissertation, or a treatise on literary theory to "instantiate a problematized dialogic" (as one is apt to read these days) it would have sunk heavily. But a golden eagle's flight to the houses of Fame and Rumor, accompanied by a brilliant lecture on sound, carries the day.

By electing not to introduce *Troilus and Criseyde* with an authenticating prologue, like those he wrote for *Duchess* and *Fowls*, Chaucer left an opening for his audience to suspect he intended Criseyde's treatment of Troilus to characterize all women. *Fame* disarms this charge, not only by offering the delightful fiction of how Geffrey acquired the intimate tidings of his Trojan lovers' story, but also by carefully deleting most of the excuses Virgil provides for his hero and, especially, by leaving out the most telling comment on Dido's self-delusion: "nec iam furtivum Dido meditatur amorem: / coniugium vocat; hoc praetexit nomine culpam" (IV.171–72), which Fyler (1979, 35) renders "nor does Dido now think about secret love; she calls it marriage, and by this name hides her fault." Only too well does the future author of the *Clerk's Tale* understand women's faithfulness to lovers who deceive them.

An important difference separates the *House of Fame* from its two dream-vision predecessors. Though the *Book of the Duchess* and the *Parliament of Fowls* undeniably include a discussion of literary expression in their thematic material, more immediate subjects command their readers' attention. The eulogy of an important lady, the narrator's patroness, determines everything in *Duchess*; the annual mating of birds, driven by the harmony of the universe, governs everything in *Fowls*. But *Fame* does not have a main subject, apart from its concern with the role literature plays in creating and sustaining the image in which any age holds the past.[10] One wonders, therefore, why Chaucer thought a poem with only a metaliterary meaning would interest his audience. The subject undoubtedly held immense importance for the poet, but it was important only insofar as he had worked it out for himself, not important to the extent that he would compose a poem about it longer than both his prior dream visions put together.[11] Not important, that is, unless the principles on which he based his poetry had been misunderstood and, as a result, the poetry itself had been ill received. Not important, unless the *House of Fame* placed on record an *Apologia pro Vita Poetica Sua* explaining his methodology, in the same way that the *Legend of Good Women* atoned for a work this methodology produced. The *House of Fame* may be an ex post facto explanation of the circumstances that led to some heinous offense, breaking off at the very point when the "gret auctorite" is about to commit his indiscretion. Chaucer leaves this "auctorite" conspicuously anonymous, causing some to believe he simply "could not identify the man."[12]

More likely, the narrator *chose* not to identify him, giving all in attendance the pleasure of identifying him by themselves. Here anonymity carries a touch of gentle humor, as many a person, perhaps in every age, leaves conspicuously unnamed someone to whom he refers, when he has confidence everyone will know it refers to himself. Such humor—here and in the *Duchess* (445–57) and in many social situations—often reveals itself by an obviously ludicrous self-aggrandizement. In *Duchess* an unnamed man is promoted to "A wonder wel-farynge knyght ... Of good mochel" (*BD* 452–54), in *Fame* to "a man of gret auctorite" (*HF* 2158). Canny listeners in both instances would recognize the combination of mock anonymity and transparent inflation as witty clues pointing to the author standing before them. As Spearing observes, "the *House* is the first of Chaucer's poems in which the narrator is realized in the specific role of poet" (1976, 82–83).[13] That Chaucer does not have his man of authority begin reciting *Troilus*, or attach a manuscript of *T&C* to his holograph of *Fame*, implies his belief that the audience already knew what these tidings were. But if Chaucer's original audience was aware of his specific indiscretion, modern readers are not.

The first words from the man of great authority, in my opinion, would have been "The double sorwe of Troilus to tellen, / That was the kyng Priamus sone of Troye, / In lovynge ... (*T&C* I.1–3). I say this because *Fame* and *Troilus* correspond to each other in much the same way that *Duchess*'s prefatory material corresponds to its narrator's exchanges with the man in black, and that *Parliament*'s prefatory matter corresponds to its scenes in Venus's garden and temple and at the bird parliament. Nor am I alone in pointing out that at least *Fame*'s Dido-Aeneas episode suggests *Troilus and Criseyde*. As early a critic as Kemp Malone implied that their strong similarity makes their differences in treatment seem strange: Chaucer's "handling of Dido and Aeneas contrasts strangely with his treatment of a like love story in *Troilus and Criseyde*, where the lovers are presented with a richness and fullness unmatched in medieval literature" (1951, 51). Even if the realization of character in *Troilus and Criseyde* reaches a greater "richness and fullness" than in *Fame*'s retelling of Virgil's Dido and Aeneas, nevertheless in Chaucer's hands, says J. L. Simmons, Dido "had become even more sympathetic than Virgil had made her" (1966, 129). Malone agrees that the stories are similar; Simmons implies that Chaucer's treatment of Dido's character is at least tending toward what he reached in Criseyde. Remarks by Bertrand H. Bronson (1960, 39–40, 49) reveal a similar, almost unconscious tendency to link the episode to *Troilus and Criseyde*:

> it seems rational to hypothesize a final tiding from the House of Rumour tending in the same direction as the Dido legend. Under the circumstances, the conclusion would be sceptical and sardonic, rather than pathetic. . . .
> We assume that the climax was the original idea from which the rest of the work germinated, and that therefore in Chaucer's conception the story of Dido was appropriate anticipatory matter. . . . The moral of the [final tiding] might have been, to adopt the words of Pandarus:
>
> O tonge, allas, so often here-byforn
> Hath mad ful many a lady bright of hewe
> Seyd "Weilaway, the day that I was born!"
> And many a maydes sorwe for to newe;
> And for the more part, al is untrewe
> That men of yelpe, and it were brought to preve.
> Of kynde non avauntour is to leve.
>
> (III.302-8)

Recent criticism has been slow to develop the full implication of the suggestion that *Fame*'s account of Dido and Aeneas foreshadows the love story Chaucer describes, despite a number of correspondences that readily surface between the Virgilian-Ovidian episode and *Troilus and Criseyde*. Each work expands an episode of the Troy legend, in particular a love affair, its subsequent betrayal by one of the principals, and the consequent sorrow of the betrayed party. In the ancient versions as well as Chaucer's, the circulation of fame greatly troubles the ladies involved: Dido after she has been betrayed, and Criseyde as she first falls in love with Troilus and, later, while slowly approaching a very different affair with Diomede and rightly recognizing what future generations will say of her betrayal and infidelity. Chaucer's treatment of the stories, in *Fame* as well as in *Troilus*, reveals a profound sympathy for both of these ladies, in contrast to their harsher treatment by others, most notably Henryson. Finally, the act of betrayal forces itself upon Aeneas in the ancient text, especially in Ovid's version, and upon Criseyde in Chaucer's poem.

Though a perfect foreshadowing of *Troilus and Criseyde* cannot be claimed for the *House of Fame*—a very different kind of work—several important similarities between the two works argue against coincidence. Each poem has deep concern for the theme of gossip, rumor, and fame. The apparent attempt to justify omniscient narration, if the eagle's lecture on sound waves in *Fame* may be called that, can apply only to *Troilus and Criseyde*, for the narrators of every other major Chaucerian poem allege personal experiences that make omniscient narration unnecessary. Then, too, the golden eagle's lecture on the stars—had we been allowed to hear it—would have been useful preparation for all those occasions "when thou redest poetrie" (*HF* 1001). Troilus's soliloquy on predestination might then have been more fully prepared for. Also curious, the name Lollius appears in only two of Chaucer's works—the *House of Fame*, where we find him among the authorities on the Trojan War (1468), and *Troilus and Criseyde*, which credits him with being the author of Chaucer's source (I.394).

Critics often acknowledge these evident points of contact between the two poems, yet pay little or no attention to another far more important area of agreement. In the enormous quantity of illuminating critical material written about *Troilus and Criseyde*, one only rarely finds the suggestion that this great love poem encodes the subject of artistic creation, as the *House of Fame* manifestly does throughout its three books. Among the familiar lines of critical argument that converge on *Troilus*—exploring character, philosophy, tragedy, theology, and preeminently psychology—the struggling artist has not been among them. In the following chapter, I shall advance the hypothesis that to consider the poem as a metaliterary construct is to reveal it as a direct descendant of the three poems explored in earlier chapters—as much a work about the creation of poetry as these dream visions are—and an even richer study of human life than has yet been seen. In doing so I do not deny other aspects of the poem that have long been admired. Rather, viewing the artistic act as an important part of the poem's meaning gains us an understanding of much that has remained mysterious, while also deepening our appreciation of what many have long praised in the poem.

Let us epitomize *Fame*'s observations on literary art. Geffrey's progress, through the courtesy of a golden eagle, takes him from one reality to another: from the literature of the past, purported to be "historical" truth, to the realm of imagination and poetic truth; from an indolent Venus and a barren desert to a wicker house of lively activity where the living noises of love's folk and their tidings fill the air; from a passive or at best a reactive temperament to a proactive engagement with all he encounters. The golden eagle transporting him from one world to the other inevitably comes with associations acquired from Virgil and Dante where similar birds symbolize literary creation. The poem's two escapes, then, first from Venus's temple of glass (119–467) and then from the House of Fame (1110–1917), apparently reject the practice of treating themes from prior writings as Chaucer's literary ancestors treated them. At length the eagle takes Geffrey to a new locale, the House of Rumor, which represents a new method of literary creation, "Based upon close observation of life and exercise of the creative imagination" (John Matthews Manly, quoted in Schibanoff 2006, 10). Thus the *House of Fame* celebrates the artistic triangle: a subject to be represented, a realistic medium in which to represent it, and the artist who does the representing.[14]

Troilus and Criseyde may be read as a poem about the same triangle Chaucer presents in the *House of Fame*, both a brilliant work of realistic romance and a practical demonstration of the theories articulated in *Duchess*, *Fowls*, and *Fame*. As we shall see, Troilus introduces the subject to be created, love, and remains an unwavering believer in its ideals; Criseyde represents the malleable material that must be elevated to this subject, capable of being crafted for the transcendent heights of love, yet amenable to something more ordinary and calculating; and Pandarus, the artificer, connects these two apexes, literally makes love happen and then, like an artist who has finished working on his artifact and must now stand aside, almost disappears.

6

Troilus and Criseyde

Previous chapters suggested that Chaucer's early dream visions, regardless of the various topics they cover, share an interest in the technical concerns of literary composition—both how it is done and what it describes.[1] These earlier poems place on record, albeit unsystematically, the poet's attitude to such questions as the oblique, stylized language of his literary predecessors, the congruence of all created things subsumed under a category he calls "love," and the broad subject of "fame." Though *Troilus and Criseyde* also touches these same subjects, it shares with the dream visions two other parallels that require special notice because Chaucer's handling, having matured very noticeably by the time he began his poem of love in Troy, may perhaps escape notice. First, mathematics has an important function in *Troilus*, as it does in two of Chaucer's dream visions, discussed in previous chapters, yet draws such casual attention that its importance has been overlooked. Second, reliance on earlier literature, from which *Duchess*, *Fowls*, and *Fame* select a central theme to emphasize, appears in *Troilus* as a subject unto itself, elevated for special scrutiny throughout the whole poem. We might name this subject the "art of reporting," which ranges in Chaucer's treatment from the fully accurate to the completely false and fanciful. Since the mathematical dimension need only be described once, and not called to readers' attention repeatedly as with the art of reporting, I propose to cover it now and thereafter move on to more conventional critical approaches.

Mathematics in *Troilus and Criseyde*

One first notices minor manifestations of mathematics, like the seven-line rhyme royal stanza that Chaucer invented specifically for the *Parliament of Fowls* and *Troilus and Criseyde*, pairing the numerological symbol 3 for divinity with the traditional symbol 4 for earthly beings, thus capturing the essence of at least one of mankind's paradoxes, the tension between fleshly impulses and theological aspirations. So too the poem's overall design, five books of different lengths, arranged as rising action to the consummation scene at the very apex of the poem and falling action thereafter. There is, however, a more fundamental mathematical presence that precisely conveys all of these paradoxes. Explicitly named, yet remaining entirely out of sight, this mathematical underpinning not only determines the length of each of the poem's five books (Hart 1981) but also provides a precise interpretive tool for the poem as a whole and for several of its key scenes.

Arising from an arcane verbal hint in book III as *Troilus* is approaching its consummation scene, an indication of the poem's underlying mathematical design takes unexpected shape in a subtle scene between Criseyde and Pandarus. While concentrating most of his verbal energy on the paradoxes of human existence, showing from several points of view the difficulty of accommodating love to both the ideals and the expediencies of daily life, Chaucer introduces a fascinating mathematical analogue to the main action. The word *dulcarnoun*, appearing twice in three lines (III.931, 933) and nowhere else in all of Chaucer, provides the "explicit warrant" called for by R. G. Peterson (1976) to justify a claim of numerical construction. Descending from Arabic and meaning "two-horned," like the related thought in English "on the horns of a dilemma," this most significant of all the poem's allusions to mathematics was appropriated in the Middle Ages as a convenient reference to Euclid's forty-seventh proposition, better known as the Pythagorean theorem (stating that in a right triangle $a^2 + b^2 = c^2$), because the famous geometric proof of this theorem resembles a two-horned beast (see figure 6.1).

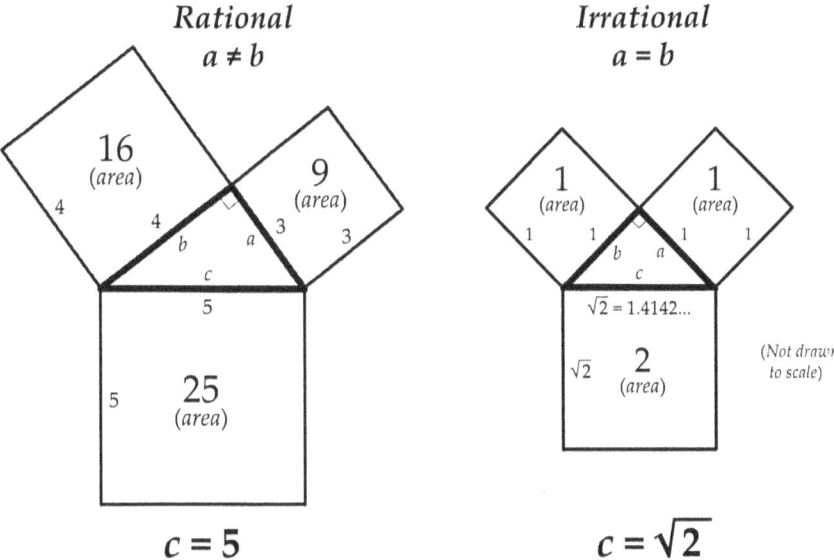

Figure 6.1. Pythagorean triangles: rational and irrational

142 / Chapter 6

Pandarus has invited Criseyde to dinner, knowing that a fierce rainstorm will force his niece to spend the night. She agrees to stay, provided he will assure her that no one is in the house who shouldn't be there. "Of course not," Pandarus dissembles, announcing shortly thereafter that Troilus has just arrived unexpectedly.

> Criseyde answerde, "As wisly God at reste
> My soule brynge, as me is for hym wo!
> And em, iwis, fayn wolde I don the beste,
> If that ich hadde grace to do so;
> But whether that ye dwelle or for hym go,
> I am, til God me bettre mynde sende,
> At *dulcarnoun*, right at me wittes ende."
>
> Quod Pandarus, "Yee, nece, wol ye here?
> *Dulcarnoun* called is 'flemyng of wrecches':
> It semeth hard, for wrecches wol nought lere,
> For verray slouthe or other wilfull tecches;
> This seyd by hem that ben nought worth two fecches;
> But ye ben wis, and that we han on honde
> Nis neither hard, ne skilful to withstonde."
>
> "Than, em," quod she, "doth herof as yow list."
>
> (III.925–39, emphases added)

Note the manipulation in this scene. Of course Criseyde knew Troilus was in the house. She might not have agreed to stay, had she thought otherwise. Still, decorum demands she keep up the pretense. When she throws up her hands "at [her] wittes ende," she uses the phrase "At dulcarnoun" in a colloquial sense, that she faces something impossible to solve, not as a reference to higher mathematics. We do something similar in modern English. Complaining of a "dilemma," we give no indication that the phrase originally meant a choice between two competing traditions or textual propositions—lemmata–as if we were preparing to publish some new edition. We speak colloquially. Similarly Criseyde, facing two courses of action, either letting Troilus come to her or declining to receive him, uses colloquially the word *dulcarnoun*, thus giving her uncle an opening. As soon as Criseyde pronounces the word in its colloquial sense, Pandarus redirects its meaning.

Not only does he seize a mathematical sense, he wrongly asserts that "dulcarnoun" alludes to a "flemyng of wrecches," a well-known reference to Euclid's fifth proposition, not his forty-seventh (Stephen Barney, *Riv Ch* 1041, note to *T&C* III.931). Dulcarnoun, he incorrectly claims, is what drives weak, lazy students out of class. But you, Criseyde, are intelligent, and this is not a difficult decision. Pandarus gives his niece a way of joining his thought, exempting herself from responsibility for what she knows her uncle will do. Then, uncle, she says, do whatever you wish (III.939).

Scholars have long focused on this apparent error in the text of the scene. Though the two theorems are similar, a huge ontological difference separates them. All solutions to the Pythagorean theorem (Euclid's proposition I.47) are expressed in rational integers. But Euclid's proposition I.5, perhaps better considered a subdivision of the Pythagorean theorem, concerns the diagonal of a square—that is, the hypotenuse of an isosceles right triangle—whose solution will never be an integer, but always an irrational number. Apparently the concept of irrational numbers so baffled weak students ("wrecches") that it had the effect of swiftly driving ("flemyng") them out of class. If Pandarus misidentifies Euclid I.5 as the reference in this Latin tag, as seems true, then whose error is it? Skeat blames Chaucer, whereas Thomas Elwood Hart argues it is "a learned joke at Pandarus's expense, but also . . . to suggest the paired relevance of both theorems to [Chaucer's] design" (1981, 138). I accept Hart's argument, although he does not pursue the *thematic* implications of Chaucer's *mathematical* design, a pursuit we might briefly take up here.

By simultaneously referencing a rational and an irrational proposition, Chaucer forces readers to compare them. Apart from revealing character, these lines introduce the scene where Troilus and Criseyde will consummate their love for the first time. The witty mathematical repartee at the beginning of the scene encourages readers to recognize the skillful effect of Pandarus's mathematical error, claiming "dulcarnoun" refers to an irrational solution, whereas it actually refers to a rational solution. In forcing a comparison of the two kinds of right triangles, Chaucer manages to create a complex metaphor for Criseyde's dilemma in wanting Troilus and yet wishing not to disclose that she wants him. He also gives readers a perfect symbol of the incompatible choices she faces near the end of the poem where ideals compete with practicality: either remaining in doomed Troy with a man she loves who cannot (or does not) defend her, or betraying him and suffering both the heartache of a lost love and an ugly reputation at the hands of future poets.

144 / Chapter 6

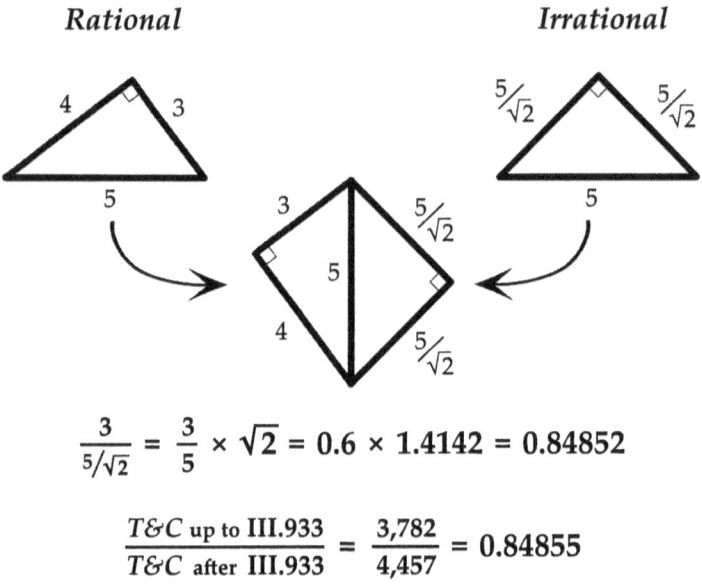

$$\frac{3}{5/\sqrt{2}} = \frac{3}{5} \times \sqrt{2} = 0.6 \times 1.4142 = 0.84852$$

$$\frac{T\&C \text{ up to III.933}}{T\&C \text{ after III.933}} = \frac{3{,}782}{4{,}457} = 0.84855$$

Figure 6.2. Pythagorean triangles: equal hypotenuse

Hart, as noted, convincingly demonstrates that the lengths of all five of the poem's books are determined by the mathematical comparison of rational and irrational triangles. One equation will suffice. In the 3-4-5 triangle on the left half of figure 6.2, the hypotenuse measures 5. If we let both triangles share the same hypotenuse with a length of 5, the two legs of the isosceles right triangle will be $5/\sqrt{2}$.

Of the three possible ratios comparing rational and irrational components,
      upper left leg, 3, to upper right leg, $5/\sqrt{2}$;
      lower left leg, 4, to lower right leg, $5/\sqrt{2}$;
      left half, [3 + 4], to right half, [$5/\sqrt{2} + 5/\sqrt{2}$]
Chaucer apparently applied the ratio of the upper legs to the full length of *Troilus and Criseyde*, 8,239 lines, to arrive at the dimensions 3,782 and 4,457. Through no coincidence, these figures locate the exact line in which Pandarus repeats the word *dulcarnoun*, 3,782 lines from the beginning of the poem and 4,457 lines before its end. As with the *Parliament of Fowls*, where mathematics underscores the perfect harmony and coherence of the created universe, imperfectly carried out or thwarted by some of its inhabitants, so too in *Troilus and Criseyde* rational and irrational triangles capture well the

irreconcilable human circumstance of lives that aim for perfection, yet fall short in misguided action.

The Art of Reporting

The art of reporting in *Troilus and Criseyde* parallels a technique Chaucer uses in his dream visions by showing a complex relationship between his announced subject and a sustained interest in the shaping of verbal records. I say "an announced subject" because, if the narrator's literal words, "The double sorwe of Troilus ... In lovynge, how his aventures fellen / Fro wo to wele, and after out of joie" (I.1–4), were a fair representation of the poem's whole matter, the curiosity raised by his promise to tell this story is likely to wane seven stanzas later when he discloses that Criseyde "forsook hym er she deyde" (I.56). Nor is the poem's subject the mere retelling of earlier accounts of these same characters in ancient Troy, as Chaucer would later do in a number of "the tales of Caunterbury" (*CT* X.1086), for Chaucer declares in the *House of Fame* that unsubstantiated accounts of the past are likely to be untrue. That other versions of the event were merely recorded earlier gives them no greater claim to truth than Chaucer's has. To be sure, these antecedent accounts of events about to be described again afford Chaucer a starting point. I suggest, however, that this very act of shaping verbal reports, the retelling of information learned earlier, or at least so claimed, becomes an important recurring theme of *Troilus and Criseyde*. The critical dialogue surrounding the poem—a kind of verbal report in its own right—tends to support this claim. In the final third of this chapter I take exception to one of these reports, a critical observation rather than a retelling of a source. I refer to the almost universal agreement noted in the previous paragraph, that Criseyde forsook Troilus.

The *Book of the Duchess*, the *Parliament of Fowls*, and the *House of Fame* typically give rise to discussions ancillary to literature, like royal succession, occasion, and to a lesser extent philosophy. Interest in *Troilus and Criseyde*, by contrast, quickly turns to the poem's pure literary dimension. Most readers would agree with Lee Patterson, for example, that the poem confirms Augustine's belief in the incapacity of any moment of secular history, whether the age of Caesar or the medieval period, to provide meaning "in terms of a providential purpose" (1991, 89). While seconding this skepticism over the probative value of history, I would press the point even further. From the critical attention the poem has attracted, one would be justified in assuming that *Troilus and Criseyde* has no historical pertinence of any kind. The critical dialogue remains almost entirely free of historiography, save for accepting ancient reports of Troy's defeat. All the rest are themes of universal occurrence, available to be plucked from antiquity and set in any age, any locale. Other than proper names, little would need adapting to set the story in, say, a Confederate state during the American Civil War, intended for a later audience who knew the South had lost. In short, the poem is nearly ahistorical.

Again, to situate *Troilus and Criseyde* in the context of the ancient poets, while certainly a literary orientation, is still very different from explaining what made Chaucer shape its final form. One useful study compares Chaucer's account of the Dido and Aeneas episode in *House of Fame* with Virgil's treatment of the same material, to show Chaucer "at once congruent ... and significantly at odds with" the Roman poet's perspective (Wetherbee 1984, 88). Another study shrewdly stresses the poet's responsibility "to disentangle and arbitrate between his sources" (Fyler 1979, 111) and his care, in having an actor in a fiction stand for its teller, to replace "Boccaccio's version of the surrogate relationship with the Ovidian one" (128). Each of these studies, and others that could be noted, call attention to valuable perspectives in Chaucer's works. Yet they do not address Chaucer's specific choices that enhance the emotional content of his poetry and the literary coherence of its scenes. We must still study Chaucer's actual lines to see how he "keep[s] the attention and interest of his audience" (Fyler, 114).

Credible Characterization, Incredible Circumstance

Let us begin by acknowledging in *Troilus and Criseyde* one of Chaucer's greatest virtues as an author, his remarkable subtlety. In nearly every scene a half dozen instances of this gentle touch could be noted for their insight, efficiency, and effect. One scene in particular, near the beginning of the poem, stands out for being initiated by the one character who would otherwise seem least likely to initiate anything, and for affording perhaps the deepest insight into this character. Criseyde normally deals assertively with her immediate circle, especially with her uncle Pandarus, yet elsewhere she reveals a demure manner, suggesting a woman accustomed to letting circumstances unfold before her. It is atypical, therefore, at the very beginning of a long chronicle of what may be the most important event in her life, when she is doubly vulnerable, bereft of an influential male's support and burdened with the name of a traitor's daughter, that she should abandon this passive nature to lay her helplessness before Hector, King Priam's son.[2] In a narrative poem of great length, this sequence remains the only act planned and executed by Criseyde herself. It must take extreme courage for her to call on Hector and plead her case before him:

> On knees she fil biforn Ector adown
> With pitous vois, and tendrely wepynge,
> His mercy bad, hirselven excusynge.
>
> (I.110–12)

This touching appeal to Troy's most formidable warrior for a clarification of her status receives in return a generous, unqualified response:

> "Lat youre fadres treson gon
> Forth with meschaunce, and ye youreself in joie
> Dwelleth with us, whil yow good list, in Troie.
>
> "And al th'onour that men may don yow have,
> As ferforth as youre fader dwelled here,
> Ye shul have, and youre body shal men save,
> As fer as I may ought enquere or here."
>
> (I.117–23)

Precisely the assurance of protection she asked for. But is it, one wonders, the reaction Criseyde hoped to receive when she planned this interview? The possibility that Criseyde had other hopes for this meeting, richer by far than Hector's assurance of political asylum, takes tantalizing shape in the narrator's spare report of her gratitude:

> And she hym thonked with ful humble chere,
> And ofter wolde, and it hadde ben his wille,
> And took hire leve, and hom, and held hir stille.
>
> (I.124–26)

Line 125 intrigues us with its suggestiveness. The phrase "ofter wolde" may, of course, merely convey the depth of Criseyde's gratitude, affirming that she would continue thanking Hector for his protection, if "his wille" implied he would welcome hearing her words again. Yet such an innocent meaning would more likely characterize the circumspect speech of a princepleaser than the heartfelt plea of a fearful widow anxious about her bodily well-being. Whatever else may be revealed of Criseyde's character, she is certainly not obsequious. On the other hand, "ofter wolde" may refer only to her appearing in Hector's presence, rather than to the grateful words she might utter on such occasions. The conditional clause that follows, "and it hadde ben his wille," would then qualify how receptive Hector might be to her frequent attendance, especially since he "saugh... that she was so fair a creature" (I.114–15), rather than how eager he would be to hear words of indebtedness repeated overly much. If, in addition to securing Hector's protection, Criseyde has taken herself to him and fallen on knees before him in order to arouse a reaction to her feminine appeal, the officiousness of his reply must be deeply disappointing.

While the sad line with which the interview concludes signals that her effort has been fruitless, even if the visit only partly sought more than official protection, Chaucer's literary purpose succeeds brilliantly. At the very least it affirms her entitlements, as strong as anyone else's in Troy, implying that no motive, political, practical, or social, can justify offering her as an exchange-prisoner in the later scheme to recover Antenor. More important by far, Criseyde's mission to Hector, if motivated as we suggest, establishes her normal feminine reaction to an appealing male while preparing well for a deep irony that occurs later, when her uncle Pandarus shares with her the news of a secret admirer who happens to be the king's son. Though designed only to pique Criseyde's curiosity, this lengthy enticement succeeds beyond her uncle's most ambitious expectation. A brief look ahead to book II shows the extraordinary effect this news has on Criseyde.

Without doubt she knows her uncle has only one interest in life, the affairs of lovers. In fact, the second sentence he utters on entering Criseyde's house, inquiring of the book she and her ladies are reading, "Is it of love?" (II.97), brings an immediate response that confirms how thoroughly she knows Pandarus, "Uncle... youre maistresse is nat here" (II.98). Thus, when she hears directly thereafter that her uncle could tell her something she would enjoy hearing (II.121), she must assume he has in mind something that concerns romance. She pleads to hear the news. But Pandarus will not reveal it. "And whi so, uncle myn? Whi so?" (II.136) she asks. Because, he says,

proudder womman is ther noon on lyve,
And ye it wiste, in al the town of Troye.
I jape nought, as evere have I joye!

   (II.138–40)

Now certain the news concerns her, and must be about love, she pretends to change the subject to various current events, "Tyl she gan axen hym how Ector ferde" (II.153). A logical question, for the current siege preoccupies the town and Hector is its greatest champion. But her uncle has already claimed his news exceeds any news of the war "wel bet than swyche fyve" (II.126). Not changing the subject at all, Criseyde merely supplies a name to the fantasy running wildly in her head. As a further indication of her growing interest in this piece of news, she agrees to dance, after having earlier declined in dismay that anyone should invite her, a widow (II.113–14), to dance. At length her eagerness to hear her uncle's news cuts off his fulsome preamble:

"Now, good em, for Goddes love, I preye,"
Quod she, "come of, and telle me what it is!"

   (II.309–10)

The opening words of this best-of-all-possible-sentences-she-could-everhear quickens an already keen excitement:

Now, nece myn, the kynges deere sone . . .

   (II.316)

A reader can almost feel the page pounding with Criseyde's heartbeat as the virtues of this king's son stretch leisurely across the next line:

The goode, wise, worthi, fresshe, and free . . .

How can Criseyde possibly contain herself when a particular trait of this son, already exercised in her behalf, receives special attention in the next line?

Which alwey for to don wel is his wone . . .

She cannot be unaware that the figure who undoubtedly fills her dreams will be named in the next line, the line beginning

The noble...

When the expected name is pronounced "Troilus" (II.319), her disappointment must be crushing. Pleasure, increasing with every word describing the ideal she has had in mind, crashes at the sound of a name different from the one she expected, a name she barely knows. How great a shock this must be to Criseyde may be gauged by the next sixty-eight lines during which Pandarus fills the air with noisy words and a burst of tears (II.320–85, 326) before she breaks her silence with a bland question, "Now em... what wolde ye devise?" (II.388).

By bringing Criseyde down to the spent emotional level she must reach on learning that Troilus, not Hector, thinks of her romantically, Chaucer creates a critically appealing parallel between the two future lovers. Pandarus will soon busy himself promoting the emotional and sexual union of Troilus and Criseyde. The expanse these future lovers must traverse, and the different behaviors of males and females on such a journey, are shown in greater relief if they begin their affair from the same point. Troilus establishes well in book I his professed indifference to love, although his obsessive interest in the subject cannot go unnoticed. But no parallel has been noted in the remarks or actions of Criseyde. Although her visit to Hector gives reason to suspect she would be more than receptive to the attentions of an admirer, her parallel to Troilus's alleged indifference to love may be inferred from her failure to draw from Hector more than a reply to her literal petition. That her stratagem does not produce the desired response implies her regret at having planned it in the first place and her resolve to steel herself against the future, a widow resigned to living alone. That resignation, like Troilus's professed indifference to love, may be a pose. For the present, however, Chaucer has brought her down to that level of blasé indifference Troilus has heretofore taken habitual pleasure in showing.

A second scene equally worthy of note for its subtlety follows shortly after Criseyde's appeal to Hector. At the feast of the Palladion in book I, Chaucer discloses complexity of character so gently it never interrupts the immediacy of the realistic scene in progress (I.155–315). The very location of this scene says much. When half the citizenry of a besieged town assemble for a religious ceremony, depend upon it, something dire is focusing their minds wonderfully.[3] That is, thoughts of the war *should* subordinate everything to the urgency pressing the Trojans, now surrounded by Greeks and pinned down within the city's walls. Of course, in places of worship everywhere, and in every age, young men all behave alike. Despite two explicit references to the rites that ought to be on everyone's mind, "temple" and "devocioun" (I.185, 187), these words enshrine Troilus's real interest at line 186, "Byholding ay the ladies of the town." Twice, then, a supercilious demeanor colors his behavior. He has no "devocioun" of the religious sort that might help Troy, and he dismisses the young ladies of the town by not even redirecting his devotion from religion to *Frauendienst*.

Subtler still is Chaucer's way of suggesting the false satisfaction that suffuses Troilus at this point in the poem. It is not ego, to which he could easily succumb, but his false wisdom that pleases him, as he contrasts his fellows with the girls whom he now indifferently surveys:

> "God woot, she slepeth softe
> For love of the, whan thow turnest ful ofte!
>
> "I have herd told, pardieux, of youre lyvynge,
> Ye loveres, and youre lewed observaunces...
> O veray fooles, nyce and blynde be ye!
> Ther nys nat oon kan war by other be."
>
> (I.195–203)

The unwarranted degree of self-assurance this wisdom brings him bursts upon us in the next two lines, "he gan caste up the browe, / Ascaunces, 'Loo! is this naught wisely spoken?'" A candidate for the Monk's wisdom in the *Canterbury Tales* predicting an "unwar strook [to] the regnes that been proude" (*CT* VII.2764), Troilus believes his insight lies in assessing the fools he knows, when in fact it points to him, the "oon" that cannot "war by other be" (I.203), about to fall so completely he will shortly be compared to "proude Bayard ... ful fat and newe shorn" (218–22).

The subtlest stroke is yet to come. Still describing the Palladion, Chaucer again writes "Ascaunces" (I.292)—the same word he used of Troilus less than a hundred lines earlier, similarly placed prominently at the beginning of a line, but now describing a very different person in a very different situation. Noticing Troilus's stare, Criseyde strikes a slightly startled, yet assertive facial expression:

> for she lat falle
> Hire look a lite aside in swich manere,
> Ascaunces, "What, may I nat stonden here?"
>
> (I.290–92)

The gloss supplied by most of Chaucer's editors (Benson, Howard, Donaldson) for *ascaunces*, "as if to say," leaves much unsaid. I do not imply the gloss is wrong, only that it offers an interpretation. It assumes body language to which the narrator ascribes conventional thought: "Loo! is this naught wisely spoken?" in Troilus's case, "What, may I nat stonden here?" in Criseyde's. The word historically refers to a slight, albeit significant, head gesture, "a lite aside" (I.291), a small turn of the head away from the direct line of vision, while keeping the eyes on the original focal point. But the gesture also connotes a cock of the head—the brow and head slightly raised to imply Troilus's self-satisfaction, a look slightly lowered to convey Criseyde's fleeting dissatisfaction.

This slight difference in their body language marks a world of difference between the two characters. Troilus sees things straight on, especially himself, though his distorted vision sees only surfaces. His head gesture exposes his chin, particularly in this temple scene where he naively struts in scorn of the war and ridicule of his contemporaries. But the views he holds are his own, uninfluenced by the thoughts of others. From that fatal moment when "His eye percede, and so depe it wente, / Til on Criseyde it smot, and ther it stente" (I.272–73), he has a clear understanding of the objective that will govern the rest of his life.

To understand the very different Criseyde, an elusive creature who may never be fathomed, perhaps demands a sensibility the equal of Chaucer's. She views herself timidly and fearfully, in guarded relation to her surroundings. Her conclusions, to the extent she arrives at any, come at the end of long sessions of worrying, weighing, and watching what others do and say. Accommodating herself to the variety of responses she elicits calls for an equally various adaptation, which Richard Lanham calls her multiple selves (1970, 22). In a similar vein, C. David Benson sees her as "an endlessly protean figure who must be created anew with each reading" (1990, 104). Talbot Donaldson, one of the finest critics of the poem, begins his analysis by calling her a "compelling mystery and challenge" (1975, 1132), yet concludes with a litany of explanations for her eventual betrayal: "mere timidity, mere opportunism, mere sensuality, mere inefficiency—even mere femininity" (1134).[4]

Criseyde's words and actions, even her thoughts, give ample evidence that all of these attempts to describe her are more than valid. These studies may overlook, however, a simpler explanation for this variety of critical responses. Hypersensitive to the opinions others have of her, though not a dissembler until much later in the poem, Criseyde takes particular pains to instill in others an impression that accords well with her own self-image, a person of impeccable character, deportment, and demeanor. In Hector's presence, she cannot reveal the inner thoughts she may have for him, nor disclose to Pandarus her disappointment that he has not brought news of Hector's feelings for her. Similarly, at the feast of the Palladion, when Troilus freezes in a fatal admiration that any attractive woman would often have experienced and instantly recognized, she acts as if Troilus's gaze had something to do with her right to attend the ceremony. She has momentary lapses, of course: when she drops her façade to demand of Pandarus the news he has been withholding from her (II.309–14); when she bursts out crying at the mention of crow's-feet under a woman's eye (II.403); when she asks "Kan [Troilus] wel speke of love?" (II.503); when she says to herself "Who yaf me drynke?" (II.651); and when she drops all pretense at the consummation scene in response to Pandarus's specific instructions (III.1100–1108). These are instances of the natural woman surfacing at moments of extraordinary intensity, the "mere femininity" Donaldson sees. She recovers quickly, never more so than the morning after the consummation, when she attempts to restore her propriety by playfully pinning blame on her uncle, though propriety is quite out of place chez Pandarus:

> How stant it now
> This mury morwe? Nece, how kan ye fare?"
> Criseyde answerde, "Nevere the bet for yow,
> Fox that ye ben! God yeve youre herte kare!
> God help me so, ye caused al this fare,
> Trowe I," quod she, "for al youre wordes white.
> O, whoso seeth yow knoweth yow ful lite."

(III.1562–68)

All these subtle marks of character—these delicate little strokes that etch deeply the marks of human emotion—obscure another characteristic of *Troilus and Criseyde*, always sensed by readers but rarely discussed by critics. Many of the poem's details strain a reader's willingness to suspend disbelief. Later in the story, for example, our faith in the ingenuity of lovers shatters in the notion that two people who love each other in secret, yet find their love threatened by external forces, would acquiesce to an exchange of prisoners and a futile hope for an improbable future reunion as their only strategy to remain together. For starters, they could marry, a thought that never presents itself realistically to them.[5] Then too, readers were already made incredulous much earlier by the uncomfortable presence of Pandarus during the initial stages of Criseyde's and Troilus's intimacy.

From the beginning of the human era men and women have been meeting each other, getting acquainted, falling in love, marrying, propagating, and nurturing, without the help of officious intermediaries telling them how to proceed. In *Troilus and Criseyde*, however, Pandarus seems to be the affair's sine qua non. Chaucer alters the details he learned from his source to make the circumstances of the affair even more unusual, indeed irregular. He not only elevates Pandarus a full generation above the lovers in *Filostrato* but makes him Criseyde's uncle, whereas Pandaro and Criseida are cousins of approximately the same age in Boccaccio. These changes produce the most shocking scene in the whole poem, when the intending lovers, under the minute direction of Uncle Pandarus, attempt to accomplish the most intimate details of sexual love. That two people in love must be shown at the moment of their initial consummation how to do what with which and to whom, as Chaucer's magically mismanaged scene in book III apparently requires, is consummately absurd. We might look at this most perplexing *reductio* of improbability, not only to see how Chaucer rarefies slapstick comedy into ineffable, timeless sublimity, but also to learn why Chaucer places the subtlest characteristics of credible human beings in the least believable circumstances.

Those whose first medieval staple was C. S. Lewis on Courtly Love[6] know well Chaucer's "long epithalamium" with its poignant moment just before the consummation, when Troilus can no longer endure the intensity of his feelings for Criseyde and swoons a sublimely courtly swoon:

Therwith the sorwe so his herte shette
That from his eyen fil there nought a tere,

And every spirit his vigour in knette,
So they astoned or oppressed were.
The felyng of his sorwe, or of his fere,
Or of aught elles, fled was out of towne;
And down he fel al sodeynly a-swowne.

(III.1086–92)

However much one might have wanted a heroic stance here, the unambiguous text will not grant it. Despite six lines of richly suggestive metaphors, the seventh, more than the Greeks, strikes down King Priam's son Troilus, like a Victorian maiden with the vapors.[7] The important critical question, of course, is not what happens but what it signifies. Why does Chaucer make Troilus faint, when his source, the *Filostrato*, has nothing like it at this point in the narrative? By not specifically addressing this question, critics imply that Troilus simply carries to a logical extreme the courtly sighing and whimpering he has displayed since first catching sight of Criseyde in the temple (I.229).[8]

There is not the least reason to doubt any of this. A venerable critical tradition from Kittredge to the present day has agreed that Chaucer draws extensively upon courtly materials, perhaps to hold them in ambivalent light. Nevertheless, one notices the imbalance. A scene lasting some fifty stanzas hardly merits a single exit line, a medical detail at that. The resolution seems simplistic and beside the point, in a poem that is much more complex in every other way than a typical poem of courtly love. To explain the scene as a courtly maneuver, a fainting spell with medical authenticity, recalls Monica E. McAlpine's observation that the narrator "struggles to comprehend the highest reaches of human love and finds the guidance provided by books wanting; he discovers a gap between the experience of his characters and the definitions of philosophers" (1978, 131).

Like the narrator McAlpine has in mind, we suspect there may be a gap between "Experience . . . [and] auctoritee " (cf. *CT* III.1). Criticism has sought Chaucer's meaning in literary, philosophic, and medical terms, while these scenes may all along have been grounded in Troilus's terms, specifically in the physiological conflict he feels at the very moment he swoons. Thus we come back to the scene again and again to see if we have not perhaps missed some important detail that might lift it from the leaves of courtly medicine to the higher reaches of Chaucer's art.

It was Lewis who first went to the heart of this scene, noting that book III contains "some of the greatest erotic poetry of the world." Unfortunately, Lewis changes direction. Having affirmed what his sensitive ear detected, he then denies what his reason found intolerable: "It is a lesson worth learning, how Chaucer can so triumphantly celebrate the flesh without becoming either delirious like Rossetti or pornographic like Ovid" (1936, 196). A close look at this scene, showing how reliable were Lewis's comparisons to Rossetti and Ovid, and how much he missed by denying them, calls first for some backtracking.

Much earlier, Pandarus had pledged himself to advance Troilus's suit with his niece (I.1023–61), later even bringing up the touchy subject of his becoming "a meene / As maken wommen unto men to comen" (III.254–55). He denied the role, of course, not because he loathed the idea of bringing Troilus and Criseyde together, but because he would not accept payment for the service (III.261). Compensated or not, Pandarus clearly intends to bring about Troilus's sexual union with Criseyde, and to control when, where, and how it will be accomplished:[9]

> "But I conjure the, Criseyde, *and oon*
> *And two*, thow Troilus, whan thow mayst goon,
> That at myn hous ye ben at my warnynge,
> For I ful wel shal shape youre comynge;
>
> "And eseth there youre hertes right ynough;
> And lat se which of yow shal bere the belle
> To speke of love aright!"—therwith he lough—
> "For ther have ye a leiser for to telle."
> Quod Troilus, "How longe shal I dwelle,
> Er this be don?" Quod he, "Whan thow mayst ryse,
> This thyng shal be right as I yow devyse."
>
> (III.193–203, emphasis added)

Note that Criseyde listens to this whole plan and, by not contradicting, implies her agreement with it. Thus Troilus waits, sequestered for long hours in Pandarus's closet, first knowing that Criseyde will spend the night there, and then spying her through "a litel wyndow" (III.601) for several more hours after she arrives. To put it mildly, he has high expectations indeed. Consider further how Troilus's excitement must rise, as rain forces Criseyde and her women to remain for the night and he receives a full report from his host along with a final encouragement: "Make the redy right anon, / For thow shalt into hevene blisse wende" (III.703–4). Not just "anon," but "right anon"! Troilus certainly suffers a powerful seizure, but by forces more urgent than Victorian vapour.

At this point Pandarus blunders, though Chaucer's hand remains sure. His exhortation to Troilus (III.703–4) appears to have worked, to judge from his lavish gratitude to Pandarus and devout prayer to every god and goddess he can bring to mind (III.706–35). But a female sensibility needs something quite different from the quick pep talk that readies a male. Accordingly, Pandarus concocts the wonderful story about Criseyde's supposed lover with the even more wonderful name Horaste. He intends the story to make Criseyde say something like the following, "If only my poor Troilus were here now, I would show him how much I love him alone!" Instead of producing its intended effect, this last-second gambit nearly loses the whole game, as Criseyde delivers forty bitter lines on "fals felicitee" (III.814) that Pandarus has difficulty redirecting to the business at hand. She promises to set things straight in the morning; Pandarus speaks of haste. She offers to send the aching lover a blue ring; Pandarus urges eros, not agape. She should make room for him not in her heart but in her bed. "Liggeth stille," Pandarus urges, "and taketh hym right here" (III.948).

Throughout this whole scene Chaucer puns more often on private parts—especially "nought" or "nothyng" for pudendum and "corage" for phallus, or at least masculine sexual energy—than anywhere else in his poetry:[10]

> Now loke thanne, if ye that ben his love
> Shul putte his lif al night in jupertie
> For thyng of nought, now by that God above,
> Naught oonly this delay comth of folie,
> But of malice, if that I shal naught lie.
> What! Platly, and ye suffre hym in destresse,
> Ye neyther bounte don ne gentilesse.[11]
>
>   (III.876–82)
>
> For ther is nothyng myghte hym bettre plese
>
>   (III.886)

> Woot ye not wel that noble and heigh corage
> Ne sorweth nought, ne stynteth ek, for lite?
>
> (III.897–98)

When Troilus finally arrives at the side of Criseyde's bed, little happens either to relieve his woe or to increase her awareness of it. In fact, few scenes in Chaucer are more hilariously incongruous than Criseyde's eighty-four-line protest of innocence, while Troilus's "corage" grows greater every second. Pandarus says it well, "Have ye no care, hym liste nought to slepe" (III.1066). First meaning: "It isn't sleep he yearns for [in your bed]." Second: "He doesn't want to be put to sleep [by your lecture]." Third: "He needs 'the nought' [in order] to sleep."

Lovers in traditional courtly literature may languish in idealized frustration forever. Those made of flesh cannot; at a certain point mechanical laws take over. Modeled more on life than on literature, Troilus has reached that moment and knows it well:

> For it thoughte hym no strokes of a yerde
> To heere or seen Criseyde, his lady, wepe;
> But wel he felt aboute his herte crepe,
> For everi tere which that Criseyde asterte,
> The crampe of deth to streyne hym by the herte.
>
> (III.1067–71)

The usual interpretation of these lines should not be discarded: "Though the sight did not pain him as would lashes of a whip, he was nevertheless anguished to hear or see Criseyde weep." But Troilus's urgent condition forces another meaning, whose key may be "the crampe of deth." Clearly not to be taken literally, "deth" must signify metaphorically a general failure or loss. But if "crampe" is also a metaphor, the sense remains entirely abstract: he feels a pressing sense of failure. That this feeling creeps or strains him about the heart scarcely makes the sense more concrete. If, however, "crampe" has literal force, then an entirely different meaning becomes possible, an alternative fully consistent with the developing scene. That literal sense, in combination with a well-known meaning of "death," may describe the tightening of the male organ prior to orgasm.[12] In this light, the metaphor "strokes of a yerde" takes on complementary meaning as well, and the five lines quoted above now evince a parallel meaning, "It did not seem to him a thrusting motion of the phallus... but he definitely felt... an approaching climax."[13]

The swooning stanza directly follows. I quote it again to have it fresh in mind:

> Therwith the sorwe so his herte shette
> That from his eyen fil there nought a tere,
> And every spirit his vigour in knette,
> So they astoned or oppressed were.
> The felyng of his sorwe, or of his fere,
> Or of aught elles, fled was out of towne;
> And down he fel al sodeynly a-swowne.
>
> (III.1086–92)

As acknowledged above, line 1092 certainly denotes a fainting spell. But to accept the fainting spell by no means precludes Troilus's loss of self-control and surrender to a premature climax, particularly if we carefully analyze the third and fourth lines. Yet these lines depend on whether "vigour" or "spirit" is the direct object of "in knette." Does every spirit contract or hold in his vigor, as Howard reads it,[14] or does his vigor "in knette" every spirit? The former has the support of grammatical convention which usually places a direct object immediately before the verb. But this rule is by no means absolute, since inverted syntax itself appears often in usual Chaucerian practice. The latter sense is supported by the logic of the next line. "They," or whatever this word signifies, seem to be in a state ("astoned," "oppressed") different from their earlier condition. It follows that whatever was acted upon in the previous line (that is, the direct object) must be the same thing signified by the recently changed "they." "They" are in a new condition because they were acted upon in a particular way. Yet the only part of the previous line with any hint of the grammatical plural is the phrase "every spirit." Hence, "every spirit" must be accusative and "vigour" nominative, giving us: "His vigour knitted every spirit in, so [that] these spirits were stunned or pressured." We still cannot translate the line with precision because "vigour" and "spirit" normally carry abstract meanings which provide little help. Nevertheless, the participle "oppressed" and the main verb "fled," two lines later, contribute an image cluster drawn from warfare. Whatever causes the oppression causes the fleeing; whatever is pressured flees. Through a process of variation, "spirit," "they," and "felyng" all refer to the same thing—a feeling of sorrow, or fear, "Or of aught elles." The phrase "aught elles" comes at us, we suspect, with a familiar Chaucerian wink. Whatever "aught elles" means, it feels pressure and ultimately flees.

We learn about this "aught elles," and coincidentally confirm our hypothesis, in the treatise in *Canterbury Tales* of another medical man, "daun Constantyn" (*CT* IV.1810) or Constantine Africanus, who explains that spirit is one of the substances in semen: "Semen consists of humor and spirit," says Constantine. Consequently,

> when semen is emitted the humor lost by the body is a substantial one, drawing its essence from the vital organs.... Hippocrates says the same thing... when we emit semen... weakness often follows.... Galen says the same thing... not only does a humor come from the organs, but the vital spirit also leaves with the semen.... For when the body is drained of these two substances... the vital spirit is dissipated; many have died in this way, and no wonder.
>
> (P. Delany 1970, 61).

It is not clear that the English word *spirit* meant semen in the late fourteenth century, as it apparently did in Shakespeare's day (cf. Sonnet 129, "Th' expense of spirit in a waste of shame / Is lust in action"). But if Troilus's "spirit" at least implies the semen in which it flows, and if "every spirit" can function as the direct object of "in knette," then line III.1088 points to an uncontrollable physiological condition as the cause of Troilus's swoon. And the entire stanza describes (with greater artistry than this discussion) the cognate accusative "flood" that prematurely "fled ... out of towne," bringing a farcical conclusion to this mismanaged assignation. Striving for the sublimity of Guillaume de Lorris's *Roman de la rose*, the characters give us a fourteenth-century fabliau in a Trojan boudoir.

The double-entendre reactions of Pandarus and Criseyde give assurance that Troilus's predicament includes Constantinus's concerns as well as Guillaume's. Since Criseyde has been slow to perceive Troilus's condition–surprisingly slow for a woman who was once married—Pandarus again assumes command, ripping off Troilus's shirt, pushing him into bed, appealing to Criseyde for help, and giving her specific instructions:

> "Nece, but ye helpe us now,
> Allas, youre owen Troilus is lorn!"
> "Iwis, so wolde I, and I wiste how,
> Ful fayn," quod she. "Allas, that I was born!"
> "Yee, nece, wol ye pullen out the thorn
> That stiketh in his herte?" quod Pandare.
>
> (III.1100–1105)

We shall shortly discuss the unusual use of plural "us" in line 1100. For the present, let us focus on the metaphor of a thorn that refers simultaneously to two different perceptions. The abstract, romantic perception sustains the motifs of courtly love: "Will you remove the impediment that makes him suffer such heartache?" The concrete, bodily perception makes a visual connection to the explicit act of intercourse toward which everything has been driving: "Will you uncover the phallus that is intended to penetrate his loved one?" Criseyde does not miss either association, as we infer from her comparison with the archetype of all fructifying instruments, the sun: "Ye, that to me," quod she, "ful levere were / Than al the good the sonne aboute gooth" (III.1107–8). Speaking as a courtly romance heroine, she means "The removal of such impediments is more desirable to me than all the benefits the sun makes possible." As a woman with urgent desires of her own she means "That thorn is much dearer to me than all the generating the sun goes about [doing]." Alas, it was "al for nought" (III.1113), as the narrator says. Yes indeed! We knew the "nought" was the objective from the beginning, as did Pandarus and Troilus certainly and Criseyde probably. We did not know the effort would all be for naught.

What fails at first often succeeds in time. From his first sighting of Criseyde in the temple, Troilus well knew he was seeking physical intercourse. Criseyde too must have known, at some point, that physical union was the immediate issue. But Chaucer knows that human beings, though made of flesh, are created for something loftier than acts available to every "sheep that rouketh in the folde" (*CT* I.1308). From the point of Troilus's swoon to the end of book III, he and Criseyde grow into their fully human dimensions. Earlier, Chaucer makes time and place a paramount concern, showing Pandarus racing from one palace to another, carrying messages back and forth, monitoring the rain, manipulating a dinner party, arranging sleeping quarters, and very nearly tolling the time. From the failed coupling forward, however, all reference to time, location, cushions, bodily details, and anything else to remind readers of those sheep in the fold vanishes from the text. Where the poem has been specific about shirts, sheets, and thorns, it now eschews the mundane, ephemeral impediments that obstruct men and women, lifting these lovers above temporal concerns, creating an experience that is "miraculous and transcendent" (Windeatt 1992, 226).[15] Troilus and Criseyde become one flesh, but no line tells us when and how they do so.

Chaucer does finally grant these lovers the privacy he denied them earlier, yet this long consummation scene at the heart of book III, like much of the entire *Troilus and Criseyde*, has that rare combination of credibility and incredibility that paradoxically permits readers a fleeting glimpse of harmony. Care should be taken, however, to distinguish those parts of the poem that accord well with our experience of how human beings actually behave from those that seem to strike a wrong note. Everything Criseyde does and says convinces us she is a genuine woman who reacts as any other woman would in similar situations. Moreover, the façade of propriety she maintains (cf. III.561–88) wins unquestioned empathy, for it is exactly what would be expected from a woman highly conscious of the opinions of others, yet also responsive to her natural inclinations. Chaucer's treatment literally announces Criseyde is an honorable woman, but also implies her preoccupation with thoughts of Troilus. Similarly, Troilus behaves as an impatient male typically acts: consumed by thoughts and urges of physical contact, as would be his similitude in book I, proud Bayard (I.216–24), were he led to a breeding barn and suitably prepared for a covering. Nor are readers alarmed at finding themselves in Criseyde's sleeping chamber—nay, in her bed—since the fabliaux scenes in *Dame Sirith*, the *Miller's Tale*, the *Reeve's Tale*, and others were standard fare in the late Middle Ages. No, the two lovers in the story make not a single unbelievable move. Still, awkwardness suffuses many a scene. Having begun at the end of book I, it increases rapidly through book II, reaching a nearly unacceptable level in book III in the consummation scene. Without question, its source is Pandarus, in particular his highly irregular attendance at the most intimate and private of human relations. His presence cannot be avoided, however, for *Troilus and Criseyde* has been following from its very beginning the demands of two seemingly unrelated genres that rarely overlap in one respect but almost completely coincide in another. To appreciate more fully this technique, which Chaucer would develop with great skill as his literary career progressed, we must look forward to one of the tales of Canterbury.

When a Work Belongs to Two Genres

The combination of true-to-life characters and preposterous situations reaches an almost untenable point for Chaucer in a work produced at the same time he wrote *Troilus and Criseyde*, or slightly later. A brief glance at this work may make the strategy he uses for *Troilus* more accessible than it would be on its own. In the early years of Grisilde's marriage in the *Clerk's Tale*, her husband Walter insists that their firstborn child, a daughter, must be put to death, falsely blaming this horrible demand on his subjects: "I moot doon with thy doghter for the beste, / Nat as I wolde, but as my peple leste" (*CT* IV.489–90). Mindful of a solemn vow she made at the time of her marriage, never to oppose anything her husband requests (351–64), Grisilde surrenders her firstborn child for what she assumes will be its death, as she does again a few years later when Walter makes the same demand regarding their firstborn son. Grisilde wrenches the heartstrings of anyone who reads how she caresses her children for the last time before surrendering them to Walter's sergeant. But she also angers these same readers for yielding to the unrelentingly cruel demands of her husband. Walter's unconscionable demand of Grisilde–unimaginable anywhere save in scripture—would easily justify her resisting the marquis, we would argue, and no one would fault her disregard of her earlier vow.

This tale, however, explores much more than dysfunctional domesticity by conveying as its second subject a Christian's struggle with the Providential Plan. In this very different, though concomitant, design, Grisilde represents Christ, "born ... in an oxe-stalle" (*CT* IV.397–98, cf. 207, 291), "from hevene sent ... Peple to save and every wrong t'amende" (440–41), who sits "as a lamb ... meke and stille" (538) and willingly surrenders temporal power to mankind in an agreement implied by the words of her earlier vow. As God will never renege on this promise of free will, however impiously and ungratefully mankind expresses this will, so Grisilde never breaks her vow to accept her husband's wishes, regardless of how cruelly he shapes them. Meanwhile, postlapsarian man, as Walter represents him, exults in his temporal power by continually tempting the limits of God's forbearance. Whereas Grisilde ought to oppose her husband within the context of a family's temporal life, she sadly yields to Walter's will within the eternal context of the

Providential Plan.[16] Chaucer structures other tales according to similar dual-genre designs: the *Knight's Tale* places a typical romance in the context of a parliament of three ages; Alisoun of Bath chases the temporal goals of wealth and appeal, while at the same time implying her preference for the lasting values of fidelity and love; the Pardoner, if we can take him at face value, uses a sacred mission to achieve tangible rewards; and the Prioress compromises nothing of a chatelaine's affecting style, while her deeply devotional tale honors the Virgin. Yet modern readers remain uncomfortable with medieval literature's simultaneous representation of the two orders that determine human life, the temporal and the eternal, or fail to understand the difference between mutable and immutable values, as Lady Philosophy would name them.

Troilus and Criseyde likewise takes simultaneous direction from two different genres. In the poem's central courtship, Criseyde, Troilus, and Pandarus remain as true to a universal understanding of human love as Hector's and Diomede's responses to Criseyde's distress—very different from each other—faithfully represent the conduct of certain males in every age, one reacting to her plea for protection, the other to her vulnerability among new surroundings in the Greek camp. At the same time, these three principals have also been crafted to answer the needs of symbolic literature, where each represents an abstraction. As the *Clerk's Tale* places its characters in the temporal context of domestic life and maternal love while also giving Grisilde divine attributes to incorporate the eternal order, *Troilus and Criseyde* too addresses the seemingly antithetical realms of the transitory and the permanent. Pandarus, Criseyde, and Troilus act believably as principals in a medieval romance, while they also represent the apexes of a literary triangle. Conventions consistent with one of these genres, though improbable in the other, are nonetheless required to support Chaucer's plan to sustain both designs. A domestic scene where an uncle sits quietly by the fire, "As for to looke upon an old romaunce" (*T&C* III.980), while an intimate scene unfolds before his very eyes, strains credulity. Yet the poem's symbolic dimension demands it. Every author who intends fully and intimately to realize such an event in literature must become part of each lover—become, as it were, their very souls. Pandarus, the great artificer who brings their love into being, shares with Criseyde and Troilus both the sublime privilege of their love and the insupportable torment of their fate.

Criseyde does not need a father named Calkas to alert readers to her shrewd ability to assess options. Though she is known almost completely for her arresting beauty and affecting demeanor, the poem tells us less about the lady herself than the effect she has on others, not least the narrator who takes three descriptions to bring her from angelic heights before landing the actual woman in Troy.[17] Few characteristics are more noticeable than her habit of scrutinizing whatever she encounters. She constantly thinks, plans, and evaluates, though acting thereafter for inscrutable reasons that may be unrelated to her earlier examination. Slow as she is to fall in love, her self-assurance suggests she might have been content to remain a widow for the remainder of her days had not Pandarus alerted her to romance and Troilus lifted her to love. That she rises during book III to heights she may never before have known, only to fall precipitously thereafter, gives her a reflection of the natural world, a persistent survivor capable of assuming whatever shape various forces fashion for her: she "behave[s] in such a way as to please the onlooker, and desire what most desires her" (Donaldson 1970, 57).

Troilus, the direct opposite of Criseyde, lacks a "calculating" temperament in the sphere of action we can observe. Born at a time when Venus "nas not al a foo / To Troilus in his nativitee" (II.684–85), he takes to his bed when first struck by love, incapable of anything but moaning in the manner of courtly lovers in romances written under the influence of Venus. Not that the man cannot reason. Quite to the contrary, before Pandarus manages to make this love affair reality, "thought" alone governs Troilus's waking and sleeping moments, a condition that persists at least to the soliloquy on predestination (IV.958–1082) that fully demonstrates his capacity as a thinker. From the moment he sees Criseyde at the feast of the Palladion (I.273), he has an idea of the perfection their love might assume, an aesthetic ideal, rather than a practical plan for achieving it. The eagle of the *House of Fame*, especially in its role as symbol of philosophy and poetry, would not inappropriately represent Troilus. So, too, the celebrated dream in which an eagle exchanges its heart for Criseyde's (II.925–31) foretells the union of the capable, shrewd, transitory, natural world of Criseyde and the rarefied, fragile, idealistic world of Troilus.

The invention of Pandarus may be Chaucer's most inspired metaphor. Wholly fictional—or at least unnecessary from one point of view, the view taken by the outside world—Pandarus is not at all a fiction from the perspective of the two lovers. Among other things, he gives concrete expression to the thoughts and desires Criseyde and Troilus experience on their own but lack the technical skill to bring into being. Pandarus and Chaucer are similar, therefore, not because they describe themselves alike or because they stand in a similar relation to the principal characters in a love story—Chaucer's being a literary relation to the lovers, Pandarus's offered as real—but because they are both makers, shapers, artists. Chaucer indeed makes poems and Pandarus makes a love affair, but Pandarus must be given credit for bringing the would-be lovers together, for engineering the entire courtship, and for joining in one flesh Troilus's idealism and Criseyde's practicality. No artist has ever had to know more about the natures of his characters, their inclinations, habits, capabilities, and limitations, than Pandarus has had to know about Criseyde and Troilus. In creating the character of Pandarus, Chaucer allows us, as it were, to perch on the shoulder of an artist at work, for it is Pandarus, rather than either of the lovers, who understands instantly that to join these two would produce—even if only for one astonishingly beautiful book III—a perfect work of art.

Pandarus performs an extremely complicated role. To say he represents a craftsman, an artificer, inadequately accounts for his skill with technique. While we have no reason to doubt he is a "frend" (I.548) of Troilus, despite the full generation separating their ages, the timing of his first appearance in the poem, directly following Troilus's brief apostrophe to a superior being variously named "God" (517, 519, 526, 533) and "Lord" (528), implies Pandarus may be more than a friend. Since these allusions and direct addresses sound like brief interjections, largely void of meaning, as in the taunt Troilus imagines from an earlier target of his ridicule, "Now, thanked God, he may gon in the daunce / Of hem that Love list febly for to avaunce" (517–18), they are apparently not to be taken as a summons to the god of Love. That is, Pandarus's sudden appearance probably does not signify that he is the god of love answering a plea to appear. Nor should we imagine that Troilus is worshiping at this god's altar when he kneels down and clasps Pandarus in his arms near the end of book I (I.1044–45). Nevertheless, Pandarus's appearance occurs at a significant moment in the progress of Troilus's thought, between those helpless moments of emotional excess after he rushes home from the Palladion to take to his bed and that point where he turns his attention to the immediate future, to thoughts of assuaging the anguish caused by his first sight of Criseyde.

The ensuing conversation between Pandarus and Troilus, closer to a sparring session than a calm discussion, cannot be very different from the internal deliberations we may assume Troilus has at this moment in his life. It seems dictated by the two roles that have identified Troilus in the poem thus far, professional warrior and sudden convert at the altar of love. Hence the role of Pandarus, at least in these early exchanges between the two men, may well approximate one of the voices of Troilus's internal debate.[18] Instead of offering "a speaking portrait of his own creator, Geoffrey Chaucer," as some have argued,[19] much of Pandarus's complex role gives voice to the inner thoughts of Troilus, later to those of Criseyde. As this scene progresses, the two sides of this internal deliberation gradually become clear, one apparently incapable of making productive moves, despite wishing to act on this sudden arrival of love, the other urging forward movement to embrace love with all the strategy and artifice Pandarus can provide.

Let us assume that in this early scene with Troilus Pandarus easily recognizes the symptoms of "lovers' malady"—all standard fare in his métier. But getting Troilus to admit the cause of his present distress poses difficulty, for such an admission would compromise this celebrated warrior's reputation for fearless action in the field. Further, it would expose him to the kind of ridicule he himself has often aimed at his fellows for dreaming distractedly under the same kind of spell. Thus Pandarus approaches his challenge from the military perspective, "Han now thus soone Grekes maad yow leene?" (I.553), followed by another taunt, on the assumption that one fearing imminent death naturally thinks of religion, "God save hem that . . . kan . . . bringe oure lusty folk to holynesse!" (558–60). The strategy succeeds, for it makes Troilus snap at his friend, "What cas . . . or what aventure / Hath gided the . . ." (568–69). Yet he does not finish this sentence as one would expect, letting the onus fall on Pandarus for his officious triviality when more important matters are occupying this warrior. No: he finishes the sentence by bringing the subject back to his woeful condition, ". . . gided the to sen me langwisshinge, / That am refus of every creature?" (569–70).

The paradoxical performance that characterizes Troilus thus far, courage in combat and lassitude in love, cannot have escaped Troilus's own notice, for in reply he excuses his surprising inability by claiming that the forces making him "refus of every creature" (570) are "Wel more than aught the Grekes han yet wrought" (578). Indeed, much later in the poem, when Pandarus scolds Troilus for a lack of "hardyment / To take a womman which that loveth the"

(IV.533–34), Troilus confirms that arguments Pandarus presents have long been in his own mind: "Al this have I myself yet thought ful ofte, / And more thyng than thow devysest here" (IV.542–43). The narrator even seems to give Pandarus a brief respite from his role as spokesman for Troilus's thoughts, for during Pandarus's press to learn the name of the woman Troilus loves, the narrator appropriates Pandarus's aphoristic style to shape these thoughts:

> to tellen nas nat his entente
> To nevere no man, for whom that he so ferde;
> For it is seyd, "Men maketh ofte a yerde
> With which the maker is hymself ybeten . . .
> Ek som tyme it is a craft to seme fle
> Fro thyng whych in effect men hunte faste;
> Al this gan Troilus in his herte caste.
>
> (I.738–49)

This similarity of form between thoughts alleged to be Troilus's and the natural mode of expression we have come to expect from Pandarus makes an outburst from Troilus a few lines later all the more surprising:

> Now pees, and crye namore,
> For I have herd thi wordes and thi lore;
> But suffre me my meschief to bywaille,
> For thi proverbes may me naught availle.
>
> (I.753–56)

Who, we wonder, has been influencing whom? Troilus may have inadvertently picked up the speech habits of his friend and advisor. But we cannot deny that Pandarus has been giving voice to Troilus's undoubted thoughts.

Further evidence that Pandarus's very words reveal the actual thoughts of others may be found in book II where Criseyde learns from her uncle that Troilus loves her, a sequence whose indirection recalls the different answer Criseyde gave earlier when Pandarus invited her to dance. The first invitation (II.110), coming *before* Criseyde knows Pandarus has important news, earns a mild rebuke. A short time later, *after* she knows this news pertains to her and probably concerns love but still has not been disclosed, she enthusiastically accepts his second invitation (221–25). Eventually Pandarus feigns surrender to his niece's insistence that he share his news and identifies

Troilus as her love-stricken admirer (319). That this news does not arouse the enthusiasm Hector's name would have summoned, we have already suggested. Now, however, let us consider the verbal dance that ensues after she learns that Troilus is her admirer, a slow minuet in which Pandarus follows a rhythm that may already have animated Criseyde on earlier occasions since becoming a widow.

Nothing untoward or risqué bears notice in the initial catalogue of reasons Pandarus gives his niece to encourage her to think kindly of Troilus. Exaggerating his friend's anguish and adding his own, as many a courtly-love expression is wont to do, he alleges that her indifference would be hazardous to their health; all beauty is bestowed for a purpose, which a failure to respond would thwart. Do not think anything improper is at issue, he argues, for kindness and pity are all he has in mind. Nor should she worry about gossip, since it is only friendship he asks. These thoughts and cautions are likely to have occurred to Criseyde on her own, or to any young woman apprised of an admirer, without any prompting from an uncle whose commitment can be assumed to coincide with her best interests. "Her best interests," that is, until she gives a small sign of accepting his reasoning: "what wolde ye devise?" (II.388). Assuming her question signals agreement with his entire plan, Pandarus leaps into the breach with an insightful if ill-advised remark:

> er that age the devoure,
> Go love; for old, ther wol no wight of the.
> . . . .
> The kynges fool is wont to crien loude,
> Whan that hym thinketh a womman berth hire hye,
> "So longe mote ye lyve, and alle proude,
> Tyl crowes feet be growe under youre yë,
> And sende yow than a myrour in to prye,
> In which that ye may se youre face a morwe!"
>
> (II.395–405)

Small wonder Criseyde "began to breste a-wepe anoon" (408), or that she conceals with transparent words a more painful explanation for her tears. An uncle urging her to enter a liaison presents less danger for her than the crow's-feet she thought only she had discovered.

If one merely suspects the underlying reason for Criseyde's tears, proof arrives 180 lines later, after Pandarus, in effect, repeats the seamy suggestion she claims sent her into tears. This second wording takes a more explicit form than the first. Where Pandarus, with an assist from thoughts that must have inspired Andrew Marvell, has earlier said only, "Go love" (396), he later says, "Ther were nevere two so wel ymet, / Whan ye ben his al hool as he is youre" (586–87). If the former words reduced Criseyde to tears, these explicit references to a carnal consummation ought to receive an even stronger response. They do not. Instead, Pandarus's sensuous proposal brings out a playful denial whose negative, "nought," takes her to an even more graphic double-entendre mirth. A little laugh at her own risqué level softens her accusation against Pandarus:

"Nay, therof spak I nought, ha, ha!" quod she;
"As helpe me God, ye shenden every deel!"

(II.589–90)

Little occurs between Pandarus's two descriptions of the union he longs to see to account for Criseyde's very different reaction to this second wording. Certainly the intervening question we looked at earlier, asked immediately after Criseyde learns that only Pandarus knows of the impending affair, "Kan he wel speke of love?" (II.503), brings a smile of expected success to Pandarus's face. But the absence of any reference to her advancing age has more significance. Pandarus's omission confirms his understanding that the tears shed earlier had nothing to do with his seamy proposal, and everything to do with what Marvell in *To His Coy Mistress* called "Time's wingèd chariot hurrying near." That her outburst has been so sudden and extreme, albeit quickly called "shock" at her uncle's ribald suggestion, implies that Pandarus's loose remark about crow's-feet gives audible expression to a thought Criseyde herself has lately worried over.

Let us not leave Criseyde's two-line response to Pandarus without noting how it captures another of Chaucer's subtle strategies. At the beginning of this study I asked readers to think of the elapsed time between the period when Chaucer was struggling to become a poet, perhaps to keep himself "fro ydelnesse" as did the man in black in *Book of the Duchess* (1155), and the years of his great literary achievement. The suggestion seems to ask for a formula or a method that might reveal a process, catch the poet in actual motion. Unfortunately, analysis of this kind is not possible, not because of a misconception that growth implies movement, or at least a dynamic state, but because no observer has a faculty for literally seeing movement, either in literature or in life. In fact, human beings see motion very much the way a camera records movement—one exposure at a time. As an eye follows a moving object, say a bird in graceful flight, the bird assuredly flies through the air without interruption, but the eye following the bird, if one can closely observe another person's eye, jerks along, registering one snapshot after another. It is not the eye, then, but the mind that resolves or interprets the eye's series of images as seamless movement. So it is with an attempt to understand literary progress, as we have been doing throughout this book. At best, we can only compare separate exposures from which we infer movement. What seems a mere analogy here between literary maturation and physical movement may be more realistic than metaphoric, especially with Chaucer, whose progress involves expansion to wider and deeper levels of meaning.

Criseyde has merely asked Pandarus how he knew of Troilus's interest in her. The long reply she receives from her uncle (II.575–88), though a carefully crafted crescendo covering at least eight points in fourteen lines, conveys only one meaning, as anyone with the least experience with Pandarus would know well. It concludes with a suggestive metaphor, "And be ye wis as ye be fair to see, / Wel in the ryng than is the ruby set," and a literal prediction, "Ther were nevere two so wel ymet, / Whan ye ben his al hool as he is youre" (II.584–87). Pandarus's speech, however, does not interest us now as much as does Criseyde's two-line reply

"Nay, therof spak I nought, ha, ha!" quod she;
"As helpe me God, ye shenden every deel!"

(II. 589–90)

Her first five words imply only that her uncle must be thinking of a courtship's full progress, while she is considering only an initial meeting. Nothing unusual in this first snapshot. But she places her denying "nought" at the end of the phrase, while the canny author chooses for this word a spelling that brings Pandarus's suggestive meaning to the ribald conclusion he has intended from the beginning. Criseyde bursts out laughing on realizing that her inadvertent diction introduces a far coarser term than does either Pandarus's coy metaphor of a ruby set in a ring or his explicit language of carnal possession. This second flash of a carnal Criseyde differs very much from the woman who, just a short time earlier, projected an image of a widow still in mourning. Yet a third snapshot develops with Criseyde's final words blaming Pandarus for this complicated movement, "As helpe me God, ye shenden every deel!" Wrong. It is not Pandarus's metaphoric images, nor his frank words, that invite the verb "shenden"; it is Criseyde's recognition that she has allowed herself to reach the level Pandarus intended for her, as her own inadvertent double entendre demonstrates. Three quick images, replicas of how the eye sees, convince a reader that Criseyde has been spiraling downward.

As these two lines illustrate by analogy, we cannot *see* subtle movement in Chaucer's maturation. Yet we are conscious it has occurred. The dreamer in *Duchess* never says, "Sir, your lines are ridiculous. Speak more directly." We can only compare his two voices, one that ties his tongue in stylized verbosity as it strives for poetry, and another that has no difficulty with ordinary conversation. When the last words from the man in black echo the mature sounds and cadences of actual thought, Chaucer no longer need show the dreamer and the man in black as different characters, as if they were competing images in an out-of-focus picture. The man in black does not so much disappear as join the dreamer in a single image. In *Parliament of Fowls* neither the narrator nor Scipio Africanus usurps the role of critic to explain that the forces keeping the heavens in harmony, expressed in numerical proportions as well as in words, are the same as those that govern man. To confirm this similarity, Chaucer permits readers to compare Scipio's wisdom with the narrator's dream; to weigh Venus's temple, including the allegorical figures surrounding it, against the verdant, fruitful, active scenes accompanying Lady Nature. The arid desert surrounding a temple at the beginning of *House of Fame*, coupled with Fame's house and its lifeless statuary, invite comparison with the bustling vitality of the House of Rumor. All these before-and-after comparisons give evidence of Chaucer's progress as a poet.

Pandarus is not alone in conveying matter obtained from other sources. Everyone in the poem has a role in reporting events, actions, and words that originate elsewhere. To take the most obvious example, the narrator says he is following the account of someone named Lollius (I.394, V.1653).[20] This may have been an attempt by Chaucer to gain respectability for his poem by naming a Latin author of the story, whose name may have been based on a mistaken (or not) translation of a line in Horace (Kittredge 1917). The entire poem, an account of an earlier author's report, is at least twice removed from the events themselves. From the opening lines of his retelling of this story, regardless of our not knowing its precise source, a reader senses disparity between the stated subject of Chaucer's great love poem and the challenge this subject presents to the narrative voice. To make "sorwe" overshadow "lovynge" presents less of a problem in a poem whose first appeal summons "Thesiphone . . . goddesse of torment" (I.1–8) than where to fix the poem's center of gravity, how the poem's principal characters face their challenges, and how the narrator faces his. No uncertainty lingers over the meaning of "the double sorwe of Troilus," despite the clarification that "double sorwe" does not mean a second sorrow compounding a former, as could be expected from its modifier, but the same sorrow experienced twice with an intervening period of "wele" (I.4). The task of reporting this story, however, remains very much a matter of uncertainty, for the narrator reveals apprehension over the outcome:

Thesiphone, thow help me for t'endite
Thise woful vers, that wepen as I write.

(I.6–7)

The grammatical subject of plural *wepen*, obviously *vers*,[21] leaves no syntactic ambiguity to cloud the arresting metaphor of tears that seep from verses in the process of being written. The very act of forming letters of the alphabet to complete the words in a verse that sheds tears evokes biological life, permitting readers and listeners to imagine actual tears. Though obviously metaphoric, the conception's literal meaning agrees so well with the understanding of poet as creator that a greater significance cannot be entirely ignored. The opening lines of *Canterbury Tales*, for example, allude to the Creation by assembling in perfect regularity water, earth, air, and fire, under conditions of hot/cold and moist/dry, to create in a gentle way the thunderous periods Genesis describes in its first chapter. We saw as well a deliberate equation between love and the creation of poetry in *Parliament of Fowls*, where "the craft so long to lerne" refers to "Love" (1–4). Let us also remember the interchangeability of love and poetry in *Book of the Duchess*, as Paula Neuss has shown, where the dreamer re-creates his much loved lady in lines of verse, and again in *Fame*, as J.A.W. Bennett, Sheila Delany, and others have pointed out, where everyone is named a "lover" (*HF* 606–99).[22] For Chaucer, a poet's relation to his craft and the work this craft produces parallels the Creator's relation to the created universe. The implications of this equation hold great significance for the narrator of these woeful verses that weep as he writes them.

Creating a Living Record

To invest a poem with life affords a narrator access to a depth of insight that may not be available without the calculated untruths of metaphor. But living creatures, even those on whom life has been bestowed in a poem, live ever in danger, as does a child who may lead an adult life her parent prayed she would avoid. Thus when Scipio Africanus says he will give the narrator of *Parliament of Fowls* "mater of to wryte" (*PF* 168), the matter expands to everything that possesses life when we look for the deepest subject of *Troilus and Criseyde*. No candidate can be excluded from the lines that seek aid from Thesiphone in the poem's second stanza:

> Help me, that am the sorwful instrument,
> That helpeth loveres, as I kan, to pleyne;
> For wel sit it, the sothe for to seyne,
> A woful wight to han a drery feere,
> And to a sorwful tale, a sory chere.
>
> (I.10–14)

Who can sort out with certainty the references in these lines? Do the first-person-singular pronouns of lines 10 and 11 and "the sorwful instrument" who helps lovers lament refer to the narrator or to the poem itself? Further complicating the poem's opening thoughts, the "woful wight" and "drery feere" of line 13 could as easily be one of the imagined "loveres" two lines earlier as the narrator, or the poem. The subject most important to the author of *Troilus and Criseyde* may not be the woe from which Troilus rises to joy, only to return again to woe, nor yet the lines of former poets and what Chaucer did to them, but the author/narrator's relation to this "sorwful tale" (I.14), especially the challenge he faces to tell it aright. For the task confronting the narrator receives as much of the poem's focus as the personal and civic tale that took place—or may have taken place—in Troy. The narrator often shows his awareness of his struggle to express material appropriately, imagining one such moment as a challenge to convey Criseyde's sorrow at her impending exchange for Antenor:

> How myghte it evere yred ben or ysonge,
> The pleynte that she made in hire destresse?
> I not; but, as for me, my litel tonge,
> If I discryven wolde hire hevynesse,
> It sholde make hire sorwe seme lesse
> Than that it was.
>
> (IV.799–804)

Verses do not literally weep, of course, however much the claim that they do adds meaning to the poet's struggle with the story he has elected to tell. The narrator's bold metaphor does, however, afford the poet a chance to acknowledge the fearsome challenge he faces to invent the revealing untruths—such are what metaphors are made of—that convey the story more accurately than his plain summary does in the poem's first five lines. For the poem's challenge is not only to unfold an intimate personal and political story in Troy, but to study the telling of various stories. Scarcely a scene passes that does not have some report, or account, or retelling of events newly shaped for a desired effect. Artful fictions are one kind of story, as when Pandarus concocts a bizarre fiction—out of thin air, one assumes—to explain how he learned of Troilus's love for Criseyde (II.498–571), a report of words spoken in sleep that not even Troilus could deny. Later he virtually dictates the first letter Troilus writes to Criseyde, urging him to eschew abstruse arguments; to blot it with a few tears; not to overuse a felicitous expression; and to avoid speech that ill suits the subject (II.1023–43). The letter is a kind of fiction, for it comes from Pandarus as much as from Troilus. Others too contribute reports more or less fictional, beginning with Troilus's own report of his love for Criseyde. Indeed, he commits himself to love on the strength of a fiction, a report he makes to himself, a visual account of Criseyde from his own imagination. Immediately after he sees Criseyde for the first time, he hastens home, throws himself on his bed to suffer lovers' malady alone, and begins to think of her

>   withouten lette,
> That, as he sat and wook, his spirit mette
> That he hire saugh a-temple, and al the wise
> Right of hire look, and gan it newe avise.

> Thus gan he make a mirour of his mynde
> In which he saugh al holly hire figure,
> And that he wel koude in his herte fynde.
> It was to hym a right good aventure
> To love swich oon.
>
> (I.361–69)

In the next stanza Chaucer gives Troilus a thought that hints at a fruitful line of inquiry. To love such a one as Criseyde, Troilus notes, would be "no shame, / Al were it wist" (I.374–75), but rather the opposite. In book II Chaucer gives the same thought to Criseyde: "Men myghten demen that he loveth me. / What dishonour were it unto me, this?" (II.730); as "this knyght ... is the worthieste, / ... it may do me no shame" (II.761–63). The striking similarity of these thoughts suggests that Chaucer intended to have Criseyde and Troilus follow parallel paths throughout the poem. The "mirour of his mynde" (I.365) that Troilus frankly admits he constructed may have a counterpart, then, in Criseyde's progress toward love. Indeed it does.

As Criseyde completes a sixteen-stanza debate with herself over the pros and cons of loving Troilus (II.701–805) and walks through her garden before retiring for the night, her attention is arrested by the "Troian song" (II.825) alluded to earlier, sung by her niece Antigone. From the noncommittal nothing-ventured-nothing-gained (cf. II.807–8) that leaves Criseyde's internal debate unresolved, Antigone's song brings her to the threshold of love:

> every word which that she of hire herde,
> She gan to prenten in hire herte faste,
> And ay gan love hire lasse for t'agaste
> Than it dide erst
>
> (II.899–902)

The narrator makes no claim that Antigone's song serves as a record of Criseyde's thoughts, yet its verses echo lines of the "Canticus Troili" (I.400–420, adapted from Petrarch's Sonnet 88) so closely as to suggest that Criseyde's progress in love in book II parallels Troilus's progress in book I, including the meditation and song that inform both of these future lovers.

It matters little that neither Criseyde's internal debate nor the mirror Troilus constructs in his mind has anything to do with love. It has everything to do with how the narrator represents character, for instance in the way he reverses sequence. Where Troilus has already committed himself to love Criseyde *before* he sings the "Canticus Troili," Criseyde begins to think of accepting Troilus *after* hearing Antigone's song. These different sequences imply a subtle difference between men and women. For a male, the beauty of a woman's face and form, however unreliable at predicting love's success, often presents an irresistible attraction. Thus Troilus yields immediately. A female feels immediate attraction too, but before committing herself to a course of action she looks for affirmation. For Criseyde, the intoxicating strains of a love song, just as irrelevant to love as Troilus's mirror, provides that affirmation. Quietly transferring Antigone's voice, "an heven ... to here" (II.826), to the "love" she celebrated, Criseyde further imagines herself as the loved one in the song, the "goodlieste mayde / Of gret estat in al the town of Troye" (II.880–81). She entirely ignores the words Antigone uses (II.890–96) that confirm the mortal strokes, the fruitless trees, and the barren pools to which the *Parliament of Fowls* refers (*PF* 134–40).

Antigone's song does not completely erase the fearful thoughts Criseyde mulls over at length; they survive in a scene she dreams shortly after retiring for the night. Words normally associated with hurtful violence, "longe clawes," "out ... he rente" (II.927–28), cause neither fear nor pain, as she dreams an eagle exchanges its heart for hers. Like the bliss and pain of love given equal attention on a gate in *Parliament of Fowls* (*PF* 127–40), Criseyde's dream attests that love is neither all joy nor all strife, as many a fiction suggests, but must balance the two equally, often at the same time.

If Chaucer did plan parallel courses for the two lovers' progress in love, neither the participants in the events of the story nor its readers have responded to them in similar ways. Troilus receives unmitigated praise from his contemporaries and modern critics alike for fidelity, *trouthe*, and a host of other virtues, as well as the oft-repeated accolade that he is the second greatest warrior in Troy. Criseyde, by contrast, has been chastised through the ages, as she knew she would be, beginning with the narrator's indictment "she forsook [Troilus] er she deyde" (I.56), continuing to Pandarus's condemnation "I hate ... Cryseyde; / And, God woot, I wol hate hire evermore!" (V.1732–33), and confirming even her own judgment:

> Allas, for now is clene ago
> My name of trouthe in love, for everemo!

> For I have falsed oon the gentileste
> That evere was, and oon the worthieste!
>
> Allas, of me, unto the worldes ende,
> Shal neyther ben ywriten nor ysonge
> No good word, for thise bokes wol me shende.
> O, rolled shal I ben on many a tonge!
> Thorughout the world my belle shal be ronge!
> And wommen moost wol haten me of alle.
> Allas, that swich a cas me sholde falle!
>
> (V.1054–64)

Her prescience was borne out soonest in the *Testament of Cresseid*, Robert Henryson's unambiguous *portrait moralisé* showing Criseyde as a leper and a beggar (Fox 1981). Shakespeare's *Troilus and Cressida* carves in stone the prevailing critical view, demeaning the entire story and giving each lover on the occasion of their perfunctory wedding an ironic foreshadowing: "As true as Troilus" (3.2.181); "As false as Cressid" (3.2.195). In the modern critical view, no assessment of Chaucer's poem would be complete that does not acknowledge Criseyde's betrayal of Troilus, while the unwavering fidelity of Troilus remains unquestioned. A hungry image haunting the walls of Troy for a loved one who never returns, Troilus well deserves the eighth sphere, nearly everyone agrees. That Criseyde's reputation has mainly been in the hands of males may account for some of this lopsided opinion, even the opinion Chaucer himself attributed to her, that no good word shall ever be written or sung about her, "for thise bokes wol me shende" (V.1060). Perhaps the mostly male authors and critics who hold such opinions would have wanted to see Criseyde pine away for the rest of her days, alone and unhappy among the Greeks, before they would grant the obvious, that her conduct differs little from Troilus's. Indeed, she may be no more guilty of wrongdoing than Troilus is; little separates his failure to defend Criseyde with a public avowal of his love for her from her failure to admit to Diomede that she and Troilus have been lovers for the past three years (V.977–78) and to return to Troy within ten days.

All this echoed opinion notwithstanding, the parallel that Chaucer seems carefully to develop between the poem's two lovers raises curiosity as to whether the poem itself does not perhaps modify this universal condemnation of one lover and praise of the other. We wonder if Troilus, too, may have some blemish to parallel the betrayal and infidelity many find in Criseyde. It would be well also to recall one of Pandarus's proverbs:

> witteth wel that bothe two ben vices:
> Mistrusten alle, or elles alle leve.
> But wel I woot, the mene of it no vice is.
>
> (I.687–89)

A curious characteristic that Troilus displays throughout the poem first shows itself at the feast of the Palladion when Criseyde's beauty nearly stops his heart (I.306–7). He does not react as many a man would by approaching her, however awkwardly, or as Diomede does in book V with a number of repellently oily lines, or at least by asking someone to introduce him to her, perhaps his close friend Pandarus who happens to be her uncle. On the contrary, he holds himself speechless, shrinking away at his first opportunity. The poem is at pains to explain that this response measures not his recessive nature but the extent of Criseyde's beauty, a rationale that is undercut by a similar reaction later in the poem when he has long been familiar with Criseyde's beauty. In King Priam's parliament (IV.141–217), convened to discuss the proposed exchange of Criseyde for Antenor, whom the Greeks have recently captured, Troilus witnesses the entire debate. He hears Hector's fruitless opposition, "she nys no prisonere" (179) and "We usen here no wommen for to selle" (182). Had Troilus added an argument or two to his brother's opposition, without compromising either Criseyde's reputation or his love for her, the parliament might have voted differently. Instead, he acts as he did earlier at the Palladion. Silence. The warrior who would never shrink from an armed opponent's challenge once again slinks away, contradicting the concern for Criseyde's well-being he has frequently sworn during love's ecstasies. Yet, by later weeping only to Pandarus and his pillow, he implies otherwise.

Another of Chaucer's well-engineered parallels sheds disconcerting light on Troilus's frame of mind. The lament uttered woefully by Troilus after hearing the parliament's decision (IV.260–336), compared with Criseyde's lament later in the same book (743–98), shows two very different responses to Troy's decision to exchange Criseyde for Antenor. To Troilus, the great tragedy of this decision lies in the sad effect the exchange will have on *him*, whereas Criseyde grieves over the devastating impact her enforced departure from Troy will have on the man she loves, barely mentioning her own sorrow. Troilus rails against Fortune for punishing *him*, not only insisting he is guiltless but saying nothing of the torment a separation will bring to Criseyde:

> What have I don? What have I thus agylt?
> How myghtestow for rowthe me bygile?
> Is ther no grace, and shal I thus be spilt?
> Shal thus Creiseyde awey, for that thow wilt?
> Allas, how maistow in thyn herte fynde
> To ben to me thus cruwel and unkynde?
>
> (IV.261–66)

When he does mention Criseyde's name, it is mostly to complain that she is being taken from him (283–87), that he will lose the comfort she once gave to ease his pain,[23] and the delight he once took in looking at her (309–10). The lament concludes with five telling apostrophes: "O wery goost . . . O soule" (302–5), meaning *his* spirit; "O woful eyen two" (309), referring to *his* eyes; "O my Criseyde" (316), lamenting *his* sorrowful soul to which Criseyde can no longer give comfort; "O ye loveris" (323), wishing them well but asking them to remember *him* when they pass *his* sepulchre (327–28); "O oold, unholsom, and myslyved man . . . O Calkas, which that wolt my bane be, / In corsed tyme was thow born for me!" (330–34), referring only to *his* hardship while ignoring the harm Calkas does to Criseyde.

Criseyde's lament (IV.743–98) certainly echoes some of the self-pity and hyperbole we hear from Troilus: a curse on the day when she met him (747–49), a recollection of him "that wont hire wo was for to lithe" (754), a despair that without him her life has no meaning (766–70), and a resolve to end her life (773–77) corresponding to Troilus's thoughts of blinding himself (299–314). Rising above all this lamentation, a strain very different from Troilus's dominates her speech, beginning with her concern for both their futures, "How shal he don, and ich also?" (757), but quickly focusing on Troilus alone:

> Who shal that sorwe slen that ye ben inne?
>
> (IV.760)

> But how shul ye don in this sorwful cas?
> How shal youre tendre herte this sustene?

But, herte myn, foryete this sorwe and tene,
And me also; for sothly for to seye,
So ye wel fare, I recche naught to deye.

(IV.794–98)

The noticeably different concerns of these two laments become more pronounced in light of the intervening scene between Pandarus and Troilus, where promising strategies are proposed for the first time in the whole course of their affair. This long interview begins, curiously enough, with Pandarus quietly moving toward Troilus's bed, as if the older man intends to become one with the younger man's most intimate thoughts. Empathy, however, remains with the past, brooding on the finality of the parliament's decision. Ever the practical man, Pandarus attempts to cast a Boethian light on what is obvious—obvious to him, that is—that the affair has come to an end, "Swich is this world! . . . / Ne trust no wight to fynden in Fortune / Ay propretee; hire yiftes ben comune" (IV.390–92). These last four words take a cryptic turn. Instead of letting the thought end by accepting the transitory nature of the world, they seem ironically to foreshadow the future, suggesting that all gifts eventually pass into someone else's possession, perhaps then on to still another. Are we, then, to place Criseyde somewhere in Chaucer's long procession of Eternal Women, arrayed before us in all the earthly and heavenly phases of Woman's devotion and desire: Grisilde, Malin, Emily, May, Alisoun of Oxford, Madam Eglentine, Prudence, Dorigen, Pertelote, Thomas's wife, Alisoun of Bath?

A different understanding is possible. If Pandarus's symbolic role as literary creator may be entertained, his regret that "oure joie" (IV.385) has come to an end similarly takes on symbolic significance. A curious expression, "oure joie," when an outsider who learned of the relationship would only have seen the joy of two, not three. In his symbolic role, however, Pandarus is as intimately aware of their love—indeed, he brought it into being—as is either Criseyde or Troilus. His first attempt to interest Troilus in the future also seems more logical from this perspective. Only a craftsman, an artificer of beautiful things, could understand the difference between the constantly shifting circumstances of a life actually lived and the permanent beauty of a work of art. Pandarus's understanding of this difference permits him to make this otherwise unfathomable observation:

> But telle me this: whi thow art now so mad
> To sorwen thus? Whi listow in this wise,
> Syn thi desir al holly hastow had,
> So that, by right, it oughte ynough suffise?
> But I, that nevere felte in my servyse
> A frendly cheere or lokyng of an eye,
> Lat me thus wepe and wailen til I deye.
>
> (IV.393–99)

As a conventional human being with a life of his own, Pandarus may speak truthfully, that he has never "felte ... A frendly cheere or lokyng of an eye." But as creator, he has shaped a compelling account that remains fixed for all time, a proprietary work of art, in which Criseyde and Troilus take poignant roles that transcend Fortune's shifting shadows. Gifted, serious creators in every medium move on to their next challenge, when a previous work is complete. For this reason Pandarus attempts to interest Troilus in becoming a leading figure in another work of love:

> This town is ful of ladys al aboute;
> And, to my doom, fairer than swiche twelve
> As evere she was, shal I fynde in som route—
> Yee, on or two, withouten any doute.
> Forthi be glad, myn owen deere brother!
> If she be lost, we shal recovere an other.
>
> (IV.401–6)

As Pandarus may suspect, and will eventually discover during a weeklong party he and Troilus attend at Sarpedoun's home (V.431–500), his suggestion falls on deaf ears. He turns his attention, therefore, to the strategy Troilus ought to have pursued weeks earlier, "Artow in Troie, and hast non hardyment / To take a womman which that loveth the" (IV.533–34). More than a tongue-lashing, this is another instance of Pandarus's giving expression to thoughts that have long troubled Troilus. Recall that we noticed his acknowledgment earlier, "Al this have I myself yet thought ful ofte" (IV.542). Even more, with these words that advise Troilus to abduct Criseyde, Pandarus announces in a formal hand-washing gesture that he is disengaging from Troilus's affair. Henceforth, Troy's second best warrior will be on his own.

Troilus, for his part, replies by protesting too much, defending his inaction with little conviction. Rather, he offers excuses, weaker by far than any one of the reasons that could—and should—prompt him to act. Again, he does nothing.

More crucial for the development of the whole poem, these are matters Criseyde herself cannot have failed to consider. She must think it unusual that Troilus has not even asked for her thoughts on how to reverse, or render moot, the sentence parliament has pronounced on her, as we know from Pandarus's query "hastow hire wil assayed?" and Troilus's astonishing answer "Nay" (IV.639–40). Or again, when the narrator admits that Criseyde cares nothing for her father, who initiated the scheme to exchange his daughter for Antenor, nor will be moved by her father's death, whenever that should occur (IV.666–68), we gain a sense of Troilus's missed opportunity. Before describing a visit to Criseyde from the ladies of Troy, and then quoting the long lament discussed above, the narrator gives a final stanza describing Criseyde's commitment to Troilus (IV.673–79), an unqualified love that suggests she would not have hesitated to run away with Troilus, had he before the parliament discussed Criseyde's fate shown the courage to protect her.

At this stage in the poem, Criseyde may already have guessed that to remain in Troy under Troilus's weak protection would not be feasible. Not that she doubts his love for her or anything he has said to her, nor that she suspects his greater concern for himself and his own happiness than for her protection. Instead of becoming Troilus's "betrayer," a name she will come to believe her future conduct deserves, Criseyde allows herself to be sent to the Greek camp—against her will, to be sure—because it is the only practical course available to her. The lament that follows (IV.743–98) serves as Criseyde's farewell—to Troy, to Troilus, and to her story. She lives on, of course, to suffer numerous painful moments, as when she gives Troilus assurance that she will return within ten days, a transparent fetch at odds with her protests of faithfulness (cf. IV.677, 1534–54, 1660–66), and with soliloquized words she imagines Troilus can hear, "foryete this sorwe and tene, / And me also" (IV.796–97).

Even more painful to hear are two replies Criseyde makes to Diomede a few days after being sent to the Greek camp. Whether they bring equal pain to Criseyde is difficult to say. Diomede plans from his first moments with Criseyde how to gain possession of her, beginning with an assertion that sounds ludicrous from so obvious a predator:

> Yeve me youre hond; I am, and shal ben ay,
> God helpe me so, while that my lyf may dure,
> Youre owene aboven every creature.
>
> Thus seyde I nevere er now to womman born,
> For God myn herte as wisly glade so,
> I loved never womman here-biforn
> As paramours, ne nevere shal no mo.
>
> (V.152–58)

Criseyde rightly does not respond to this lubricious claim. By the tenth day, however, her resistance to Diomede's bid to be her man weakens:

> "But as to speke of love, ywis," she seyde,
> "I hadde a lord, to whom I wedded was,
> The whos myn herte al was, til that he deyde;
> And other love, as help me now Pallas,
> *Ther in myn herte nys, ne nevere was.*"
>
> (V.974–78, emphasis added)

That Criseyde can even formulate these words would normally be impossible to believe, but for the intimations Chaucer has given "that this immortal-seeming creature was most subject to time and to change" (Donaldson 1970, 59). As the daughter of an accomplished calculator, she responds adroitly to her changed fortunes in Troy, to her probable disappointment with Hector's formal promise to give aid, to Pandarus's startling news of Troilus's interest in her, to Troilus's silence in her hour of most need, and now to Diomede's evident interest. Thus, when Diomede resolves to declare himself to her on her fourth day in the Greek camp, while he thinks figurative thoughts of bringing her into his net and fishing her with hook and line, Criseyde is undoubtedly preparing herself for the next chapter in her life.

To show that this new acquaintance is not unlike Criseyde, at least in some ways, Chaucer gives Diomede the very words Criseyde herself used in book II when deciding to accept Troilus's attention. Criseyde then said, "He which that nothing undertaketh, / Nothyng n'acheveth, be hym looth or deere" (II.807–8). More than five thousand lines later Diomede offers the same aphorism in an identical circumstance: "But for t'asay, . . . it naught n'agreveth, / For he that naught n'asaieth naught n'acheveth" (V.783–84). Confirmation that this is not a mere coincidence comes in a second linguistic signal. Much earlier, shortly before Criseyde enumerates the pros and cons of accepting Troilus as her suitor, but immediately after she sees him ride by her window and says "Who yaf me drynke?" (II.651), the narrator thrice exonerates her of the charge that she is a sudden lover (II.667, 673, 679). Not coincidentally, this same narrator calls her next suitor "this sodeyn Diomede" (V.1024). No matter that Criseyde seems not to be a sudden lover, while sudden hardly does justice to Diomede's alacrity, the narrator puts the word in the air, speaking of both the Trojan woman and the Greek warrior. Steeled by these broad hints, a reader does not respond with surprise to Criseyde's final hurtful comment:

> But syn I se ther is no bettre way,
> And that to late is now for me to rewe,
> *To Diomede algate I wol be trewe.*
>
>   (V.1069–71, emphasis added)

Let us note, as if to gain support for the narrator's defense of Criseyde at every turn, that these lines record Criseyde's ambivalence. She knows "I have hem don dishonour" (V.1066), but she also knows that it has not been entirely her fault. Even before she left Troy, she could see that "ther is no bettre way" (V.1069). But what is the point of seeking excuses, for she knows, too, her actions have sullied her *trouthe*. The pain of her loss remains.

In the parallel paths Chaucer gives the principal characters in his great study of human love, he places before readers a profound point about human beings, captured well in two Boethian passages, *Consolation* II.m.8 and V.pr.3, one of which appears tangentially in *Parliament of Fowls*, the other quoted in some manuscripts of *Troilus and Criseyde*.[24] Taken together, these passages identify an undeniable paradox. One passage alleges that since all created things are bound together by an irresistible force, human beings too are attracted to each other and impelled forward in expectation of perfect harmony and eternal happiness (*Boece* II.m.8). The second passage avers a predestined fortune condemning objects to dissolution and creatures to misery (*Boece*, V.pr.3). The first half of this paradox scarcely needs defense; by nature we humans are social creatures. Add the fact of our being divided into two sexes, necessarily attracted to each other to sustain the species, and the premise becomes self-evident. Its corollary, paraphrased in Troilus's soliloquy on predestination (IV.958–1082) is another matter. Yes, everyone will one day reach life's end. But since many lives are far more rewarding than death's sorrow can diminish, an inevitable condemnation to misery and dreamless dust cannot be universal. Thus Chaucer omits the philosophic puzzle Boethius uses to rebut the second half of the paradox: Are we not all predestined, if God by definition knows what we will freely choose to do, even before we do it? By electing not to paraphrase *Boece* V.pr.4–6, the sections of the *Consolation* where Boethius's "conditional necessity" defends belief in free will, Chaucer permits Troilus to pin humanity to a paradox. Thus the similar paths he designs for these two Trojans—whom he introduces to love, raises to a rare experience achieved by only very few, and then lets blunder into losing what they have cherished—create not a story of a faithful male and a faithless female but two instances of human beings who deserve a love that predestined ill-fortune snatches from them. Two nearly indistinguishable examples of humanity enjoy a brief period of love, and then must suffer the paradox under which all humanity seems destined to live.

To be "bounde with love" (*Boece* II.m.8, lines 14–15), as Boethius called the impulse to sustain forever the harmony and joy Criseyde and Troilus have together, cannot succeed in the normal, earthly way the lovers would wish. Not even Pandarus can make it last forever, for only in Eden and Arcady is the beautiful at one with the real. He cannot—or will not—return to restructure the world as he once did. To him, the worries of both lovers are lost in irrelevance; let others make the affair he has already made and left. In its place a different kind of stability brings Chaucer's poem to its close. Whatever loveliness and beauty Criseyde possessed finally slips through her grasp. However lofty the height to which she rose when Troilus and love awakened her emotions, she sinks by degrees to what her world guides her to be: a tactician, a supplicant, a loved one, a playing piece in a board game, and finally a sad woman. Having once been a spouse, then Troilus's beloved, we last see her on the verge of a match no tragedian will celebrate in song. In the kindest view, she pledges herself to her only available protector, albeit a pledge consigned to a concessive clause and a protector marked by sudden opportunism. A rival view measures her by the traitor who begot her and the traitor for whom she is exchanged. Like Nature herself, Criseyde reaches the stability of cyclic change, ever present, ever available to be shaped again.

Nor can Troilus bring Criseyde back. Occupying in the matter-form spectrum the opposite end from Criseyde, he appears useless in the practice of human love, despite his great prowess on the field. If it is possible to hold firmly an ideal that is only vaguely understood, he commits himself to an idea of perfection marked by a stable, never-changing love fashioned in the mirror of his own mind.[25] Guided by the artistry of one who instinctively understands well the importance of what the House of Rumor represents, Troilus and Criseyde become, however briefly, a perfectly matched, sublimely beautiful pair "bounde with love." At the end of their literary romance, they become permanent exaggerations of their own natures. Criseyde, a lady worthy of a verse with Villon's snows of yesteryear—beautiful when falling and nourishing to the plains of next season and to the poets of later ages—easily enters the cold, ethically compromised world in which she finds herself. Troilus, translated out of time, not to become an object of pleasure for the lords and ladies of Byzantium but to escape the world's disappointing limits, ascends to a permanent heaven and laughs down at a world that knows itself but slenderly. As symbols eluding the paradox Boethius describes, they bring together the transitory nature of flesh and the permanence of an ideal held fast, making themselves and the poem in which they live sweeter, unheard melodies forever new.

Appendix A

Parallel Structures of *Duchess*, *Fowls*, and *Fame* with its Tidings of Love

Duchess	*Fowls*	*Fame*
Pre-dream	**Pre-dream**	**Pre-dream**
Emotional state of narrator: lethargic, unable to discriminate, sad, suffers from insomnia.	Emotional state of narrator: seeks knowledge, especially regarding "love," later understood to mean "harmony."	Emotional state of narrator: perplexed over the variety of dreams and their causes.
External influence: a book. Reads Ovid's story of Ceyx, Alcione, and Morpheus. Learns that Morpheus governs sleep and sends dreams.	External influence: a book. Reads and summarizes Cicero's *Somnium Scipionis* on universal harmony. Still missing what he sought, but has something he was not seeking.	External influence: a dream. Recalls and praises highly a dream he had on December 10.
Sleep arrives from fatigue.	Sleep arrives from fatigue, loss of light.	Remembers he fell asleep "wonder sone."
Has a wonderful dream, impossible to interpret.		Has the best dream anyone ever dreamed.
Dream setting	**Dream setting**	**Dream setting**
Dreams he awakens in a bedroom. Hears the harmony of birdsong. Walls covered with story of Troy, *Roman de la rose*.	Dreams that Africanus appears to him as a reward for reading *Somnium Scipionus*.	Dreams he is in Venus's temple of glass. Walls covered with *Aeneid* showing destruction of Troy and Dido-Aeneas story.
Horn summons dreamer to hunt led by Octovyen. Hart escapes; horn blows a forloyn.		Digression on males false to women. Summarizes last six books of *Aeneid* in fifteen lines. Exits temple of Venus for desert wasteland. "Crist . . . Fro fantome and illusion me save."

Guide	Guide	Guide
Whelp, almost caught, leads dreamer to forest of artifice.	Africanus takes dreamer to gate leading to garden and Venus's temple. Reward for studying the *Somnium*, revered by Macrobius.	Golden eagle swoops down, seizes dreamer, takes him aloft. Eagle: reward for faithful, albeit fruitless, service to Venus and Cupid, to increase his knowledge and his ability. Eagle lectures dreamer on sound waves, eventually depositing him at House of Fame.
Symbolic alternatives *Artificial* Presentation of Love in *Roman de la rose*. Windows shut. Artificial forest, a locale that suits a man in black. Stilted use of language in poems and in speech of man in black.	**Symbolic alternatives** *Artificial* Fearful words in black over gate. Temple of Venus's allegorical figures, like statuary, mainly showing love's sorrows. Artificial speeches declaimed by three tercel eagles who violate Nature's law.	**Symbolic alternatives** *Artificial* Sterile landscape outside glass temple of Venus. Fame's castle and tower on a rock of ice. Fame's caprice in assigning reputations. Busts of authors from the past, all associated with Troy legend.
Natural Harmony of birdsong outside windows. Activity of the hunt. Dreamer's use of direct, unadorned language.	*Natural* Appealing words in gold over gate. Verdant garden outside temple of Venus. Birds of lower degree selecting their mates.	*Natural* Actions and lessons of golden eagle. Agreement with intuitions of prior writers who explained the universe. Activity and sounds of House of Rumor.

Resolution:	Resolution:	Resolution:
Endorsement of natural representation	Endorsement of natural representation	Endorsement of natural representation
Long, stilted monologues by man in black frustrate the dreamer.	Hyperbolic, stilted proposals of three tercel eagles fail to win a mate, while angering other birds.	["A man of gret auctorite" recites T&C, fiction about realistic lovers who grow from earthly attraction to harmonious perfection, then lose this ideal.
Mathematical tour de force: conversation between dreamer and man in black encodes harmony versus disharmony. At length, dreamer skillfully draws man in black to declare in plain language that his lady is dead.	Mathematical tour de force: four encoded proportions of mathematics agree with the harmony of nature. Lady Nature approves lower birds' selection of mates. A picked group of bird singers celebrates with a joyous roundel. All the birds fly away until next year	[Mathematical tour de force: tension between rational and irrational triangle alludes to contradictory nature of Man. [Though Nature endures by successions, flawed humanity cannot. Criseyde and Troilus become permanent images of, respectively, humanity's lesser capitulations and higher aspirations.]

Appendix B

The Golden Proportion

The proportion known successively as the cut (in the ancient world), the divine proportion (Middle Ages), the golden section (after Kepler), and *phi* (twentieth century) was probably discovered ca. 400 B.C. The word *proportion* signifies an equivalence of two ratios, $a \div b = x \div y$. Though "division into extreme and mean ratio," as *phi* is defined, indicates a specific point on a line, creating two segments that are in a golden ratio, neither of these two segments can be precisely measured. Nor can their ratio to each other be precisely shown with whole numbers (that is, shown with numbers that are integers unto themselves, like $^4/_5$ or $^{11}/_{25}$, both of which resolve in terminating decimals, 0.8 and 0.44, respectively). *Phi* is a nonterminating decimal, called by mathematicians "irrational," meaning not amenable to whole-number ratio. It is commonly indicated to the fifth decimal place, 1.61803 . . . , with the three dots signifying an infinite number of decimal places. *Phi* can, however, be easily plotted geometrically. In figure B.1, point C, constructed from the diagonal across two equal squares, is the golden cut of line AB.

The algebraic equation for φ, discovered long after it was identified by Pythagorean geometry, depends on the square root of 5, another irrational number whose decimal equivalent is 2.23606. Since fourteenth-century mathematicians in Europe were incapable of working with irrational numbers, they normally substituted the rational convergent $^{20}/_9$ (2.22222 . . . in modern mathematics) for the square root of 5.

When a line is divided geometrically at its precise golden cut, and only then, a remarkable relationship exists among its three magnitudes—the shorter segment, the longer segment, and the whole line. The magnitude of the shorter segment, multiplied by φ, produces the magnitude of the longer segment, and this longer segment, multiplied by φ, produces the length of the whole line. It follows that if the original whole line is extended by a length equal to the longer segment, this extension becomes the shorter segment of a new *phi* relationship in which the original whole line is now the

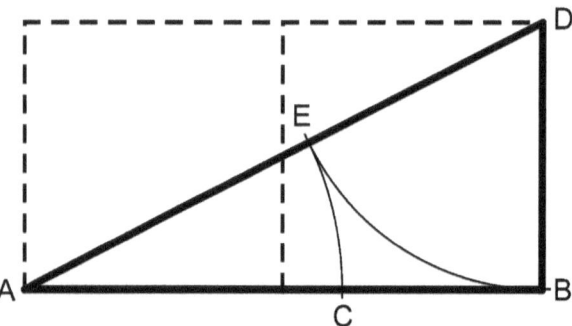

Figure B.1. Geometric construction of the divine porportion

longer segment. In turn this longer segment can also be folded out to create yet a third demonstration. And so on to the threshold of infinity.

For a proportion to be called *phi*, it must satisfy two equations. The first is an additive equation: $a + b = c$. The second requires equality between two ratios, for which a simple equation from Euclid is the most convenient demonstration. The Middle Ages learned its Euclid from Nicomachus of Gerasa, whose tenth mean provides the equation that proves a divine proportion among three magnitudes a, b, and c (where $a > b$ and $b > c$):

$$\frac{a-c}{a-b} = \frac{b}{c}$$

In every age since the divine proportion was discovered, mathematicians have been captivated by both its elegance and its occurrence everywhere in nature. *Phi* is the only ratio whose square is itself plus 1 and whose reciprocal is itself minus 1. It governs the fifth Platonic solid, a dodecahedron, thought to be the first manifestation of matter when the Creator converted virtue into essence.[1] The Parthenon was apparently constructed according to this proportion, as were the sculptures of Phidias, the first letter of whose name gave Mark Barr the thought in the early twentieth century to use φ as its mathematical symbol. The two parts of Horace's *Ars poetica* (lines 1–294, discussing the craft of poetry, and lines 295–476, on the interaction between poet and critic) are separated from each other at the poem's precise golden cut (Le Grelle 1949, 142–56; Duckworth 1962, 76–77). In this instance, mathematics underscores Horace's thematic point, that the craft of poetry, the middle term, is the means by which the lesser extreme, poets and critics, achieve the greater extreme, literature.

Virgil's *Georgics I*, said by the editor of the Loeb edition to be "perhaps the most carefully finished production of Roman literature" (Fairclough 1978, x), divides its poetic lines into five sections:

    37.5 161 55 204.5 51.5

The poet's aim was evidently to demonstrate mathematically the natural harmony of the universe. The line totals 161 and 204.5 leap out from sections 2 and 4, which discuss technical farming matters, as the total number of days in a year, understood by the ancient world to be 365½. The divine proportion is demonstrated with the three remaining magnitudes, 55 as the lesser extreme at the center of the design, the mean 89 (37.5 + 51.5) split up to bracket the whole design, and the sum of 55 and 89, or 144, as the greater extreme. These numbers yield results extremely close to *phi*: 89 ÷ 55 = 1.61818 and 144 ÷ 89 = 1.61797. Virgil provides, therefore, an accessible demonstration of universal harmony in the rhythms of the celestial spheres and the yearly cycles of farming.

Many of the carpet folios of early medieval book art use *phi* as their controlling design (Stevick 1982, 1994). Medieval cathedrals were often constructed with *phi* as their principal proportion (Simson 1956; Hiscock 1999). Chaucer's contemporary, the *Pearl*-poet, designed the unique MS Cotton Nero A.x according to *phi* (Condren 2002). Leonardo da Vinci and Albrecht Dürer frequently employed *phi* in the Renaissance. *Phi* also shows up in countless natural phenomena: in the fascinating chambered nautilus, in the petals of a pinecone, in the seeds of a sunflower, in the arrangement of leaves around a stalk, in the spirals of hurricanes and galaxies. The modern era, too, has increasingly recognized *phi* as an aesthetically pleasing presence. Salvador Dalí's *Sacrament of the Last Supper*, heavily based on the golden proportion (Livio 2002, 9), seems to honor *phi* more obviously than it celebrates Christ. In this instance a connection is unmistakable, since Dalí places above Christ's head part of a giant dodecahedron, within which a partial figure alludes to Leonardo da Vinci's *Vitruvian Man*, a drawing long accepted as homage to both the Roman architect Vitruvius and the proportions that were the foundation of his architectural designs. Finally, in an almost unnatural gesture, Dalí positions the thumb and index fingers of Christ's right hand both as a *v*, the Roman symbol for 5, and as the modern symbol for square root, √, acknowledging that the algebraic equation for *phi* uses the square root of 5 as its basic component.

As noted in chapter 2's discussion of *Book of the Duchess*, Chaucer allots total lines to his five "dialogues" (the brief conversational exchanges between dreamer and man in black, separating the latter's "monologues") almost exactly as Virgil does for the five sections of his *Georgics I*. While Virgil represents the rhythms of nature in two sections totaling 365.5 lines to equal the days that span a year, the heavenly rhythms are arrayed in sections of 55 lines and 89 lines, giving a total of 144 lines. Although he displays it differently, Chaucer uses this same series of numbers, 55, 89, and 144, in the *Duchess* (see chapter 2) to endorse one kind of poetic style over another. And at the end of the *Parliament of Fowls*, discussed in chapter 3, he uses yet another series, 11, 18, and 29, to display the same golden proportion as a way of expressing consummate harmony in the universe.

Notes

Chapter 1: Introduction

1. The quoted line that begins this chapter is the famous opening sentence of Francis Bacon's essay "On Truth," also quoted by David Lawton (1985, 31) in connection with Chaucer's Pardoner. Bacon was perhaps inspired by Chaucer's reference to Pilate's words in *Lenvoy de Chaucer a Bukton*, where Christ's silence may indicate a refusal to admonish Pilate, for "No man is al trewe" (4). Boethius explicitly names "love" as the fundamental harmony of the universe and everything in it (II.m.8.13–16). For Chaucer's translation of this passage, see note 6 to chapter 3. All quotations of Chaucer's prose and poetry throughout this book, unless otherwise noted, are from *The Riverside Chaucer*, 3rd ed. (1987), abbreviated *Riv Ch*.

2. Chaucer may never have heard the name Ockham, much less been influenced by him. Nevertheless, the litany of natural forces that constitute "love" in Boethius's and Chaucer's lexicon implies agreement with Ockham's philosophy, for which see Spade 1994, including a translation of d. 2, qq. 4–8.

3. Quotations of *Dream of the Rood* are from *The Vercelli Book*; see Krapp 1932, 61–65.

Chapter 2: *Book of the Duchess*

1. Very little certainty informs the dating of Chaucer's individual poems. Nevertheless the current consensus assumes that the *Legend of Good Women* is "a product of Chaucer's artistic maturity, written not long after ... *Troilus and Criseyde*" (*Riv Ch* 587). The *Retraction* to the *Canterbury Tales*, containing a very complete bibliography of Chaucer's major works, including "the book of the Duchesse" (*CT* X.1086), must have been written near the end of Chaucer's life.

2. For a fuller, and certainly wittier, discussion of the poem's titles, see Steve Ellis (1995) who argues for a restoration of what he says was "Chaucer's own title: the *Death of Blanche the Duchess*" (257).

3. In the Oxford Guides to Chaucer, in Minnis's *The Shorter Poems* (1995), the chapter on the *Book of the Duchess* begins with a discussion of the sincerity and affection of marital love among royals in the fourteenth century, with moving references to Philip Larkin's poem "An Arundel Tomb," and with particular emphasis on the marriage of Gaunt and Blanche. The first connection between this marriage and Gaunt's presence as the man in black in Chaucer's poem occurs five pages into this discussion, in a subordinate clause, as a fact not open to question: "Gaunt's best side

is presented to the beholder: here is one who is not numbered in the roll of common men. And this is, of course, precisely what the *Book of the Duchess* shows and says, inasmuch as its Man in Black is an idealized figure of Gaunt" (77).

4. See the thorough discussion of the relationship among the texts in Helen Phillips's 1982 edition, 65–66, as well as two discussions by N. F. Blake (1981, 1986) arising from a consideration of the authenticity of lines 31–96, which appear only in Thynne's edition of 1532.

5. Edwards 1989, 65–66. The wording of this quoted passage may give the erroneous impression that John of Gaunt was Chaucer's patron at the time of Blanche's death in 1368. But there is no evidence that Chaucer came under even the partial patronage of Gaunt until 1374 at the earliest. The little evidence available suggests Chaucer was continuously in the household of Edward III and, while she lived, Queen Philippa from 1367 through the spring of 1374.

6. If Chaucer is using "fantasy" here as the Greeks understood φαντασμα (cog. fantasm, i.e., L. *visum*), corresponding to the fifth of Macrobius's five types of dream, the apparition, then the main difference between "fantasy" and "ymagynacioun" is that the former "comes upon one in the moment between wakefulness and slumber" (Stahl 1952, 88), whereas the latter is not associated with dreaming. The nightmare and the apparition (the fourth and fifth types of dream) were not worth interpreting, according to Macrobius (I.iii), since they have no prophetic value. By contrast, the first three types, the enigmatic dream (*somnium*), the prophetic vision (*visio*), and the oracular dream (*oraculum*), were thought to foretell the future, at least in part.

7. J. J. Anderson calls attention to the terms of a similar dichotomy, though giving them different names, "doer" and "thinker" in one place, "experience" and "authority" immediately thereafter (1992, 220). Suggesting that the narrator of *Fowls* is a thinker, whereas the dreamer of *Duchess* is a doer, his interpretation of the narrators of these two poems differs from the one proposed here. The narrator of *Duchess*, in my opinion, begins in a passive state, whether intellectually sensitive or not, and progresses to an active state, whereas Anderson does not focus on the progress of either narrator, however contrasted they are to each other, but sees each narrator as consistent throughout.

8. The important reference to an eight-year illness (37) occurs in the much debated lines 31–96 which appear only in Thynne and in a late addition to Fairfax. Though all editors accept the lines as probably authentic, N. F. Blake (1986), finding no compelling evidence for this attribution, regards them as suspect, a position very different from doubting their authenticity. But see the convincing rejoinder to Blake's suspicion by Helen Phillips (1986).

9. See Machaut, *Le Remede de Fortune*, 1467–69, *Le Dit dou Lyon*, 57–67. Note

also the kindred metaphor in Jaufré Rudel's Chanson II, "E no'n puesc trobar mezina" (10), where "mezina" means primarily medicine.

10. See also T. A. Shippey's interesting article on three measured sections in *BD*, 62–214, 1145–1297, and, after a convincing argument, 290–442, which have 153 lines each, an allusion to the Miraculous Draught of Fishes (John 21:11), where Simon Peter takes 153 fish in one haul after the risen Christ tells him where to throw his nets. As Shippey says, "153 is the Number of Salvation, in the end one of the most familiar and popular relics of scholarly commentary" (1996, 197).

11. According to Benson's notes (*Riv Ch* 1137), "After [line] 479 Th[ynne] has *And thus in sorwe lefte me aloon*, rejected by all eds. except [Koch and Dickerson]. To retain the traditional numbering the next line is called 481." Thus the poem has a total of 1,333 lines, not 1,334 as the numbering of its last line implies.

12. By arguing for her understanding of the "central message of the *Book of the Duchess*, that language inevitably fails to capture the 'real'" (16), Kiser implicitly disagrees with my contention that the Black Knight's expression alone is elusive, not the reality he intends to re-create. Her admission that the narrator and the man in black are partly identical, however, narrows considerably the distance between our respective views.

13. Cf. the fine article by Michael B. Herzog (1988), who sees *BD* as a search for artistic vision: "The *Book of the Duchess* is not only a part of Chaucer's pilgrimage toward a theory of art, it is the essential and formative first step. . . . Chaucer's early narrative works have not been recognized for the crucial role they play in the poet's search for his artistic vision" (269).

14. Though Kolve mentions readers more often than authors in advancing the central thesis of *Chaucer and the Imagery of Narrative* (*passim*, but esp. chap. 2), namely that medieval readers would have responded visually to a text, this generalization—as sweeping as it is well supported—must apply equally to those who *produce* literature as to those who hear or read it.

15. In view of the many passages the *Book of the Duchess* borrows from three of Guillaume de Machaut's poems (*Dit de la fonteinne amoureuse*, *Jugement dou Roy de Behaingne*, and *Remede de Fortune*) and one of Jean de Froissart's (*Paradys d'Amours*), passages conveniently identified in the notes to the Riverside edition, Robert R. Edwards prefers to call this meeting between the poem's dreamer and the man in black "an active poetic dialogue with his contemporaries and predecessors" (1989, 67).

The interpretation proposed here, that it is a conversation between Chaucer and his younger self, does not greatly differ from Edwards's. It does add the autobiographical dimension depicting Chaucer's progress as a poet, from the time when he perhaps echoed the contemporaries and predecessors Edwards has in mind, to the present time of the poem when his verses already create the sounds and thoughts of everyday

Londoners. I disagree, however, with the claim that Chaucer's replies to previous poetic styles should be called "escape narratives" (Schibanoff 2006, 27), and that the style he was beginning to favor should be called "blunt" (Ian Robinson 1972, 16–17). More accurately, the style of troubadour lyrics and courtly literature "escaped," or was truant, from the underlying culture of the medieval period, falsifying the culture in the process. Chaucer merely restores literal meaning to descriptions of perfectly normal human activity that had been much adulterated by an earlier, orotund style.

16. In addition to works formally titled "Debate Between Self and Soul," I include *Pearl* and Boethius's *Consolation of Philosophy* in the category of an internal dialogue.

17. Chaucer's familiarity with Machaut's poetry and extensive indebtedness to him has long been well known. In addition to an introductory comment in *The Riverside Chaucer*—"*The Book of the Duchess* was strongly influenced by French poetry, notably *Le roman de la rose* and the works of Froissart and Machaut. A number of passages are closely translated, and the form of *The Book of the Duchess* owes much to Machaut's *Jugement dou Roy de Behaingne*" (966)—Colin Wilcockson, the Riverside editor of *BD*, mentions Machaut's name or his poems eighty times in the explanatory notes (966–76).

18. "Gaunt's marriage put him directly in line for the throne of Castile and Leon. From 1371 on, his privy seal bore the royal arms of Castile and Leon, impaling the royal arms of France and England quarterly. From 1372, 'he had, with Edward III's permission, assumed the title of king of Castile and Leon and had been regularly addressed by it'" (Schless 1985, summarizing Armitage-Smith 1904, app. VII, 456–57, and quoting Steel 1941, 107). Cf. Pearsall: Gaunt "styled himself 'Roy de Castille et de Leon Duc de Lancastre' in all documents from 1372 to 1388" (1992, 52).

19. Challenges to identifying the man in black as John of Gaunt have been few. One of the strongest comes from Huppé and Robertson in *Fruyt and Chaf*, 51–53. See also Helen Phillips's sensible statement "Despite the wordplay (which functions somewhat as a monogram, extraneous to the work of art), the love and grief expressed in the poem are general rather than specific. Its three main characters—the lady White, the Knight and the narrator—are not the Duchess, the Duke and Chaucer. They are figures of a wider reference . . . not directly representing any particular real-life situation" (1982, 6). But her later observation falls in step with the traditional interpretation, despite its subjunctive mood: "The kings of Bohemia and Navarre appear in the works bearing their names, and the plight of the lover doomed to exile in [*Fonteinne amoreuse*] stands for the contemporary situation of the Duc de Berry, rather as the grief of the Knight in [*Book of the Duchess*] may stand for the contemporary situation of John of Gaunt" (23).

20. John N. Palmer is paraphrasing here the argument I first advanced in 1971 and reiterated in 1975 in a reply to his article of 1974.

21. Facts of publication for the four exemplars in modern editions may be found in the bibliography later in this book, three under "MS." and the fourth under "Thynne."

22. The Fairfax MS has 19 paragraphs, Tanner 9, and Bodley only 2, one at the beginning of the poem and the second at the beginning of the dream sequence in line 291. Thynne's 95 paragraphs are close in number to the 87 separate paragraphs in *The Riverside Chaucer*.

23. Modern editors have had varying responses to Thynne's paragraph symbol and indentation at line 1311 and indentation at 1314. John Hurt Fisher (1989) does not indent at either 1311 or 1314; Talbot Donaldson (1975) and Helen Phillips (1982) indent at 1311 but not at 1314; neither Phillips nor Donaldson prints ¶ at 1311; A. C. Baugh (1963) does not indent at 1311 but does indent at 1314.

24. In *Chaucer Life-Records* Crow and Olson give chapter 10 the title "Chaucer's Connexion with the House of Lancaster, 1374 onwards."

25. Cf. Huppé and Robertson: "the line of description, 'Upon hys berd but lytel her' (456), seems hardly designed to flatter. . . . the beard was considered the 'ornament of a man's face,' and a sign of masculinity. To say that John's beard had 'little hair' would hardly have been tactful" (1963, 52).

26. In a very well researched article, Arthur W. Bahr (2000) attaches to his first sentence an instructive note, remarkable for both its caution and its disregard of this same caution: "The precise extent of John of Gaunt's 'patronage' of Chaucer is an unresolved issue. Derek Pearsall rightly cautions against making too much of their association, noting that . . . there is no evidence of the kind of sustained, intimate relationship between the two men that William Godwin implies [in his biography of Chaucer]. Nevertheless, since Chaucer must have written the *Book of the Duchess* with Gaunt's knowledge, if not his positive encouragement . . . 'patronage' seems the appropriate word for their relationship within the limited context of this poem's composition" (1992, 56). Bahr's assumption here, that Chaucer composed the *Duchess* at least with Gaunt's knowledge, differs from my belief that the poem was Chaucer's deft strategy for seeking his patronage.

27. The assumption that Chaucer was in Spain in 1366 rests on thin evidence, and that he was at the battle of Najera on no evidence at all. The safe-conduct granted to one "Geffroy de Chanserre [or Chauserre] escuier englois" for the period from February 22 to May 24, 1366 (*Ch L-R* 64–66) may well be a reference to Chaucer. If true, it establishes only that he was in Spain at the same time the battle of Najera was being fought, not that he was at this battle. Pearsall believes Chaucer was on some secret mission involving the affairs of Charles of Navarre concerning Pedro of Castile and the challenge Pedro's half brother Enrique was making for the throne of Castile and Leon. That Gaunt was to become an interested party, marrying Pedro's daughter Constanza five years later, may encourage the belief that Chaucer must have been in contact with Gaunt during this time. See Pearsall 1992, 51–55.

28. Jean Froissart (ca. 1337–ca. 1405) of Hainault enjoyed the patronage of Queen Philippa from 1361 until her death.

29. See Phillips 1982, 6: "The Fairfax manuscript bears in a sixteenth century hand the words 'made by Geffrey Chawcyer at ye request of ye duke of lancastar: pitiously complaynynge the deathe of ye sayd dutchesse/blanche/,' but this . . . has unfortunately no earlier corroboration."

30. Though arguing for a very different interpretation of the *Duchess* than is advanced here, David Lawton accepts for the poem's composition a later date than has been traditionally understood, indeed some considerable time after Blanche's death.

31. Among the many who discuss Chaucer's audience, see in particular Richard F. Green (1980) and Paul Strohm (1989, 47–51, esp. n. 14).

32. Thundy further argues (99 ff.) that the version of *Book of the Duchess* that we now have may have been finished in 1400, or later if the traditional date of Chaucer's death is incorrect.

33. Compare *Behaingne* 193–201 (text and Palmer trans.) with *Book of the Duchess* 481–86.

N'a mon las cuer jamais bien ne vendra,	[Nor will any good ever come to my sad heart,
N'a nul confort n'a joie n'ateindra,	Nor any comfort, any joy ever touch it,
Jusques atant que la mort me prendra,	That is til death will take me,
Qui a grant tort	Death who has greatly
Par devers moy, quant elle ne s'amort	Wronged me, in that she did not bring herself
A moy mordre de son dolereus mort,	To bite me with her mortal sting
Quant elle m'a dou tout tollu et mort	When of everything she stripped me by killing
Mon dous amy	My lover sweet,
Que j'amoie de fin cuer et il my.	Whom I loved with a tender heart as he did me.]

   Allas, deth, what ayleth the,
That thou noldest have taken me,
Whan thou toke my lady swete,
That was so fair, so fresh, so fre,
So good that men may wel se
Of al goodnesse she had no mete!

34. Compare *Behaingne* 177–87 (text and Palmer trans.) to *BD* 599–612:

Lasse, dolente! Or est bien a rebours.	[Alas! What sorrow! Now the opposite is true.
Car mes douceurs sont dolereus labours,	For what was sweetness now is painful suffering,
Et mes joies sont ameres dolours,	What was joy is now bitter hurt,
Et mi penser,	And my thoughts,
En qui mes cuers se soloit deliter	In which my heart did once take delight
Et doucement de tous maus conforter,	And sweetly found solace for every hurt,
Sont et seront dolent, triste, et amer.	Are painful, bitter, sad, and will so remain:
En obscurté	In darkness
Seront mi jour, plein de maleürté,	Will my days remain, filled with misadventure,
Et mi espoir sans nulle seürté,	And my hope without any certainty,
Et ma douceur sera dure durté	And my sweetness will become a lasting hardness]

My song ys turned to pleynynge,
And al my laughtre to wepynge,
My glade thoghtes to hevynesse;
In travayle ys my ydelnesse
And eke my reste; my wele is woo,
My good ys harm, and evermoo
In wrathe ys turned my pleynge
And my delyt into sorwynge.
Myn hele ys turned into seknesse,
In drede ys al my sykernesse;
To derke ys turned al my lyght,
My wyt ys foly, my day ys nyght,
My love ys hate, my slep wakynge,
My myrthe and meles ys fastynge

35. Though Herzog (1988, 277–79) concludes his discussion of *Book of the Duchess* by suggesting that the poem is a study in the relation between poetry and reality, he overlooks the possibility that "fers" may also refer to the literal queen. On this point, see also Gabriel Josipovici (1971 77).

36. Calculating from the notes in *Riv Ch*, 81 lines from Machaut influenced in one way or another, sometimes word for word, the 152 lines of monologue 1.

37. The possibility that line 960 refers to a time before Gaunt married Blanche does not accord with the absence of some word with temporal meaning, for example, "As fer as I *then* had knowynge." The thesis advanced here argues, of course, that the man in black was not the lady's husband but a surrogate of Chaucer at twenty-four, attempting to create a tribute to Queen Philippa.

38. Edward III married Philippa of Hainault in 1328, within his first year of kingship at age sixteen, two years older than his wife. Philippa died in 1369 at age fifty-five.

39. A fondness for end-stopped lines, for comparisons, and for catalogues of feelings characterizes what may have been the original draft of *Duchess*. For example, see 563–72, 599–617, 848–77, 919–47.

40. The French phrase *la dame lointaine* is mine, meant to recall a particular genre, often represented by Jaufré Rudel's most celebrated chanson, "Lanquan li jorn son lonc en may" [When the days are long in May]. The Provençal phrase *amor de loing* (or *soi de loing*; or *pres mi loing*; or *auzels de loing*) occurs ten times in Rudel's thirty-five-line poem. The sentiment of this troubadour song is often referred to as *l'amor de lonh* (in modern French, *l'amour lointain*). I am not suggesting that Chaucer was familiar with the troubadours, though he may have known of them. And yet, his situation as the man in black in *Book of the Duchess* exactly parallels the position of most troubadours who were primarily dedicated to their poetic craft, and also dependent on patronage. I have argued elsewhere (Condren 1972) that several troubadours, especially among those celebrating *fin' amor*, took as their covert subjects the poet's desire to complete his poem.

41. In Pierre Bec's convenient *Anthologie*, 71–73, see the *joc partit* (text by K. Bartsch) between "Peirol" and "Bernatz," the latter assumed to be Bernard de Ventadour.

42. R. G. Peterson's powerful challenge appeared first in 1976, when he suggested three tests, as summarized by Hart (1981, 131): "explicit warrant of authorial intent, relevance to content, and consistency with cultural context." In the following year in the Forum section of *PMLA* (92: 126–29), Peterson, S. K. Heninger Jr., Daniel Laferrière, and Thomas Elwood Hart engaged in an interesting discussion on the same subject.

The case for Chaucer's knowledge of mathematics was made long ago by persuasive scholars: Walter Clyde Curry (1960), Robert M. Jordan (1967), Chauncey Wood (1970), Derek Brewer (1978), and many others. The instinctive resistance to this self-evident dimension in Chaucer remains as strong as it is inexplicable.

43. Some readers may disagree slightly with the specific lines I indicate in table 2.4

for the beginnings and endings of dialogues and monologues. For example, Russell Peck (1970) notes that dialogues A and B have 44 lines each, whereas I see 44 lines in dialogue A and 45 in dialogue B. The disputed line is 758, which I would call the concluding line of dialogue B. "A Goddes half!" (758), obviously expressing gratitude at the dreamer's promise to listen attentively, belongs to the conversation of the two men, dialogue B, rather than to the subject of the knight's monologue 2.

Table 2.4 has nine items, with a beginning and ending for each to be considered. Of the eighteen points of possible disagreement, only five require an explanation. 1) Though the actual words exchanged between the dreamer and the unnamed man begin at 519, I begin counting the lines of dialogue A at line 514, five lines earlier, because 514–18 describe the body language of the two participants. 2) Monologue 1 begins at 558, in my opinion, while others may see it beginning at line 559. My rationale is to consider the descriptive lines "With that he loked on me asyde, / As who sayth, 'Nay, that wol not be'" (558–59) as another instance of body language and an imagined remark assigned to the man in black, both of which describe the facial expression with which he begins his long description of his sorrow. 3) Lines 710–13 belong to neither a dialogue nor a monologue since they reveal an inner reflection of the dreamer himself that has nothing to do with the exchanges between the two men or the self-revelations of the man in black. 4) The seam between the end of dialogue C and the beginning of monologue 3 is arguable. I have elected to consider line 1052 the first line of the monologue because, at most, only the interjection "With myn?" could be called part of the dialogue, whereas the succeeding words, "Nay, alle that hir seyen, / Seyde and sworen hyt was soo" (1052–53) initiate the hyperbole—the "gabbe" (1075)—that extends for another twenty-two lines. 5) Line 1144, perhaps the one most subject to demur, I choose to place in monologue 4 not only because the preceding line has a ring of finality, bringing dialogue D to a close, but also for its marked departure from the light subject of the preceding lines in favor of the seriousness the man in black brings to the assertion of absolute truth in his immediately succeeding remarks.

44. There is a potential exception to the claim that no allusion to number can be found in the monologues of the man in black. Based on a convincing discussion of editorial emendation regarding paragraph indenting, T. A. Shippey (see note 10 above) argues that there are three distinct sections in the *Duchess* that have precisely 153 lines each. Since this is the number of fish caught by the apostles when the risen Christ was manifesting himself to them, Augustine's discussion of this passage in the *Tractates of John* calls 153 the number of salvation. None of the monologues of the man in black has precisely 153 lines. But two of them, number 1 with 152 lines and number 4 with 154, straddle this number. In a poem with many allusions to life after death, it is not impossible that Chaucer was attempting to suggest for Blanche, the

sustained subject of the poem, a close approach to salvation, and for himself several personal goals, not least the salvation of everyone represented in the poem as well as the survival of his literary work long after his own end.

45. The higher learning in the Middle Ages, following a straight line from Martianus Capella through Boethius and down to the fifteenth century, understood the seven liberal arts to have two divisions, the trivium and the quadrivium. The trivium contained the three language arts: grammar as a foundation and two applied arts that shared this foundation, rhetoric and logic (see Russell 1998). The quadrivium, consisting of the foundational arithmetic and three applied arts, music, geometry, and astronomy, was held together by the mathematics of Pythagoras. See R. W. Southern (1979) and the essays by Southern, d'Alverny, and Beaujouan in Benson and Constable (1982).

46. For an unexplained reason, all commentators on Kepler's coinage seem to have switched his names for Pythagoras's two great discoveries in geometry. In *Mysterium cosmographicum*, Kepler writes "geometry possesses two treasures: the ratio of the hypotenuse in the right triangle to the legs, as well as division in extreme and mean ratio." A footnote amplifies: "The former, which states that in a right-triangle the sum of the legs squared is equal to the hypotenuse squared, I would like to compare to a gold-nugget; the other, relating to proportional division, I would like to call a gemstone." Everyone in mathematics, when not using modern *phi*, now refers to the latter as "the golden proportion" or "the golden section." See Kepler 1938–, 1: 2, 81, quoted in Herz-Fischler 1987, 175.

47. Virgil's five-part design does not include a 4.5-line poetic "table of contents," covering all four books of his treatise on farming, which lie outside the numerical design for his first book, *Georgics I*.

48. The initial discussion of *Georgics I* as a work with a mathematical design was by G. Le Grelle (1949). More than a decade later, while discussing Virgil's use of mathematical design in the *Aeneid*, George Duckworth (1962, 76–77) showed that Horace's *Ars Poetica* was a work based on the golden proportion.

49. A lively, thorough account of these events may be found in the Donald R. Howard biography *Chaucer*, 217–22.

Chapter 3: *Parliament of Fowls*

1. The lone exception, John Hurt Fisher (1989, 564–65, 582), basing his decision on historical arguments regarding Richard II's betrothal, and on *Fame* as an "appropriate transition" to *Troilus and Criseyde*, prints *Fame* after *Fowls*. Although I tend to agree with Fisher's implied conclusion, that *Fowls* predates *Fame*, the arguments on which he rests this opinion are very different from those offered here.

2. In a learned, persuasive article that anticipates many of the arguments advanced here, Helen Cooper (1999, 59) apparently accepts Skeat's proposal (1894, 1: lxiii) of

1383–84 as the date of *Fame*'s composition. Cf. Minnis (1995, 171), arguing from the increasing influence of Italian literature on Chaucer during the 1380s: "Personally I believe that the *House of Fame* just might have been composed after *Troilus and Criseyde*."

3. The misstatements alleged to be errors may not be errors at all. First, Chaucer incorrectly calls Scipio a "kyng" (*HF* 916). Though Scipio never held this precise title, medieval English uses the term imprecisely. The title may only testify to Chaucer's accurate translation of Guillaume de Lorris's "roi Cipion" (10) in *Roman de la rose*. Second, the technically incorrect claim that Scipio saw hell and heaven in his dream (*HF* 917–18) may only be interpretive references, respectively, to whirling about in pain and coming to a blissful place, allusions that *Fowls* (78–84) leaves free of theological connotation. Finally, the statement that Macrobius "wrot al th'avysyoun" (*BD* 285) that Scipio dreamed may only reflect the title of the book Macrobius produced.

Apparently no one doubted that the encyclopedic knowledge conveyed by Macrobius was of greater value than the fanciful dream created by Cicero. Indeed most telling is the first page of the first printed edition of the *Commentary*, from 1472, reproduced by Stahl as a frontispiece. Centered at the top of this elegantly printed page appear the following words in a late medieval display script that looks very like a title: "Macro · de · republica ·." Not only was this book produced without the text of Cicero's *Somnium*, its title seems to credit Macrobius as the author of *De republica* and thus of the *Somnium* which concludes that treatise. In short, Macrobius's name may well have been used to refer to the entire manuscript, *Somnium* as well as *Commentary*, even by those who knew that Cicero wrote the former and Macrobius wrote only the latter. Note that Cicero's name does not even appear in the subtitle of the first printed edition, though Cicero's title, *Somnium Scipionis*, appears there: "MACROBII AVRELII THEODOSII VIRI CONSVLARIS ET ILLVSTRIS IN SOMNIVM SCIPIONIS EXPOSITIONIS QVAMELEGANTISSIMAE LIBER PRIMVS." The *Commentary* obviously had a career quite independent of, and more important than, Cicero's *Somnium*, as the names Freud and Jung are more prominent in the modern era than any of the dreams or dreamers they comment on. Apparently if someone in the late fourteenth century wished to learn about mathematics, music, astronomy, and geometry he would probably have sought the easily understood, comfortable "dilettante's grasp" (Stahl, 56) in the *Commentary* of Macrobius, rather than the detailed, erudite, difficult science that characterizes the writings of Theon of Smyrna, Geminus, Cleomedes, Chalcidius, Martianus Capella, and Boethius (Stahl, 55–56).

4. Critics disagree slightly over the specific lines that divide the *Parliament*, but are of one mind that the poem has "three chief episodes within the poem" (Clemen 1964, 125). The divisions Victoria Rothschild (1984) sees in the poem create a commemorative calendar of the leap year 1384: 12 stanzas to represent the months in

the year; 52 stanzas for weeks; 29 stanzas to indicate the 29 days of February in that year; and 100 total stanzas to count the 100 days from January 1 to Easter Sunday on April 9. She notes further that the first mention of "Seynt Valentynes day" (309) occurs in stanza 45, corresponding to February 14, the 45th day of the year. The argument advanced here agrees completely with Rothschild's points of division, but sees a different—perhaps an additional—reason for these divisions.

5. By using Jamesian words—"presents" to refer to the first half of the narrator's dream, "represents" in reference to the second—I hope to suggest that Chaucer shares Henry James's preference for representation.

6. That the popular understanding of "love" is but one among many meanings that Boethius attributes to the word may be inferred from the concluding passage, *metrum* 8, of book II of the *Consolation*, quoted here in full from Chaucer's translation:

> That the world with stable feyth varieth accordable chaungynges; that the contrarious qualities of elementz holden among hemself allyaunce perdurable; that Phebus, the sonne, with his goldene chariet bryngeth forth the rosene day; that the moone hath comaundement over the nyghtes, whiche nyghtes Esperus, the eve-sterre, hath brought; that the see, gredy to flowen, constreyneth with a certein eende his floodes, so that it is nat leveful to strecche his brode termes or bowndes uppon the erthes (that is to seyn, to coveren al the erthe)— al this accordaunce [and] ordenaunce of thynges is bounde with love, that governeth erthe and see, and hath also comandement to the hevene. And yif this love slakede the bridelis, alle thynges that now loven hem togidres wolden make batayle contynuely, and stryven to fordo the fassoun of this world, the which they now leden in accordable feith by fayre moevynges. This love halt togidres peples joyned with an holy boond, and knytteth sacrement of mariages of chaste loves; and love enditeth lawes to trewe felawes. O weleful were mankynde, yif thilke love that governeth hevene governede yowr corages.

7. Cf. Rowe, "the love which created and sustains the universe, the love 'that al maist circumscrive,' is repeatedly represented in [*Troilus and Criseyde*] as a love which binds" (1976, 74).

8. Muscatine confidently claims that the *Parliament* cannot "support the theory that makes of it a sober philosophical tract" (1957, 122), an opinion with which I must respectfully disagree if he means the emphasis to fall on "philosophical." If, on the other hand, the emphasis is placed on "tract," Muscatine is correct; the *Parliament* is certainly not a tract.

9. Cf. Emsley, "Another main theme of the *Parliament* is the idea of harmony" (1999, 141). See also Paul A. Olson's elegant article (1980) which, but for its limitation to the social and civic orders, also gives due attention to the importance of universal harmony.

10. To my mind, the fourteen neutral or positive references to harmony occur in lines 1–4, 8, 38, 47, 59, 60, 62, 72, 75, 77, and 83; the five references to disharmony are found in 65, 78, 79, 80, and 82.

11. Opening stanzas 19 and 20 (*PF* 127, 134), Chaucer's "Thorgh me" echoes Dante's initial words over the gate to Hell, "Per me" (*Inf* III.1). There is nothing in Chaucer to equal the devastating line with which Dante concludes his inscription, "Lasciate ogne speranza, voi ch'intrate" (*Inf* III.9) [Abandon every hope, you who enter here].

12. See, for example, Paul A. Olson, "the inclusion of a 'Parlement' is not fictional decoration but the representation of that vehicle through which late medieval man found it most possible to develop his sense of sociality and conviviality" (1980, 53). See also Cowgill 1975, 316–19.

13. Thus far, the subject that has interested the majority of commentators on the *Parliament*, namely the occasion that prompted Chaucer to compose his poem, has not been discussed. I intend no disservice to the authors of much fine work on this subject, not least Larry D. Benson (1982), for some occasion may well have been in Chaucer's mind when he set about creating the *Parliament*. But that occasion has little or nothing to do with poetic achievement. Like Pericles' funeral oration, the Old English *Battle of Maldon*, Shakespeare's sonnets, Milton's "Lycidas," Pope's *Rape of the Lock*, Swift's *Modest Proposal*, and many another work that unquestionably (or probably, or possibly) arose from an historical event, Chaucer's *Parliament of Fowls* transcends by far whatever event occasioned its creation.

14. Though a critical consensus on the significance of the roundel at the end of the poem seems unlikely, in view of the wide variety of opinion, James Dean's suggestion (1986) that it brings "artistic conclusiveness" to the poem comes closer to the arguments advanced here than most other readings. However, we do disagree in our interpretations of the poem as a whole.

15. Evidence that Chaucer may have had in mind some song other than "Now welcome, somor" comes from a title that appears in some manuscripts of the Parliament: "Qui bien aime a tard oublie" [Whoever loves well forgets slowly], which happens to be the first line of one of Machaut's songs.

16. In Hughes and Abraham 1960, see Reaney, 15–30, on the profound influence Machaut had on musical innovation during the third quarter of the fourteenth century. Later in this work Ficker writes that music in England remained "almost unaffected by the daring novelties introduced by the French *ars nova* composers, such as Vitry and Machaut" (134). Nevertheless, Machaut's influence on English court life when Queen Philippa was his patron, and on literature after his death in 1377, gives reason to infer that the subsequent remark by Reaney applies to England as well as to France.

17. The number of lines in the first fitt totals 502 if counting begins where the

Knight begins speaking at line I.853, that is, if we take direction from authorial transition rather than from post-Chaucerian editorial breaks. Chaucer's holographs were probably composed in continuous lines, without the editorial separations and headings shown in Thynne and in modern editions. The headnote, *Heere bigynneth the Knyghtes Tale. / Iamque domos patrias, Scithice post aspera gentis / Prelia, laurigero, &c.*, has always been assumed by critics to be an editorial insertion. So too elsewhere in *Canterbury Tales*.

18. High praise for the *Parliament of Fowls* remains undiminished through the years. Dorothy Everett called it "the most perfect of Chaucer's Love Visions" (1955, 102); John M. Fyler wrote that it "is Chaucer's most sophisticated comment on the world ruled by Nature; indeed, it is in many respects the thematic epitome of his poetry" (1979, 81–82); and Alastair Minnis has declared the work "not only finished, but highly polished" (1995, 262). I do, however, take partial exception to David Lawton's Wildean description of *Parliament* as a "polished inconsequentiality" (1985, 43).

For a shrewd, sensitive discussion of the rhyme-royal stanza, see Barry Windeatt (1992, 354–59).

19. In Stahl, for example, discounting for the moment book I chapter 6, where Macrobius discusses individual numbers, the remaining thirty-nine chapters of books I and II average 18 numbered sections each. But book I chapter 6 has 83 numbered sections, 79 of which discuss the number seven. The next largest chapter has only 36 sections.

20. To the Middle Ages, the name of an interval (e.g., fourth, fifth, and octave) signifies the number of staff positions enclosed by the interval. For example, to strike F and B on a piano, skipping G and A, would constitute a fourth, because the entire interval includes the upper and lower tones as well as the skipped tones, or four whole tones in all.

21. "Ita enim elementa inter se diversissima, opifex tamen deus ordinis opportunitate conexuit ut facile iungerentur" (Macrobius I.6.25) ["For thus, in spite of the utter diversity of these elements, the Creator harmonized them so skillfully that they could be readily united" (Stahl, 105)].

22. Macrobius takes his understanding of the Creation from Plato, as expressed throughout the *Timaeus*, and transmits it through the whole of book I chapter 6 of the *Commentary*. His words conveying the essence of the universe's harmony bear close examination: "Et ita fit ut singula quaeque elementorum duo sibi hinc inde vicina singulis qualitatibus velut quibusdam amplectantur ulnis: aqua terram frigore, aerem sibi nectit umore; aer aquae umecto simili et igni calore sociatur; ignis aeri miscetur ut calido, terrae iungitur siccitate; terra ignem sicco patitur, aquam frigore non respuit" (Macrobius I.6.27) ["And so it happens that each one of the elements appears to embrace the two elements bordering on each side of it by single qualities:

water binds earth to itself by coldness, and air by moisture; air is allied to water by its moisture, and to fire by warmth; fire mingles with air because of its heat, and with earth because of its dryness; earth is compatible with fire because of its dryness, and with water because of its coldness" (Stahl, 105)].

23. "Illud vero quod est inter aquam et aerem Harmonia dicitur, id est apta et consonans convenientia, quia hoc spatium est quod superioribus inferiora conciliat et facit dissona convenire" (Macrobius I.6.38).

24. In addition to Guzzardo, see John Freccero (1965) and Charles S. Singleton (1965).

25. A roundel normally consists of a three-line refrain that opens and closes the song and two or more interposed stanzas of either two or three lines each that separate the medial repetition(s) of the refrain. Lacking manuscript authority for the way Chaucer wanted the roundel to appear, since no exemplar includes a roundel, Skeat apparently assumed that Chaucer intended as many stanzas of *Fowls* as possible to fit the seven-line rhyme royal. Hence his *Oxford Chaucer* (1894–97) prints the opening lines of the roundel thus: the three-line refrain, a two-line stanza, and the first two lines of the refrain. By dropping the third line of the refrain, he achieved the seven lines needed to match Chaucer's rhyme royal stanza. To complete the roundel, Skeat could do nothing but produce a six-line stanza: a three-line roundel stanza followed by the concluding three-line refrain. The result is a roundel of thirteen lines, probably not faithful to the way the song would have been sung. In his anthology *Chaucer's Poetry* (1975), Donaldson prints the line that Skeat omitted, "And driven away the longe nyghtes blake," giving eight lines to the roundel's first stanza. He then finishes the roundel as Skeat does: a three-line stanza and the three-line refrain, for a stanza of six lines. Donaldson succeeds, therefore, in fitting the fourteen lines of the roundel as it was probably sung in Chaucer's day—that is, not omitting any lines of the refrain—into the same number of lines that two stanzas of rhyme royal would have occupied, reaching 700 lines for the poem as a whole.

26. Macrobius I.vi.34; Stahl, 106, emphasis in original. Cicero's comment is at V.2; Stahl, 74. Stahl observes: "The number seven receives the greatest attention from Macrobius, as it does in the arithmologies, mainly because it marks the lunar quarters, which, according to widespread ancient (and surviving) superstition were supposed to control menstruation, gestation, and the critical periods of diseases" (108n). See also note 19.

27. To demonstrate the geometric proportion that measures the poem as a whole (if this note may look ahead briefly), Chaucer divides his one hundred stanzas into three distinct parts by creating obvious transitions at stanzas 17, 70, and 100, which are not included in a comparison of the lengths of the three parts. But when demonstrating the difficult harmonic proportion that part II encodes, he must sacrifice consistency by also discounting stanza 18 (whereas he included it to demonstrate

the geometric proportion) and by including stanza 70 (after discounting it for the geometric proportion). These departures are the only mathematical aberrations in Chaucer's otherwise brilliant and complex design.

28. Though Macrobius was probably the Middle Ages' principal source of knowledge of Neoplatonic number theory, the concept of harmony, which derives from number, can be traced back to Plato, mainly his *Timaeus*. See the accessible translation and commentary by F. M. Cornford (1937), esp. 43–52.

29. For a full discussion of the mathematical design of British Library MS Cotton Nero A.x, the unique manuscript containing *Pearl*, *Purity*, *Patience*, and *Sir Gawain and the Green Knight*, see Condren 2002.

30. Rowe is referring to *Timaeus* 32b–c in connection with his discussion of the *Knight's Tale* and deriving his summary of medieval concepts of harmony (34 ff.) from Cornford's commentary in *Plato's Cosmology*, 43–52, and from Wetherbee (1972, 34–35).

31. A proportion is understood mathematically as an equivalence between two ratios, $a : b = x : y$. When the proportion is also a series—that is, when the two middle terms (b and x in the previous sentence) are the same—the proportion $a : b = b : c$ is usually written as a series, $a : b : c$. A geometric proportion is understood in mathematics as a numerical series in which each number exceeds or diminishes its predecessor by the same fixed rate. The numbers 2, 8, 32, and 128, for example, are in a geometric series where each number, multiplied by 4, produces the next number in the series.

32. To appreciate how difficult it would have been for Chaucer to calculate to an extreme degree of precision while using only unit fractions, consider that the modern decimal 1.8125 would have been represented in the late fourteenth century thus: $1 + \frac{1}{2} + \frac{1}{4} + \frac{1}{16}$, but written in the even more cumbersome Latin symbols i + i/ii + i/iv + i/xvi.

33. The necessity of excluding stanza 17 to demonstrate the geometric proportion embracing the entire poem, and then reintroducing this stanza to show the arithmetic proportion encoded in part I, certainly must be reckoned an imperfection of some kind. So, yes, Chaucer probably fell short of his ideal to produce his design without a single blemish. I would suggest, however, that Chaucer did not commit an error. Quite simply, he could not have reached this ideal within any unit numbering system. See note 27.

34. To be precise, an arithmetic progression is not a proportion but a series, a string of numbers each of which surpasses its predecessor by a fixed amount, as in the series 2, 4, 6, 8, 10 . . . , or 5, 10, 15, 20, 25 . . . , or the like.

35. For a political discussion of the *Parliament* that sees the lower-class birds challenging the upper-class, see David Aers (1986).

36. Complete discussions of the divine proportion are readily available (e.g.,

Herz-Fischler 1987). Appendix B offers a brief explanation intended for audiences not familiar with discussions of mathematics.

37. *De divina proportione*, chap. 5, translation from Herz-Fischler, 171–72.

38. Letter to Joachim Tanckius, 1608, in Kepler 1938–, 16: 154–65, quoted in Herz-Fischler, 174.

39. For a scholarly study of the examples cited here and many others, all well known to mathematicians, see Herz-Fischler. A discussion for popular audiences is offered by Mario Livio in *The Golden Ratio*.

40. According to G. Le Grelle (1949), Virgil designed *Georgics I* as a representation of the golden proportion to show the harmony between the progress of a year and the progress of the seasons, especially those propitious for farming. And Charles Singleton (1965) persuasively demonstrates a complicated numerical symmetry based on the number seven, at the exact center of Dante's *Commedia*, that emphasizes the turning point reached when the journeying pilgrim contemplates the proper understanding of Love. See also Guzzardo, appendix I, "The Numbers Seven and Thirteen in the Structure of the *Commedia*."

41. The discovery of a calendar in Spenser's *Epithalamion* was made by A. Kent Hieatt (1960), 365 years after the poem's first publication.

42. Cf. Emsley, "Chaucer offers a poem that praises the very ordinariness of marriage among commoners" (147).

43. As remarked in note 4 to this chapter, these parallels with the calendar have all been advanced by Victoria Rothschild in a convincing article that has received less attention than it deserves. Most of the magnitudes to which she refers are discussed above as they pertain to proportion, rather than to the calendar. Two other suggestions by Rothschild—the forty-five days to St. Valentine's Day, first mentioned in the forty-fifth stanza, and the poem's hundred stanzas equaling the hundred days from January 1 to Easter in the leap year of 1384—do not figure in the numerical arguments advanced here. See also H. A. Kelly (1986), who suggests the English actually celebrated a Genovese Saint Valentine's Day on May 1, 2, or 3. But note as well the rebuttal arguments of Minnis (1995, 258–60).

44. I wish to thank David Lawton for inviting me to give the first public expression of the numerical arguments contained in this chapter at the London Congress of the New Chaucer Society in 2000, during its sixth-centennial commemoration of Chaucer's death.

Chapter 4: *House of Fame*

1. Prologue to the *Fall of Princes* (fol. 8b). It is only assumed that this phrase refers to the *House of Fame*.

2. Full discussions of the critical responses to *House of Fame* may be found in monographs by B. G. Koonce (1966), Sheila Delany (1972), John M. Fyler (1979),

Piero Boitani (1984), J. A. W. Bennett (1986), and Robert R. Edwards (1989). See also Spearing (1976) and Minnis (1995).

3. First suggested by J. M. Manly, in the Kittredge Festschrift (1913).

4. For example, the fascinating proposal of Larry D. Benson (1987) gives greater insight into the political maneuvers for the hand of Anne of Bohemia than critical analysis of the *Parliament of Fowls*. One of Benson's observations, addressed specifically to the formel's refusal to choose a suitor but apt as well for the poem as a whole, paradoxically acknowledges the subordinate nature of historical contexts for "occasional" poems: "The poetic reasons for the formel's reluctance to choose are probably to be sought not in the historical circumstances but in the poem itself" (*Riv Ch* 384).

5. See Wetherbee for a complementary discussion of how Chaucer's narrator in *Troilus* declares that poem subject "to the standards of the great poets—Homer, Vergil, and the rest—[while] at the same time implicitly setting himself apart from the historiographic tradition of Benoit and Guido, who had undertaken to correct the Homeric-Vergilian version of the story of Troy, and . . . tipping the balance back again, toward poetic rather than 'historical' truth" (1984, 24).

6. To date, the only possible (though not necessarily probable) source suggested for Dido's mention of a man's three mistresses (*HF*, 305–10) is a Provençal poem by Daude de Pradas. Robert M. Estrich notes that in Daude's poem "Amors m'envica e·m somo," the poet claims "he is especially blest by love. He has achieved three women: a *dompna* . . . *per mais valer*; a *piucella*; and a *soudadeira*, whom he will grant *ab pauc de querer tot so c'Amors vol a jazer*" (1940, 344). On a potentially symbolic significance for these three loves, Estrich does not comment.

7. For Evrart de Conty, Minnis refers readers to F. Guichard Tesson, "Evrart de Conty, auteur de la 'Glose des Eschecs amoureux'" *Le Moyen français* 8–9 (1981), 111–48. For the text of Evrart's work, see Françoise Guichard Tesson and Bruno Roy, *Le Livre des Eschez amoureux moralisés: Edition critique* (Montreal: CERES, 1994). Minnis's translation has relied on Joan Morton Jones, "The Chess of Love [Old French Text with Translation and Commentary]" (Ph.D. diss., University of Nebraska, 1968).

8. The narrator's claim for the uniqueness of his dream in *Fame* (59–63) differs from the assertion in *Duchess* (276–79)—by a different kind of surrogate narrator, to be sure—that no one can interpret his dream properly. The *Parliament* makes no claim for either the transparency or the obscurity of its dream.

9. Only in the *House of Fame* does Chaucer precisely record a date on which he experienced a dream that he then made the subject of a poem. The *Parliament* does mention "Seynt Valentynes day" (309), but this is the date *in* the dream, not the date *of* the dream. On the date of St. Valentine's Day in the fourteenth century, see note 43 to chapter 3.

Helen Cooper connects December 10 with the second Sunday of Advent in the year 1384, the only year during Chaucer's tenure as controller of customs when the second Sunday of Advent and December 10 coincided. Preachers were instructed to deliver on that Sunday a homily, drawn from Luke 21: 25–33, on the second of the "four last things," namely "judgment" in the list death, judgment, hell, and heaven (Cooper 1999, 39, 63–64). This interesting suggestion does not preclude the possibility, argued below, that December 10 might also have been the day on which Chaucer gave a public reading of the poem he refers to as a dream and praises with comic extravagance (59–65, quoted in my text).

10. For a rather different view, see Winthrop Wetherbee: "More than any other of Chaucer's works the *House of Fame* is a poem about poetic tradition. A brief review of its complex and cerebral allegory can help us understand what was at stake for Chaucer when he sought to come to terms with the great poetry of the past" (18). And again, "The pity that Dido's Ovidian passion inspires in the dreamer ... is the index to a kind of alienation, a lack of moral orientation, which ... constitutes [*House of Fame*'s] serious theme" (19).

11. On the eagle's associations and powers, see Fyler 1979, 46–49, and Minnis 1995, 201–3.

12. The *Middle English Dictionary* shows that "tydyng" and "tale" could be used interchangeably in the fourteenth century: "tidinge, 1.(a) that which one tells, the oral or written relation of an event or a series of events purporting to be true; tale, i.(a) a report of an occurrence or an event." See Goffin 1943.

13. For a close rival to the eagle's lecture, see the gloriously absurd scientific debate that arose, and still receives occasional discussion, over the precise nature of the "spontaneous combustion" that causes the death of Mr. Krook in Dickens's *Bleak House*, chapter 32.

14. See, for example, Minnis 1995, 204–7.

15. On the question of Shakespeare's sexuality, the most satisfying comment is Stephen Booth's "William Shakespeare was almost certainly homosexual, bisexual, or heterosexual. The sonnets provide no evidence on the matter" (Shakespeare, *Sonnets*, 548).

16. See also Clemen, 98 and note 1.

17. In his *Book of Minerals*, Albertus Magnus states that beryl makes husband and wife agree in marriage, that it confers cleverness (76), and that under its form as *diacodos* it is "so effective in calling up phantasms that magicians use it a great deal" (86). Robert Burton reflects the same tradition in the *Anatomy of Melancholy*: "the Beryl, it much avails to a good understanding" (568) as well as reconciling men and wives (865). Myths about the stone continue to survive, for W. B. Yeats wrote that "beryl was enchanted by our fathers that it might unfold the pictures in its heart,

and not to mirror our own excited faces, or the boughs waving outside the window" (1924, 201).

18. Despite a contrary opinion by John Fyler (*Riv Ch* 998), I have long believed that this "English Gaufride" identifies the poet himself, a belief anticipated by E. K. Rand and J. S. P. Tatlock and shared, most recently, by Helen Cooper (1999, 58–59), though Cooper reveals a slight hesitation: "English Gaufride would make still better sense as a name for Chaucer among the poets of Troy *if he had already written, or was at work on Troilus and Criseyde*; it is because of this poem that Lydgate counts him among the Trojan authorities" (59, emphasis added). Her contrary-to-fact conditional clause is exactly what I argue in chapters 4 and 5. If Cooper were to accept the argument I advance there, that Chaucer wrote *House of Fame* after he had completed and recited *Troilus and Criseyde*, she would have no reason to hesitate, for Lydgate's remark would then be literally true, as Cooper says.

19. According to Laurence K. Shook, the "whole new approach to the Art of Poetry" offered by the *House of Fame* suggests that "poems are made not out of love but out of sound" (1968, 349). This interesting suggestion requires a distinction between the sounds of the world which become, in this new theory, the poet's source of material, and the sounds of his finished poem. Father Shook locates the "workshop" of this sound—the representation of the poet's shaping these sounds into finished poetry—"in Fame's House" (349), rather than in the House of Rumor, as I propose.

20. I base this conclusion on the assumption that the narrator of the *House of Fame*—called Geffrey by the eagle (729)—in fact represents Geoffrey Chaucer, regardless of whatever combination of qualifications modern criticism wishes to place on him. This identification has never been questioned.

21. The quoted words allude to Abrams, *The Mirror and the Lamp*. In the following sentence, "onlie begetter" is taken from the heading to Shakespeare's *Sonnets*.

22. The quoted phrase is from line 60 of "Ode to Psyche," the earliest of Keats's great odes, written in 1819. Although no evidence suggests that the shape and appearance of Chaucer's House of Rumor influenced Keats's image, the two poets seem to have used the figure for the same purpose. If Chaucer imagines the House of Rumor as the place where the creative activity of his own poetic processes occurs—"Non other auctour alegge I" (314)—so Keats shapes "Psyche" as the declaration of his intent "by my own eyes inspired" (43) to embark upon the period of his major poetry.

Chapter 5: The Missing Tidings of the *House of Fame*

1. The *Cook's Tale*, *Squire's Tale*, *Tale of Sir Thopas*, and *Monk's Tale* are not, in my opinion, unfinished works, in the sense that Chaucer intended to complete them for the *Canterbury Tales* but never got around to it. Chaucer terminated the

first of these for thematic reasons, as I have argued elsewhere (1999, 26–27), and called upon the Franklin, Harry Bailly, and the Knight to interrupt, respectively, the Squire, Chaucer the Pilgrim, and the Monk in order to spare the pilgrims further boredom.

2. The narrator's first rejection is implied by his response to a question about the fame he may be seeking: "'Nay, for sothe, frend,' quod y; / 'I cam noght hyder, graunt mercy, / For no such cause, by me hed!'" (1873–75). The second rejection concerns the kind of "newe tydynges" (1886) the eagle assured Geffrey he would learn: "But these be no suche tydynges / As I mene of" (1894–95), a reaction that prompts the eagle to take him to the House of Rumor.

3. Windeatt may be taken as representing the majority in assuming "Englyssh Gaufride" (*HF* 1470) refers unambiguously to Geoffrey of Monmouth, for in summarizing the names listed by Chaucer in *HF* 1466–70 he translates "Englyssh Gaufride" without comment as "Geoffrey of Monmouth" (38). Helen Cooper represents the minority in arguing that the reference is to Chaucer himself; see note 18 to chapter 4.

4. John M. Fyler, as editor of *HF* for *The Riverside Chaucer*, accepts Robinson's dating: "*The House of Fame* . . . shows the beginnings of the Italian influence on Chaucer's poetry, and it draws not only on Dante but on Boccaccio's poetry, which Chaucer is generally believed not to have known until after his journey to Italy in 1378. . . . Such considerations led Robinson to place the work . . . after *The Book of the Duchess* and before *Anelida* and *The Parliament of Fowls*. . . . The usually suggested date is 1379–80" (*Riv Ch* 347). The argument Fyler adopts from Robinson establishes only a terminus a quo. That a greater Italian influence is thought to govern *Anelida* and *Fowls* than *Fame* gives reason for selecting a terminus ad quem earlier than either *Anelida* or *Fowls*. But since the dates for *Anelida* and *Fowls* are as difficult to assign as a date for *Fame*, a terminus ad quem may be impossible to determine. To my knowledge, only J. Stephen Russell (1995), in a brief but persuasive argument that *HF* 935–49 is "thick with allusions to the Peasants' Revolt and particularly to the catastrophic events of June 1381," accepts a date as late as 1381 for the *House of Fame*'s terminus a quo.

5. Cf. the opening sentence of M. C. E. Shaner's introduction to the poem: "*The Legend of Good Women* is a product of Chaucer's artistic maturity, written not long after (and purportedly as an atonement for) *Troilus and Criseyde*" (*Riv Ch* 587).

6. *Troilus and Criseyde* had to have been completed, or very nearly so, before the death by execution of Thomas Usk in April 1388, for Chaucer's poem is mentioned in Usk's *Testament of Love*, the date of which is uncertain but obviously earlier than April 1388.

7. See, for example, Sheila Delany (1972, 48–57), whose remarks on the Dido-Aeneas episode call for frequent comparison to the *Legend*, including the obser-

vation that Chaucer's treatment of Dido in both *Fame* and *Legend* follows Ovid's sympathetic view of Carthage's queen, rather than Virgil's dispassionate narrative. See also Allen 1956, 400.

8. If independent evidence compelled us to accept for *Fame* a 1379–80 date of composition, which of course is not the case, the question critics do not ask could be stated with a different emphasis: If *Fame* was written in 1379–80, and if *Troilus and Criseyde* occupied Chaucer during most of the 1380s, with no major intervening work, would it not seem obvious that Chaucer thought of *Fame* as the prologue to *Troilus and Criseyde*? But the witty, light touch of *Fame* persuades me that it was not written before *Troilus*. Its evident skill rather shows a poetic maturity similar to what is displayed in the *T&C* of the 1380s, implying that it could have been composed after *T&C* to answer that poem's critics in the same way the *Legend of Good Women* replies in a hasty, less witty way.

9. The "auctour" of line 314 is ambiguous. If the word refers to Dido, suggesting that the lament to follow comes from the queen herself, not from any ancient author, it strains credulity, since the poem has not yet introduced the golden eagle's explanation of how a fourteenth-century writer could overhear a speech already eighteen centuries old. On the other hand, if the audience has no difficulty accepting "dream" as a metaphor signifying a poet's own creation, and readily understands the eagle's explanation of sound waves as a witty defense of authorial omniscience, then "auctour" in line 314 would refer to Chaucer. Lines 311–14 are Chaucer's insistence, then, that he alone composed Dido's lament.

10. Though I disagree with several of Robert M. Jordan's statements about *Fame*'s lack of referentiality (1967, 24), in my opinion he rightly centers Chaucer's poem in a discussion of compositional choices, or as Minnis puts it, succinctly summarizing Jordan, "Chaucer is not so much writing about the world as writing about writing about the world" (1995, 219). See also Martin Irvine (1985, 850–76) and Winthrop Wetherbee (1984, 17–20).

11. *Book of the Duchess* has 1,333 lines (though numbered 1334), *Parliament of Fowls* has 699 (though probably intended by Chaucer to have 700), whereas *House of Fame* has 2,158, not counting the missing tidings, whatever these tidings would have been.

12. J.A.W. Bennett 1968, xii–xiii, as summarized by John M. Fyler in the notes to *The Riverside Chaucer*, 990.

13. Spearing does not extend the role of poet to either the "gret auctorite" in *Fame* or the wel-faring "man in blak" in *Duchess*, as I do here for the former and in chapter 2 for the latter.

14. That Chaucer understood well the apexes of this triangle, without the benefit of Meyer Abrams's *The Mirror and the Lamp*, should surprise no one.

Chapter 6: *Troilus and Criseyde*

1. The chapters referred to discuss three of the four dream visions Chaucer wrote. The fourth, the *Legend of Good Women*, together with its F and G prologues, though often noted allusively or *en passant*, is not discussed in a separate chapter because its transparent references to Chaucer's *Troilus and Criseyde*, as well as the author's witty atonement for that work's alleged misrepresentations, make further exegesis unnecessary in the present study.

2. Criseyde's interview with Hector is almost entirely original with Chaucer. The *Filostrato* notes in only four lines that Criseyde sought Hector's protection (Windeatt, 55).

3. An allusion to Dr. Johnson's famous remark may be unfair at this point; the prediction that every living Trojan "will be hanged in a fortnight," or one similar to it, does not come until V.883–89. Nevertheless, from the beginning readers have had their minds focused on Troy's defeat.

4. It is interesting to note how different the portraits Chaucer gives his major women characters are from those he gives his leading men. To oversimplify (a defect I hope to correct in a future study), his men are types, almost clichés of certain kinds of men. The composite figure of the dreamer and the man in black in the *Duchess*, as well as the Knight, Nicholas, the Reeve, Walter, January, the Host and the Narrator in *Canterbury Tales*, and a variety of lesser figures all behave in predictable ways. Only the Pardoner eludes understanding, perhaps because his masculinity may be undeveloped. On the other hand, Chaucer's main women are highly complex, continually driven by mutually contradictory values. The Wife of Bath and the Prioress come immediately to mind, but Griselda too has a profundity not often seen in literature or life, as does Dorigen. Even Malin in the *Reeve's Tale* and the wife in the *Shipman's Tale* have some little uniqueness. Perhaps Criseyde is Chaucer's triumph in this regard. On this and related subjects, see Carolyn Dinshaw (1989), Sheila Delany (1983), and Elaine Tuttle Hansen (1992), among others.

5. In *Love and Marriage in the Age of Chaucer* (1975), Henry Ansgar Kelly develops the thesis that Criseyde and Troilus are already married canonically since they complete each of the several acts needed for making a clandestine marriage theologically lawful. This may well be true, as far as the canons are concerned. But *Troilus and Criseyde* is not a treatise; it appeals to readers for its compelling presentation of two people who fall in love, become consummate lovers, and later suffer the ill fortune of separation. Readers know instinctively, not canonically, that Troilus's speeches are sincere, as are Criseyde's up to the point where she realizes she must leave Troilus. These same instincts recognize immediately what Diomede represents, a slick opportunist whose cloying speeches are capable only of manipulating, not loving, despite a potential canonicity in his relations, too, with Criseyde.

6. The words *Courtly Love* echo the title of the first chapter in C. S. Lewis's *The Allegory of Love*.

7. To give a precise explanation of Troilus's condition, Donald R. Howard (1976, 141–42) glosses line III.1088 with a detailed report, based on medieval medical knowledge: "Each of the three bodily spirits contracted or held in (*in knette*) its power (*vigour*), with the result that he faints (line 1092). Earlier (1: 306–7), Troilus felt faint because of failure of the 'vital Spirit' or 'spirit of the heart,' which controls pulse and breath. Now the 'natural spirit' (liver) and 'animal spirit' (brain) also contract. The passage reflects medieval medical theories. Evidently what happens inside Troilus is that a powerful emotion in his heart blocks the flow of the spirits from the liver to the brain. Hence his tears cannot flow (1087), he cannot feel emotion (1090–91), and ultimately cannot sustain consciousness."

8. An exception is Jill Mann, who refines the point: "The developing relationship between Troilus and Criseyde is conceived and described in terms of power, and ... the shifts and transformations in the way each of them either exerts or refuses to exert power over the other lead to the achievement of a mature and complex relationship on which the consummation can fittingly be based." According to Mann, Troilus's "swoon demonstrates, in the clearest possible way, his subjection to Criseyde and to his love of her" (1980, 319–20, 328).

9. I depart from *The Riverside Chaucer* to adopt from several manuscripts (with Donaldson, Howard, Shoaf, and others) the italicized words at III.193–94. By reading the bridge connecting "the, Criseyde" (III.193) and "thow Troilus" (III.194) with the majority of manuscripts and early editions (12 of 19 extant authorities), I accept Chaucer's particular emphasis that both Criseyde and Troilus are in Pandarus's presence to hear this speech.

10. A convincing work on "nothing" as a pun on pudendum was done by Thomas Pyles, "Ophelia's 'Nothing'" (1949). See also Paul Jorgensen's "Much Ado About Nothing" (1962). These critics discuss later work than Chaucer's, but the suitability of the pun to many of Chaucer's lines makes it impossible to believe that the meaning did not also exist in Middle English. The case for "corage" is made by Chaucer himself, in his frequent use of the word in contexts where the allusion is obvious. See *CT* I.11, IV.1254, 1725, 1759, 1808, VII.3452.

11. With punning liberty, line III.882 may mean either "you do neither kindness nor gentleness" or "your nether bounty does no gentleness."

12. "Death," a frequent Renaissance metaphor for orgasm, has not been widely shown to have this potential meaning in the fourteenth century. Nevertheless, it is more likely that it did have this meaning in certain contexts than that it did not: (a) by Shakespeare's day this special meaning had become a well-worked metaphor, presupposing a long prior development; (b) an orgasm's sudden arrival, followed by an almost total decrease of energy, makes it difficult to imagine the metaphor

"death" not attaching to so climactic a moment (cf. *la petite mort*); (c) the secondary meaning proposed here for "death" so enriches the phrase "the crampe of deth" and the whole swooning scene that it would be foolish to imagine it had not occurred to Chaucer.

13. Of Chaucer's thirteen other uses of *yard*, meaning "stick," at least one has clear phallic suggestiveness; see *CT* I.1387.

14. See note 7.

15. Here one can agree entirely with Barry Windeatt's language, and with the lines he quotes from Troilus to confirm his description, "I not myself naught wisly what it is, / But now I feele a newe qualitee—/ Yee, al another than I dide er this" (III.1653–55). I do take exception, however, to his earlier opinion "It is the charge of jealousy, of tainting with jealousy a true understanding of love, that brings on Troilus' swoon" (225).

16. It is impossible to determine whether Chaucer's sources for the *Clerk's Tale* include the level of meaning summarized here, or whether Chaucer alone added this exegetical level by making strategic additions and emphases. I offer a more detailed defense of this reading in *Chaucer and the Energy of Creation*, 125–35. Recently the *Clerk's Tale* has been attracting new-historicist attention. In particular, see two companion pieces in the 2001 Festschrift to Del Kolve: Glending Olson, "The Marquis of Salazzo and the Marquis of Dublin," and Charlotte C. Morse, "Griselda Reads Philippa de Coucy," the former an essay on Richard II's relationship with Robert de Vere, the latter on de Vere's repudiation of his wife.

17. Donaldson notes that the first three descriptions of Criseyde (I.99–105, I.169–82, I.281–94) leave readers "so charmed . . . that we readily forget that we still know nothing about her except that she is charming" (1970, 57).

18. That Pandarus perhaps represents, among other things, the thoughts and feelings of two other characters in the same work in which he himself appears is not as improbable as it may seem. Some of the most celebrated works of Middle English literature and its sources employ the same strategy discussed here. Boethius's *Consolation of Philosophy*, Martianus Capella's *Marriage of Philology and Mercury*, the *Parliament of Three Ages*, *Pearl*, and others have characters who articulate competing views within a single consciousness. In Chaucer's *Wife of Bath's Tale* too, the old hag and the young knight-rapist represent, respectively, the irreconcilable truths and artful fictions of the Wife herself.

19. The quotation is from Neville Coghill (1967, 76). See also the 1965 study by George Williams, an attempt to see everything Chaucer wrote as a roman à clef and to see Pandarus *as* Chaucer (76–77).

20. Interest in discovering the identity of this Lollius has occasioned much speculation but produced little certainty. Although scholars generally accept Boccaccio's *Filostrato* as the poem's main source, Chaucer may not have known it was Boccaccio

who authored the actual text he had before him. The most likely explanation for the appearance of the name Lollius in Chaucer's *House of Fame*, 1468, and *Troilus and Criseyde*, I.394, V.1653, was first advanced by Kittredge (1917): that it came from a line at the opening of Horace's *Epistles*, or possibly an assumed reconstruction of Horace's line. See Stephen Barney's brief summary of this reasoning in his introduction to *Troilus and Criseyde* (*Riv Ch* 1022). Barry Windeatt, the most thorough commentator on the subject, seems to favor the theory that Chaucer used the name to fake a more respectable source than the one he was actually following (37–41).

21. Monosyllabic words ending in *r* + a consonant were invariably neuter in Middle English and had the identical form in the nominative singular and plural, e.g., "His hors were goode" (*CT* I.74).

22. See the last four paragraphs of chapter 2.

23. I take the "woful soule" of line IV.317 as a reference to Troilus, though some readers may argue that lines 319–21 refer to Criseyde as the one who habitually brought comfort to Troilus's pain. The previous stanza, complaining that she who once was his light is now extinguished, prepares for the same kind of thought at lines 317–18, describing how she used to minister to Troilus. Moreover, the relative clause "that thus crieth," amplifying "thilke woful soule," seems to refer to a lament that has just been heard, which could only be Troilus's lament, since Criseyde is not present in the scene.

24. Book II.m.8 of Boethius's *Consolation* is discussed in chapter 3 and quoted in full in note 6 to that chapter. Book V.pr.3 of the *Consolation*, discussing predestination, strongly influences Troilus's soliloquy in IV.958–1082. The passage does not appear in the *Filostrato* or in some of the manuscripts of *Troilus*. Although Boethius extends these passages to include all of nature, here we shall discuss only human life, as does Chaucer in *Troilus*.

25. Talbot Donaldson, one of the most sensitive and loving interpreters of the ending of *Troilus and Criseyde*, empathizes with the narrator who "makes one last effort to resolve the tension in his mind between loving a world he ought to hate and hating a world he cannot help loving" (1963, 42).

Appendix B

1. All medieval interpretations and speculations on Creation are ultimately traceable to Plato's *Timaeus* (passim, esp. 52d–92c), from the discussion of the Empedoclean theory of elements and their insertion into the Pythagorean theory of number, to the concluding discussion of quadrupeds and the deepest sea creatures. See as well the commentaries by A. E. Taylor (1928) on the *Timaeus* and by Macrobius (Stahl, 94–177) on Cicero's *Somnium Scipionis*, which is also indebted to the *Timaeus*.

Works Cited

Abrams, M. H. 1953. *The Mirror and the Lamp: Romantic Theory and the Critical Tradition*. New York: Oxford University Press.
———, ed. 1993. *The Norton Anthology of English Literature*. 6th ed. 2 vols. New York: Norton.
Acker, Paul. 1994. "The Emergence of an Arithmetical Mentality in Middle English Literature." *ChauR* 28: 293–302.
Aers, David. 1986. *Chaucer*. Brighton, Sussex: Harvester.
Alanus de Insulis. 1973. *Anticlaudianus*. Translated by James J. Sheridan. Toronto: Pontifical Institute of Mediaeval Studies.
———. 1980. *The Plaint of Nature [De planctu naturae]*. Translated by James J. Sheridan. Toronto: Pontifical Institute of Mediaeval Studies.
Albertus Magnus. 1967. *Book of Minerals*. Translated by Dorothy Wyckoff. Oxford: Clarendon.
Allen, Robert J. 1956. "A Recurring Motif in Chaucer's *House of Fame*." *Journal of English and Germanic Philology* 55: 393–405.
Alverny, Marie-Thérèse d'. 1982. "Translations and Translators." In Benson and Constable, *Renaissance and Renewal*, 421–62.
Anderson, J. J. 1992. "The Narrators in the *Book of the Duchess* and the *Parlement of Foules*." *ChauR* 26: 219–35.
Armitage-Smith, Sydney. 1904. *John of Gaunt, King of Castile and Leon, Duke of Aquitaine and Lancaster, Earl of Derby, Lincoln, and Leicester, Seneschal of England*. London: Constable.
Bahr, Arthur W. 2000. "The Rhetorical Construction of Narrator and Narrative in Chaucer's the *Book of the Duchess*." *ChauR* 35: 43–59.
Beaujouan, Guy. 1982. "The Transformation of the Quadrivium." In Benson and Constable, *Renaissance and Renewal*, 463–87.
Bec, Pierre, ed. 1966. *Petite Anthologie de la lyrique occitane du Moyen âge: Initiation à la langue et à la poésie des troubadours, textes avec traductions* ... 4th ed. Avignon: Aubanel Père.
Behaingne. See Machaut 1984.
Bennett, J. A. W. 1968. *Chaucer's "Book of Fame."* Oxford: Clarendon.
Bennett, Michael J. 1997. "The Historical Background." In *A Companion to the Gawain Poet*, edited by Derek Brewer and Jonathan Gibson, 71–90. Cambridge: D. S. Brewer.
Benson, C. David. 1990. *Chaucer's "Troilus and Criseyde."* London: Unwin Hyman.

Benson, Larry D. 1982. "The Occasion of *The Parliament of Fowls*." In *The Wisdom of Poetry*, edited by Larry D. Benson and Siegfried Wenzel, 123–44. Kalamazoo, Mich: Medieval Institute Publications.

———. 1986. "The Love-Tydynges in Chaucer's *House of Fame*." In *Chaucer in the Eighties*, edited by Julian N. Wasserman and Robert J. Blanch, 3–22. Syracuse, N.Y.: Syracuse University Press.

———. 1987. *See* Chaucer 1987.

Benson, Robert L., and Giles Constable, eds. 1982. *Renaissance and Renewal in the Twelfth Century*. With Carol D. Lanham. Oxford: Clarendon.

Biblia sacra. Holy Bible Translated from the Latin Vulgate. 1949–50. New York: Catholic Book Publishing.

Blake, N. F. 1981. "The Textual Tradition of *The Book of the Duchess*." *English Studies* 62: 237–48.

———. 1986. "*The Book of the Duchess* Again." *English Studies* 67: 122–25.

Bloomfield, Morton. 1964. "Authenticating Realism and the Realism of Chaucer." *Thought* 39: 335–58.

Boccaccio, Giovanni. ca. 1340. *Il Filostrato*. Translated by Nathaniel Edward Griffin and Arthur Beckwith Myrick. Philadelphia: University of Pennsylvania Press, 1929.

Boethius (Anicius Manlius Severinus Boethius). ca. 525. *De Consolatione Philosophiae*. Edited by Ludwig Bieler as *Anicii Manlii Severini Boethii Philosophiae Consolatio*, CC Ser. Lat. 94.1 (Turnhout: Brepols, 1957). Translated as *Boece* by Geoffrey Chaucer in *The Riverside Chaucer*, 395–469. Modern translations include *The Theological Tractates, and The Consolation of Philosophy*, translated by H. F. Stewart and E. K. Rand (London: Heinemann, 1918), and *Boethius: The Consolation of Philosophy*, translated by V. E. Watts (Baltimore: Penguin, 1969).

Boitani, Piero. 1984. *Chaucer and the Imaginary World of Fame*. Cambridge: D. S. Brewer.

Bowers, Bege K., and Mark Allen, eds. 2002. *Annotated Chaucer Bibliography, 1986–1996*. Notre Dame, Ind.: University of Notre Dame Press.

Bowers, John M. 2001. *The Politics of "Pearl": Court Poetry in the Age of Richard II*. Cambridge: D. S. Brewer.

Boyer, Carl B. 1989. *A History of Mathematics*. 2nd ed. Revised by Uta C. Merzbach. New York: John Wiley.

Brewer, Derek. 1978. *Chaucer and His World*. New York: Dodd, Mead.

Bronson, Bertrand H. 1934. "Chaucer's Hous of Fame: Another Hypothesis." *University of California Publications in English* 3: 171–92.

———. 1960. *In Search of Chaucer*. Toronto: University of Toronto Press.

Bruyne, Edgar de. 1969. *The Esthetics of the Middle Ages*. Translated by Eileen B. Hennessy. New York: Frederick Ungar.

Burrow, John A. 1971. "'Sir Thopas': An Agony in Three Fits." *Review of English Studies*, n.s., 22: 54–58. Reprinted in *Essays on Medieval Literature* (Oxford: Clarendon), 61–65.
Burton, Robert. 1621. *Anatomy of Melancholy*. Edited by Thomas C. Faulkner, Nicolas K. Kiessling, and Rhonda L. Blair. Commentary by J. B. Bamborough. 6 vols. Oxford: Clarendon, 1989–2000.
Calabrese, Michael A. 1994. *Chaucer's Ovidian Arts of Love*. Gainesville: University Press of Florida.
Capella, Martianus. 1969. *De Nuptiis Philologiae et Mercurii*. In *Martianus Capella*, edited by Adolphus Dick, revised by Jean Préaux. Stuttgart: Teubner.
———. 1977. *The Marriage of Philology and Mercury*. Translated by William Harris Stahl and Richard Johnson, with E. L. Burge. New York: Columbia University Press.
Carruthers, Mary J. 1987. "Italy, *Ars Memorativa*, and Fame's House." *Studies in the Age of Chaucer: Proceedings, No. 2, 1986*, 179–88.
———. 1990. *The Book of Memory: A Study of Memory in Medieval Culture*. Cambridge: Cambridge University Press.
Chamberlain, David. 1970. "The Music of the Spheres and *The Parlement of Foules*." *ChauR* 5: 32–56.
Chaucer, Geoffrey. 1894–97. *The Complete Works of Geoffrey Chaucer*. Edited by Walter W. Skeat. 7 vols. Oxford: Clarendon.
———. 1957. *The Works of Geoffrey Chaucer*. 2nd ed. Edited by F. N. Robinson. Boston: Houghton Mifflin. Now superseded by *The Riverside Chaucer*.
———. 1963. *Major Poetry*. Edited by Albert C. Baugh. New York: Appleton-Century-Crofts.
———. 1975. *Chaucer's Poetry: An Anthology for the Modern Reader*. 2nd ed. Edited by E. T. Donaldson. New York: Ronald Press.
———. 1976. *Troilus and Criseyde and Selected Short Poems*. Edited by Donald R. Howard and James Dean. New York: New American Library.
———. 1982. *Chaucer: The Book of the Duchess*. Edited by Helen Phillips. Durham: Durham and St. Andrews Medieval Texts.
———. 1987. *The Riverside Chaucer*. 3rd ed. Edited by Larry D. Benson. Boston: Houghton Mifflin.
———. 1989a. *The Complete Poetry and Prose of Geoffrey Chaucer*. 2nd ed. Edited by John Hurt Fisher. New York: Holt, Rinehart and Winston.
———. 1989b. *Troilus and Criseyde*. Edited by R. A. Shoaf from the text of A. C. Baugh. East Lansing, Mich.: Colleagues Press.
Chaucer Life-Records. 1966. Edited by Martin M. Crow and Clair C. Olson. Oxford: Clarendon.

Cherniss, Michael D. 1987. *Boethian Apocalypse: Studies in Middle English Vision Poetry*. Norman, Okla.: Pilgrim.
Clark, Mary T. 1958. *Augustine: Philosopher of Freedom*. New York: Desclée.
Clemen, Wolfgang. 1964. *Chaucer's Early Poetry*. Translated by C. A. M. Sym. New York: Barnes and Noble.
Coghill, Nevill. 1967. *The Poet Chaucer*. 2nd ed. London: Oxford University Press.
Condren, Edward I. 1971. "The Historical Context of the *Book of the Duchess*: A New Hypothesis." *ChauR* 5: 195–212.
———. 1972. "The Troubadour and His Labour of Love." *Mediæval Studies* 34: 174–95.
———. 1975. "Of Deaths and Duchesses and Scholars Coughing in Ink." *ChauR* 10: 87–95.
———. 1999. *Chaucer and the Energy of Creation: The Design and Organization of the "Canterbury Tales."* Gainesville: University Press of Florida.
———. 2002. *The Numerical Universe of the "Gawain-Pearl" Poet: Beyond Phi*. Gainesville: University Press of Florida.
Connolly, Margaret. 1994. "Chaucer and Chess." *ChauR* 29: 40–44.
Cook, Theodore Andrea. [1914] 1978. *The Curves of Life: Being an Account of Spiral Formations and Their Application to Growth in Nature, to Science, and to Art; with Special Reference to the Manuscripts of Leonardo da Vinci*. New York: Dover.
Cooper, Helen. 1999. "The Last Four Things in Dante and Chaucer: Ugolino in the House of Rumor." *New Medieval Literatures* 3: 39–66.
Cornford, Francis Macdonald, trans. 1937. *Plato's Cosmology: The Timaeus*. With running commentary. New York: Harcourt, Brace.
Cowgill, Bruce Kent. 1975. "The *Parlement of Foules* and the Body Politic." *Journal of English and Germanic Philology* 74: 315–35.
Curry, Walter Clyde. 1960. *Chaucer and the Mediaeval Sciences*. Rev. ed. New York: Barnes and Noble.
Dante Alighieri. 1970–75. *The Divine Comedy*. Vol. 1, *Inferno* (1970); vol. 2, *Purgatorio* (1973); vol. 3, *Paradiso* (1975). Translated by Charles S. Singleton. Princeton: Princeton University Press.
Delany, Paul. 1970. "Constantinus Africanus' *De Coitu*: A Translation." *ChauR* 4: 55–65.
Delany, Sheila. 1972. *Chaucer's "House of Fame": The Poetics of Skeptical Fideism*. Chicago: University of Chicago Press.
———. 1983. *Writing Women: Women Writers and Women in Literature, Medieval to Modern*. New York: Schocken.
Delasanta, Rodney. 1969. "Christian Affirmation in *The Book of the Duchess*." *PMLA* 84: 245–51.

Dinshaw, Carolyn. 1989. *Chaucer's Sexual Poetics*. Madison: University of Wisconsin Press.

Donaldson, E. Talbot. 1963. "The Ending of Chaucer's *Troilus*." In *Early English and Norse Studies: Presented to Hugh Smith*, edited by Arthur Brown and Peter Foote, 26–45. London: Methuen. Reprinted in *Speaking of Chaucer* (New York: Norton, 1970), 84–101.

———. 1970. "The Masculine Narrator and Four Women of Style." In *Speaking of Chaucer*, 46–64. New York: Norton.

———. 1975. *See* Chaucer 1975.

———. 1985. *The Swan at the Well: Shakespeare Reading Chaucer*. New Haven: Yale University Press.

D'Ooge, Martin Luther, trans. 1926. *Introduction to Arithmetic*, by Nicomachus of Gerasa. With studies in Greek arithmetic by Frank Egleston Robbins and Louis Charles Karpinski. New York: Macmillan.

Duckworth, George Eckel. 1962. *Structural Patterns and Proportions in Vergil's "Aeneid": A Study in Mathematical Composition*. Ann Arbor: University of Michigan Press.

Edwards, Robert R. 1989. *The Dream of Chaucer: Representation and Reflection in the Early Narratives*. Durham, N.C.: Duke University Press.

Ellis, Steve. 1995. "The Death of the *Book of the Duchess*." *ChauR* 29: 249–58.

Emsley, Sarah. 1999. "'By evene acord': Marriage and Genre in the *Parliament of Fowls*." *ChauR* 34:139–49.

Estrich, Robert M. 1940. "A Possible Provençal Source for Chaucer's *House of Fame*." *Modern Language Notes* 55: 342–49.

Everett, Dorothy. 1955. *Essays on Middle English Literature*. Edited by Patricia Kean. Oxford: Clarendon.

Fairclough, H. Rushton, ed. and trans. 1978. *Virgil*. Vol. 1: *Eclogues, Georgics, Aeneid 1–6*. Rev. ed. Loeb Classical Library. Cambridge, Mass.: Harvard University Press.

Ferster, Judith. 1985. *Chaucer on Interpretation*. Cambridge: Cambridge University Press.

Ficker, Rudolf von. 1960. "The Transition on the Continent." In Hughes and Abraham, *Ars Nova*, 134–64.

Fisher, John Hurt. 1989. *See* Chaucer 1989a.

Fox, Denton, ed. 1981. *Testament of Cresseid*, by Robert Henryson. In *The Poems of Robert Henryson*, 111–31. New York: Oxford University Press.

Freccero, John. 1965. "Infernal Inversion and Christian Conversion (*Inferno* XXXIV)." *Italica* 42: 35–41.

French, W. F. 1949. "Medieval Chess and *The Book of the Duchess*." *Modern Language Notes* 64: 261–64.

Froissart, Jean. 1975. *Le Joli Buisson de Jonece*. Edited by Anthime Fourrier. Paris: Klincksieck.

———. 1982. *Le Paradys d'Amours*. In *Chaucer's Dream Poetry: Sources and Analogues*, edited and translated by B. A. Windeatt, 41–57. Cambridge: D. S. Brewer.

Fyler, John M. 1979. *Chaucer and Ovid*. New Haven: Yale University Press.

———. 1992. "Chaucer, Pope, and the *House of Fame*." In *The Idea of Medieval Literature: New Essays on Chaucer and Medieval Culture in Honor of Donald R. Howard*, edited by James M. Dean and Christian K. Zacher, 149–59. Newark: University of Delaware Press.

Ghyka, Matila. 1946. *The Geometry of Art and Life*. New York: Sheed and Ward.

Ginsberg, Warren. 2002. *Chaucer's Italian Tradition*. Ann Arbor: University of Michigan Press.

Goffin, R. C. 1943. "Quiting by Tidings in the *Hous of Fame*," *Medium ævum* 12: 40–44.

Green, Richard Firth. 1980. *Poets and Princepleasers: Literature and the English Court in the Late Middle Ages*. Toronto: University of Toronto Press.

Guillaume de Lorris and Jean de Meun. ca. 1230–ca. 1280. *Le Roman de la rose*. Translated in part by Geoffrey Chaucer as *The Romaunt of the Rose* in *The Riverside Chaucer*, 686–767.

Guzzardo, John J. 1987. *Dante: Numerological Studies*. New York: Peter Lang.

Hansen, Elaine Tuttle. 1992. *Chaucer and the Fictions of Gender*. Berkeley and Los Angeles: University of California Press.

Hart, Thomas Elwood. 1981. "Medieval Structuralism: 'Dulcarnoun' and the Five-Book Design of Chaucer's *Troilus*." *ChauR* 16: 129–70.

Hawthorne, Nathaniel. 1850. "The Customs House." In *The Scarlet Letter*, 2nd ed., edited by Sculley Bradley et al., 26–29. New York: Norton, 1978.

Heath, Sir Thomas. 1921. *A History of Greek Mathematics*. 2 vols. Oxford: Clarendon.

Henryson, Robert. *Testament of Cresseid*. See Fox.

Herrick, Robert. 1648. "The Argument of His Book." In Abrams, *Norton Anthology*, 1: 1355–56.

Herz-Fischler, Roger. 1987. *A Mathematical History of Division in Extreme and Mean Ratio*. Waterloo, Ont.: Wilfrid Laurier University Press. Reissued as *A Mathematical History of the Golden Number* (Mineola, N.Y.: Dover, 1998).

Herzog, Michael B. 1988. "The *Book of the Duchess*: The Vision of the Artist as a Young Dreamer." *ChauR* 22: 269–81.

Hieatt, A. Kent. 1960. *Short Time's Endless Monument: The Symbolism of the Numbers in Edmund Spenser's "Epithalamion."* New York: Columbia University Press.

Hill, John M. 1974. "The *Book of the Duchess*, Melancholy, and That Eight-Year Sickness." *ChauR* 9: 35–50.

Hiscock, Nigel. 1999. *The Wise Master Builder: Platonic Geometry in Plans of Medieval Abbeys and Cathedrals*. Aldershot: Ashgate.
Howard, Donald R. 1976. *See* Chaucer 1976.
———. 1987. *Chaucer, His Life, His Works, His World*. New York: Dutton.
Hughes, Dom Anselm, and Gerald Abraham, eds. 1960. *Ars Nova and the Renaissance: 1300–1540*. Vol. 3 of *New Oxford History of Music*. London: Oxford University Press.
Huntley, H. E. 1970. *The Divine Proportion: A Study in Mathematical Beauty*. New York: Dover.
Huppé, Bernard F., and D. W. Robertson Jr. 1963. *Fruyt and Chaf: Studies in Chaucer's Allegories*. Princeton: Princeton University Press.
Irvine, Martin. 1985. "Medieval Grammatical Theory and Chaucer's *House of Fame*." *Speculum* 60: 850–76.
Jaufré Rudel. 1978. *The Songs of Jaufré Rudel*. Edited by Rupert T. Pickens. Toronto: Pontifical Institute of Mediaeval Studies.
Jordan, Robert M. 1967. *Chaucer and the Shape of Creation: The Aesthetic Possibilities of Inorganic Structure*. Cambridge, Mass.: Harvard University Press.
Jorgensen, Paul A. 1962. "Much Ado About Nothing." In *Redeeming Shakespeare's Words*, 22–42. Berkeley and Los Angeles: University of California Press.
Josipovici, Gabriel. 1971. *The World and the Book: A Study of Modern Fiction*. Stanford, Cal.: Stanford University Press.
Keats, John. 1819. "Ode to Psyche." In Abrams, *Norton Anthology*, 2: 788–90.
Kelly, Henry Ansgar. 1975. *Love and Marriage in the Age of Chaucer*. Ithaca, N.Y.: Cornell University Press.
———. 1986. *Chaucer and the Cult of Saint Valentine*. Leiden: Brill.
Kepler, Johannes. 1938–90. *Gesammelte Werke*. Edited by Max Caspar and Franz Hammer. 20 vols. Munich: Beck.
Kiser, Lisa J. 1991. *Truth and Textuality in Chaucer's Poetry*. Hanover, N.H.: University Press of New England.
Kittredge, George Lyman. 1917. "Chaucer's Lollius." *Harvard Studies in Classical Philology* 28: 47–133.
Klassen, Norman. 1995. *Chaucer on Love, Knowledge, and Sight*. Cambridge: D. S. Brewer.
Kolve, V. A. 1984. *Chaucer and the Imagery of Narrative: The First Five Canterbury Tales*. Stanford, Cal.: Stanford University Press.
Koonce, B. G. 1966. *Chaucer and the Tradition of Fame*. Princeton: Princeton University Press.
Krapp, George Philip, ed. 1932. *The Vercelli Book*. Vol. 2 of *Anglo-Saxon Poetic Records*. New York: Columbia University Press.

Lanham, Richard A. 1967. "Game Play and High Seriousness in Chaucer's Poetry." *English Studies* 48: 1–24.

———. 1970. "Opaque Style and Its Uses in *Troilus and Criseyde*." *Studies in Medieval Culture* 3: 169–76.

Lawton, David. 1985. *Chaucer's Narrators*. Cambridge: D. S. Brewer.

Le Grelle, G. 1949. "Le Premier Livre des Géorgiques, poème pythagoricien." *Études classiques* 17: 139–235.

Leicester, H. Marshall. 1974. "The Harmony of Chaucer's *Parlement*: A Dissonant Voice." *ChauR* 9: 15–34.

———. 1990. *The Disenchanted Self: Representing the Subject in the Canterbury Tales*. Berkeley and Los Angeles: University of California Press.

Lewis, C. S. 1936. *The Allegory of Love: A Study in Medieval Tradition*. Oxford: Clarendon.

Leyerle, John. 1971. "Chaucer's Windy Eagle." *University of Toronto Quarterly* 40: 247–65.

Livio, Mario. 2002. *The Golden Ratio: The Story of Phi, the World's Most Astonishing Number*. New York: Broadway Books.

Lydgate, John. [1924–27] 1967. *The Fall of Princes*. Edited by Henry Bergen. 4 vols. EETS e.s. 121–24. London: Oxford University Press.

Lynch, Kathryn L. 1988a. "The *Book of the Duchess* as a Philosophical Vision: The Argument from Form." *Genre* 21: 279–305.

———. 1988b. *The High Medieval Dream Vision: Poetry, Philosophy, and Literary Form*. Stanford, Cal.: Stanford University Press.

Machaut, Guillaume de. 1908. *Oeuvres de Guillaume de Machaut*. Edited by Ernest Hoepffner. 3 vols. Paris: Société des Anciens Textes Français.

———. 1984. *The Judgment of the King of Bohemia = Le Jugement dou Roy de Behaingne*. Edited and translated by R. Barton Palmer. New York: Garland.

———. 1988. *Le Jugement dou Roy de Behaingne; and, Remede de Fortune*. Edited by James I. Wimsatt and William W. Kibler. Athens: University of Georgia Press.

———. 1993. *The Fountain of Love = La Fonteinne Amoureuse, and Two Other Love Vision Poems*. Edited and translated by R. Barton Palmer. New York: Garland.

Macrobius. 1952. *Commentary on the Dream of Scipio*. Edited and translated by William Harris Stahl. New York: Columbia University Press.

———. 1981. *Macrobii Ambrosii Theodosii Commentariorum in Somnium Scipionis Libri Duo*. Edited and translated by Luigi Scarpa. Padua: Liviana.

Malone, Kemp. 1951. *Chapters on Chaucer*. Baltimore: Johns Hopkins Press.

Manly, J. M. 1913. "What Is Chaucer's *Hous of Fame?*" In *Anniversary Papers by Colleagues and Pupils of George Lyman Kittredge*, edited by Fred N. Robinson, William A. Nielson, and Edward S. Sheldon, 73–81. Boston: Ginn.

Mann, Jill. 1980. "Troilus' Swoon." *ChauR* 14: 319–35.

———. 1991. *Geoffrey Chaucer*. Atlantic Highlands, N.J.: Humanities Press International.
Martianus Capella. *See* Capella, Martianus.
McAlpine, Monica E. 1978. *The Genre of Troilus and Criseyde*. Ithaca, N.Y.: Cornell University Press.
Middle English Dictionary. 1954–. Edited by Hans Kurath, Sherman M. Kuhn, John Reidy, and Robert E. Lewis. Ann Arbor: University of Michigan Press.
Miller, Robert P., ed. 1977. *Chaucer: Sources and Backgrounds*. New York: Oxford University Press.
Minnis, A. J. 1995. *The Shorter Poems*. With V. J. Scattergood and J. J. Smith. Oxford Guides to Chaucer. Oxford: Clarendon.
Minnis, A. J., and A. B. Scott, eds. 1991. *Medieval Literary Theory and Criticism, c. 1100–c. 1375*. With David Wallace. Rev. ed. Oxford: Clarendon.
Morse, Charlotte C. 2001. "Griselda Reads Philippa de Coucy." In Yeager and Morse, *Speaking Images*, 347–92.
MS Bodley 638. 1982. *Manuscript Bodley 638: A Facsimile: Bodleian Library, Oxford University*. Introduction by Pamela Robinson. Variorum edition. Norman, Okla.: Pilgrim.
MS Fairfax 16. 1979. *Bodleian Library, MS Fairfax 16*. Introduction by John Norton-Smith. London: Scolar.
MS Tanner 346. 1980. *Manuscript Tanner 346: A Facsimile: Bodleian Library, Oxford University*. Introduction by Pamela Robinson. Variorum edition. Norman, Okla.: Pilgrim.
Muscatine, Charles. 1957. *Chaucer and the French Tradition: A Study in Style and Meaning*. Berkeley and Los Angeles: University of California Press.
Neuss, Paula. 1981. "Images of Writing and the Book in Chaucer's Poetry." *Review of English Studies*, n.s., 32, no. 128: 385–97.
Nicomachus of Gerasa. *See* D'Ooge.
Ockham, William of. *See* Spade.
Olson, Glending. 2001. "The Marquis of Saluzzo and the Marquis of Dublin." In Yeager and Morse, *Speaking Images*, 325–45.
Olson, Paul A. 1980. "*The Parlement of Foules*: Aristotle's *Politics* and the Foundations of Human Society." *Studies in the Age of Chaucer* 2: 53–69.
Ovid. 1977. *Metamorphoses*. Translated by Frank Justus Miller. Revised by G. P. Goold. Loeb Classical Library. Cambridge, Mass.: Harvard University Press.
Pacioli, Luca. 1956. *De divina proportione*. Fontes Ambrosiani 31. Milano: Silvana.
Palmer, John N. 1974. "The Historical Context of the *Book of the Duchess*: A Revision." *ChauR* 8: 253–61.
Palmer, R. Barton. *See* Machaut.

Patterson, Lee. 1991. *Chaucer and the Subject of History*. Madison: University of Wisconsin Press.
Pearsall, Derek. 1992. *The Life of Geoffrey Chaucer: A Critical Biography*. Oxford: Basil Blackwell.
Peck, Russell A. 1970. "Theme and Number in Chaucer's *Book of the Duchess*." In *Silent Poetry: Essays in Numerological Analysis*, edited by Alastair Fowler, 73–115. London: Routledge and Kegan Paul.
Pelen, Marc M. 1976. "Machaut's Court of Love Narratives and Chaucer's *Book of the Duchess*." *ChauR* 11: 128–55.
Peterson, R. G. 1976. "Critical Calculations: Measure and Symmetry in Literature." *PMLA* 91: 367–75.
Peterson, R. G., S. K. Heninger Jr., Daniel Laferrière, and Thomas Elwood Hart. 1977. Forum. *PMLA* 92: 126–29.
Phillips, Helen. 1981. "Structure and Consolation in the *Book of the Duchess*." *ChauR* 16: 107–18.
———. 1982. *See* Chaucer 1982.
———. 1986. "*The Book of the Duchess*, Lines 31-96: Are They a Forgery?" *English Studies* 67: 113–21.
Plato. 1961. *The Collected Dialogues of Plato, Including the Letters*. Edited by Edith Hamilton and Huntington Cairns. New York: Pantheon.
———. *Timaeus*. *See* Taylor.
Pyles, Thomas. 1949. "Ophelia's 'Nothing.'" *Modern Language Notes* 64: 322–23.
Reaney, Gilbert. 1960. "*Ars Nova* in France." In Hughes and Abraham, *Ars Nova*, 1–30.
Riedel, F. C. 1928. "Chaucer's House of Fame." *Journal of English and Germanic Philology* 27: 441–69.
Robbins, Rossell Hope, ed. 1975. *Chaucer at Albany*. New York: Burt Franklin.
Robinson, F. N. 1957. *See* Chaucer 1957.
Robinson, Ian. 1972. *Chaucer and the English Tradition*. Cambridge: Cambridge University Press.
Roman de la rose. *See* Guillaume de Lorris and Jean le Meun.
Rothschild, Victoria. 1984. "*The Parliament of Fowls*: Chaucer's Mirror Up to Nature?" *Review of English Studies*, n.s., 35, no. 138: 164–84.
Rowe, Donald W. 1976. *O Love, O Charite! Contraries Harmonized in Chaucer's "Troilus."* Carbondale: Southern Illinois University Press.
Rowland, Beryl. 1993. "The Artificial Memory, Chaucer, and Modern Scholars." *Poetica* 37: 1–14.
Rudel, Jaufré. *See* Jaufré Rudel.
Russell, J. Stephen. 1988. *The English Dream Vision: Anatomy of a Form*. Columbus: Ohio State University Press.

———. 1995. "Is London Burning? A Chaucerian Allusion to the Rising of 1381." *ChauR* 30: 107–9.
———. 1998. *Chaucer and the Trivium: The Mindsong of the Canterbury Tales*. Gainesville: University Press of Florida.
Schibanoff, Susan. 2006. *Chaucer's Queer Poetics: Rereading the Dream Trio*. Toronto: University of Toronto Press.
Schless, Howard. 1985. "A Dating for the *Book of the Duchess*: Line 1314." *ChauR* 19: 273–76.
Schuman, Samuel. 1976. "The Circle of Nature: Patterns of Imagery in Chaucer's *Troilus and Criseyde*." *ChauR* 10: 99–112.
Shakespeare, William. 1977. *Shakespeare's Sonnets*. Edited by Stephen Booth. New Haven: Yale University Press.
———. 1992. *The Complete Works of Shakespeare*. 4th ed. Edited by David Bevington. New York: HarperCollins.
Shippey, T. A. 1996. "Chaucer's Arithmetical Mentality and the *Book of the Duchess*." *ChauR* 31: 184–200.
Shoaf, R. A. 1989. *See* Chaucer 1989b.
Shook, Laurence K. 1968. "*The House of Fame*." In *Companion to Chaucer Studies*, edited by Beryl Rowland, 341–54. Toronto: Oxford University Press.
Simmons, J. L. 1966. "The Place of the Poet in Chaucer's *House of Fame*." *Modern Language Quarterly* 27: 125–35.
Simson, Otto von. 1956. *The Gothic Cathedral: Origins of Gothic Architecture and the Medieval Concept of Order*. New York: Pantheon.
Singleton, Charles S. 1965. "The Poet's Number at the Center." *Modern Language Notes* 80: 1–10. Reprinted in *Essays in the Numerical Criticism of Medieval Literature*, edited by Caroline D. Eckhardt (Lewisburg, Pa.: Bucknell University Press, 1980), 79–90.
Southern, R. W. 1979. *Platonism, Scholastic Method, and the School of Chartres*. Reading, Berks.: Reading University Press.
———. 1982. "The Schools of Paris and the School of Chartres." In Benson and Constable, *Renaissance and Renewal*, 113–37.
Spade, Paul Vincent, ed. 1994. *Five Texts on the Mediaeval Problem of Universals: Porphyry, Boethius, Abelard, Duns Scotus, Ockham*. Indianapolis: Hackett.
Spearing, A. C. 1976. *Medieval Dream-Poetry*. Cambridge: Cambridge University Press.
Spenser, Edmund. 1595. *Epithalamion*. In Abrams, *Norton Anthology*, 1: 738–48.
Stahl, William Harris. *See* Macrobius.
Steel, Anthony. 1941. *Richard II*. Cambridge: Cambridge University Press.
Stevick, Robert D. 1982. "A Formal Analogue of Elene." *Studies in Medieval and Renaissance History* 5: 47–104.

———. 1994. *The Earliest Irish and English Bookarts: Visual and Poetic Forms Before A.D. 1000*. Philadelphia: University of Pennsylvania Press.
Stone, Brian, trans. 1983. *Geoffrey Chaucer: Love Visions*. London: Penguin.
Strohm, Paul. 1989. *Social Chaucer*. Cambridge, Mass.: Harvard University Press.
Taylor, A. E. 1928. *A Commentary on Plato's Timaeus*. Oxford: Clarendon.
Thundy, Zacharias P. 1995. "The Dreame of Chaucer: Boethian Consolation or Political Celebration?" *Carmina Philosophiae: Journal of the International Boethius Society* 4: 91–109.
Thynne, William. 1969. *Geoffrey Chaucer, The Works, 1532: With Supplementary Materials from the editions of 1542, 1561, 1598, and 1602*. Edited by Derek S. Brewer. London: Scolar.
Vickery, Gwen M. 1995. "*The Book of the Duchess*: The Date of Composition Related to Theme of Impracticality." *Essays in Literature* 22: 161–69.
Virgil (Publius Virgilius Maro). *See* Fairclough.
Walker, Denis. 1983. "Narrative Inconclusiveness and Consolatory Dialectic in the *Book of the Duchess*." *ChauR* 18: 1–17.
Wetherbee, Winthrop. 1972. *Platonism and Poetry in the Twelfth Century: The Literary Influence of the School of Chartres*. Princeton: Princeton University Press.
———. 1984. *Chaucer and the Poets: An Essay on Troilus and Criseyde*. Ithaca, N.Y.: Cornell University Press.
Williams, George. 1965. *A New View of Chaucer*. Durham, N.C.: Duke University Press.
Windeatt, Barry. 1992. *Troilus and Criseyde*. Oxford Guides to Chaucer. Oxford: Clarendon.
Wood, Chauncey. 1970. *Chaucer and the Country of the Stars: Poetic Uses of Astrological Imagery*. Princeton: Princeton University Press.
Yates, Frances. 1966. *The Art of Memory*. Chicago: University of Chicago Press.
Yeager, Robert F., and Charlotte C. Morse, eds. 2001. *Speaking Images: Essays in Honor of V. A. Kolve*. Asheville, N.C.: Pegasus.
Yeats, W. B. 1924. "The Symbolism of Poetry." In *Essays*, 188–202. London: Macmillan.

Index

Abrams, M. H., 216n21, 218n14
Aers, David, 212n35
Alanus de Insulis, 117; on accepting reports *vs.* seeing truth, 113; Nature's laws: sexual violation of, 71
Albertus Magnus: and beryl stone, 215n17
Allen, Robert J., 117, 217–18n7
d'Alverny, Marie-Thérèse, 206n45
Anelida and Arcite: and the dating of *HF*, 217n4; as incomplete, 125

Bacon, Francis, 1, 197n1
Beaujouan, Guy, 206n45
Behaingne: as a much-used source for *BD*, 45, 48, 199n15; *BD* compared with, 202n33, 203n34
Bennett, J.A.W., 102
Benson, C. David, 152
Benson, Larry D., 97, 152, 214n4
Blake, N. F., 30, 198nn4 & 8
Blanche of Lancaster, 22, 23, 28–29, 205n44; death of, 10–11, 31–32, 34–35, 197n2, 198n5, 202n30; identified in *BD* by puns, 34; and Philip Larkin's "An Arundel Tomb," 197n3; and the ring at *BD* 1273, 54
Boccaccio, Giovanni, 221–22n20; *Filostrato*: altered by Chaucer for *T&C*, 146, 154; *Filostrato*: as main source for *T&C*, 221–22n20
Boethius (Anicius Manlius Severinus Boethius), 69; agreement with Ockham, 197n2; as fictive persona in *Consolation*, 6; as a founder of the quadrivium, 206n45
—*Consolation*: as a dream vision, 6; as internal dialogue, 200n16; love defined in, 208n6
Boitani, Piero, 213–14n2
Book of Revelation, 5
Book of the Duchess, 3; alleged error at line 455, 10–11; Ceyx and Alcione in, 16–19, 40; dialogues in, 3, 4, 43, 55–7; early names of, 8; immortality in, 14, 17, 95, 135, 205n44; as influenced by *jeupardyes* and *joc partit*, 55–56, 204n41; internal debate in, 3–4, 22; John of Gaunt in, 9–11, 22–31, 34, 54, 60–61, 97, 197–98n3, 198n5, 200nn18–19, 201nn26, 27, 204n37; man in black in, 22–37; misinterpreted, 22–28; manuscript evidence for eight-year illness in, 29–30; monologues by man in black in, 3, 43, 44–57, 60, 128, 191, 204–6nn43, 44; and Queen Philippa, original addressee, 30–32; as representing two personas of Chaucer, 22, 29–30, 52–53; revised by Chaucer ca. 1376, 59; self-dialogue, 3–4; sorrowing insomnia, 11–15; speculations on Chaucer's presence in, 35–36; as traditionally interpreted, 8, 32–34
Boyer, Carl B., 4, 80
Brewer, Derek, 204n42
Bronson, Bertrand H., 17, 137
Burrow, John A., 77
Burton, Robert, 215n17

Canterbury Tales, 2, 30, 67, 76, 97, 115, 120, 129, 130, 151, 160, 173, 197n1, 209–10n17, 216 17n1, 219n4; *Gen. Prol.* as authenticating frame for, 129; importance of audience in, 2; mathematics in, 76; *Retraction* in, 8, 120, 130, 197n1; self-representation in, 22, 54; as unfinished, 125
Capella, Martianus, 69, 113, 117, 221n18; as founder/shaper of higher learning in the Middle Ages, 206n45; as a more learned scientist than Macrobius, 207n3; on reading or hearing *vs.* seeing or experiencing for oneself, 113
Carruthers, Mary J., 18
Chaucer, Geoffrey: as both dreamer and man in black in *BD*, 22, 29; in conversation with self á la Machaut, 40–41; date of birth, 35, 36–37; and "Englyssh Gaufride" (*HF* 1470), 120, 217n3; ludicrous self-aggrandizement of narrator in *BD* and auctoritee in *HF*, 136; and mathematics, 76–77; poetic maturation revealed in still-life images, 170–71. See also *Anelida and Arcite, Book of the Duchess, Canterbury Tales, House of Fame, Legend of Good Women, Parliament of Fowls, Troilus and Criseyde*
Crow, Martin M., 32, 201n24

236 / Index

Cicero: agreement in the *Somnium* with Plato and early medieval philosophers, 68–69

Christ, 1, 197n1; represented by Salvador Dalí in *Sacrament of the Last Supper*, 195–96; symbolized by Grisilda in *Clerk's Tale*, 163

Clemen, Wolfgang, 16, 38, 45, 67, 96, 103, 106, 207–8n4, 215n16

Clerk's Tale: as an example of literature following two genres, 163–64; and new historicism, 221n16

Coghill, Nevill, 221n19

Condren, Edward I. 195, 204n40, 212n29

Cook, Theodore Andrea, 57

Cook's Tale, 216–17n1

Cooper, Helen, 63, 101, 206–7n2, 214–15n9, 216n18, 217n3

Creator/Creation, 3, 78–79, 93, 128, 138, 173–74; Pandarus as literary creator, 181–82

Dante Alighieri: eagle in *Purg.* (ix.19–33), 110; echoed in Chaucer's planning process, 95; and inscription over the gate to Hell, 70; and mathematics, 79

Delany, Sheila, 51, 134, 217–18n7

Delasanta, Rodney, 14

Dinshaw, Carolyn, 219n4

Divine proportion (golden section, *phi*), 3–4, 57–60, 83–84, 92–94, 193–96

Donaldson, E. Talbot, 46, 80, 201n23, 211n25, 222n25

Dream visions, 4–7, 19–22, 189–91; Chaucer's central figures in, 6–7; *Gilgamesh*, 4; *Pearl*, 6

Duckworth, George Eckel, 194, 206n48

Edwards, Robert R., 10–11, 198n5, 199n15

Ellis, Steve, 197n2

Emsley, Sarah, 208n9

Estrich, Robert M., 214n6

Everett, Dorothy, 210n18

Fairclough, H. Rushton, 195.

Ferster, Judith, 113

Fisher, John Hurt, 201n23, 206n1

Fox, Denton, 178

Freccero, John, 211n24

Froissart, Jean, 30, 34, 199–200n15, 200n17, 202n28

Fyler, John M., 132, 146, 217n4

Goffin, R. C., 215n12

Golden section. *See* divine proportion

Green, Richard Firth, 202n31

Guillaume de Lorris, 160, 207n3

Guzzardo, John J., 79, 213n40

Hansen, Elaine Tuttle, 16, 26, 219n4

Hart, Thomas Elwood, 141, 143, 204n42

Hawthorne, Nathaniel, 114

Heath, Sir Thomas, 57, 90, 91

Henryson, Robert, 138, 178

Herrick, Robert, 64–66, 75

Herz-Fischler, Roger, 206n46, 212–13nn36–39

Herzog, Michael B., 199n13, 203n35

Hieatt, A. Kent, 213n41

Hill, John M., 11

Homer, 112, 214n5

House of Fame, 2, 4, 7; Chaucer's atypical reference to, 126; critical reception of, 96–98; Dido-Aeneas episode, 98, 99, 101, 105–8, 120, 129, 131–37, 146, 214n6, 215n10, 217–18n7, 218n9; atypical ending of as "unfinished" poem, 125–26; "Lollius" in, 138, 172, 221–22n20; man of great authority in, 4, 125, 128–29, 136; missing tidings in, 7, 63, 98, 129–31; parallel paths of narrators in *BD*, *PF*, and *HF*, 98; as parallel to Chaucer's earlier poetry, 98–101; as prologue for *T&C*, 132–34; scholarly inquiry into dreams, dismissed in, 102–3; structural echoes of *BD* and *PF* in, 126–29

Howard, Donald R., 67, 152, 159, 206n49, 220n7

Huppé, Bernard, 29, 200n19, 201n25

Immortality, 14, 95, 100, 135, 205–6n44

Jaufré Rudel, 198–99n9, 204n40

Jean de Meun. *See* Guillaume de Lorris

Jordan, Robert M., 204n42, 218n10

Keats, John, 124, 216n22

Kelly, Henry Ansgar, 213n43, 219n5

Kepler, Johannes, 3, 57, 93, 193, 206n46, 213n38

Kittredge, George Lyman, 155, 172, 214n3, 221–22n20
Knight's Tale, 212n30; death as consistent with Nature's plan, 72; love as broadly defined in *Timaeus*, 68; mathematics in, 77; as a tale in two genres, 164
Kolve, V. A., 18, 20, 199n14, 221n16,
Koonce, B. G., 213n2,
Krapp, George Philip., 197n3

Lady Nature, 2, 42, 67, 71–74, 77–79, 86–94, 127–28, 172, 186, 190, 191, 210n18
Lanham, Richard A., 152
Lawton, David, 9, 45, 197n1, 202n30
Le Grelle, G., 194, 206n48, 213n40
Legend of Good Women, 8, 30, 97, 106, 112, 115, 129, 130–35, 197n1, 217n5, 218n8, 219n1; as incomplete, 125; and missing tidings of *HF*, 129; as parallel to *HF* and *T&C*, 132–33; remembrance as knowledge in *LGW* Prol., 117; same period as *HF* and *T&C*, 63
Leicester, H. Marshall, 67, 68
Lewis, C. S., 38, 154, 156, 220n6
Leyerle, John, 134
Livio, Mario, 195, 213n39
Love, 1; as celestial harmony, 119; as interchangeable with poetry, 3, 6, 51–52, 173
Lucan, 95, 131
Lydgate, John, 96, 216n18
Lynch, Kathryn L., 42

Machaut, Guillaume de, 34, 52, 113, 198–99nn9,15, 200n17, 204n36, 209nn15–16; as source for *BD*, 42, 45, 46, 48; composer of rondeaux and motets, 75; self-depiction in internal dialogues, 22; influence on English court life, 209n16; self-disparagement of, 30
Macrobius, 18, 23, 63, 68, 75, 76–77, 83, 99, 207n3, 210n19, 210n21, 211n23, 211n26, 212n28, 222n1; connection between the *Somnium* and mathematics, 96; five dream types, 198n6; mathematical method and the Creation, 79; mathematics as principal *Commentary* subject, 77; motives for composing the *Somnium*, 76; the number seven, 80; Platonism, source of,

68; as putative author of the *Somnium*, 207n3; and the *Timaeus*, 210n22
Malone, Kemp, 136–37
Manly, J. M., 139, 214n3
Mann, Jill, 220n8
Martianus. *See* Capella, Martianus
Marvell, Andrew, 170
Mathematics: Macrobius' importance to, 68; and Nicomachus of Gerasa, 194; and the number seven, 77, 210n19, 211n26; Pythagorean theorem as "dulcarnoun," 141; significance of the number 144, 56–57; the trivium and the quadrivium, 206n45
McAlpine, Monica E., 155
Merzbach, Uta C. *See* Boyer, Carl B.
Miller's Tale, 77, 114, 115
Minnis, A. J., 18, 63, 102, 197–98n3, 210n18, 213n43, 213–14n2, 214n7, 215nn11,14, 218n10; dating of *HF*, 206–7n2; and Evrart de Conty, 102; poetic style of *HF* praised, 134
Missing Tidings of *House of Fame*, 125–39. See also *House of Fame*
MS Bodley 638, 8, 25, 29, 30, 201n22
MS Fairfax 16, 8, 25, 29, 30, 201n22, 202n29; and lines 31–96 of *BD*, 198n4
MS Tanner 346, 8, 25, 29, 30, 201n22; and gap for insertion of *BD* lines 31–96, 29
Muscatine, Charles, 208n8; discordances in *PF*, 67

Neuss, Paula: on relation of dream and creative act, 51, 173
Nicomachus of Gerasa, 58, 90, 194
Number seven, 77, 80, 84, 210n19, 211n26, 213n40
Numerical design, 3, 55, 77, 81, 84, 95. *See also* divine proportion, golden section, and *phi*

Ockham, William of, 1, 197n2
Olson, Glending, 221n16
Olson, Paul A., 208n9, 209n12
Ovid, 16–21, 29, 32, 37–41, 59, 69, 95, 106, 108, 120, 131–32, 134, 137, 138, 146, 156, 189, 215n10, 217–18n7; and narrator of *BD*, 15

Pacioli, Luca, 93
Palmer, John N., 10, 200n20; Blanche's death date, 31; discussion of "this kyng" (*BD* 1314), 24

Palmer, R. Barton, 202n33; and Machaut's concern for establishing his identity, 22; 203n34
Parliament of Fowls 1, 2; arithmetic progression in, 78, 79, 84, 85, 212nn33, 34; Cicero's *Somnium Scipionis* in, 67, 69, 77, 79, 83–85, 129, 189, 207n3, 222n1; class rivalries in, 212n35; disharmony in, 70–72, 78, 88, 100, 191, 209n10; divine proportion in, 3, 76, 79, 83, 84, 92–94, 212–13n36; geometric progression in, 79, 84, 211–12n27, 212nn31, 33; harmonic progression in, 79, 84, 86, 90–91, 211–12n27; harmony of bird song, 19, 66, 70, 72, 73, 74–75; harmony of the universe in, 1, 2, 4, 68–71, 78–79; music of the spheres, 80; numerical design in, 81–83; roundel as pure expression of harmony in, 68, 74–75, 79, 84, 93–94, 128, 191, 209n14, 211n25
Patterson, Lee, 145
Patron/patronage, 31, 32–34, 36–37, 46, 61, 100, 118, 135, 198n5, 201n26, 202n28, 204n40, 209n16; Caesar Augustus, patron of Virgil, 21, 26; John of Gaunt, patron to Chaucer, 26
Pearsall, Derek, 200n18, 201nn26,27; on Chaucer as page to Elizabeth de Burgh, 27–28
Peck, Russell A., 205n43
Peterson, R. G., 204n42; and claim of numerical design, 55, 141
Phi (φ), 57–58, 82, 93–94, 193–96, 206n46
Philippa, wife of Edward III, 46; death of, 30–35; inappropriate descriptions of, 47; Louis de Mâle, exchange of letters with 10; original addressee of *BD*, 31–32, 36, 50, 52, 54, 61
Phillips, Helen, 10, 39, 202n29; on the Black Knight's eight-year illness (*BD* 37), 198n8; on grief in *BD*, 200n19; on indenting *BD* 1311 and 1314, 201n23; on presumed scribal error at *BD* 455, 9; on the relationship among *BD*'s exemplars, 198nn4, 8
Pilate, Pontius, 1, 197n1
Pyles, Thomas, 220n10

Reeve's Tale, 77, 162, 219n4
Retraction, 8, 120, 130, 197n1
Riedel, F. C., 97
Robinson, F. N., 24; and dating of *HF*, 217n4
Robinson, Ian., 199–200n15

Roman de la rose. *See* Guillaume de Lorris.
Rothschild, Victoria, 82; on *Parliament of Fowls* as 1384 commemorative calendar, 207–8n4, 213n43
Rowe, Donald W., 208n7, 212n30; and importance of geometric progression to Pythagorean theory, 82
Rowland, Beryl, 18
Russell, J. Stephen, 4, 206n45; on influence of 1381 Peasants' Revolt on *HF*, 935–49, 217n4; on the visionary in dream literature, 5–6

Scattergood, V. J., *See* A. J. Minnis
Schibanoff, Susan, 139, 199–200n15; on Black Knight in *BD* as John of Gaunt, 9
Schless, Howard, 200n18
Shakespeare, William, 114, 160, 178, 209n13, 215n15, 216n21, 220–21n12
Shipman's Tale, 125, 219n4
Shippey, T. A., 199n10, 205n44
Shoaf, R. A., 220n9
Shook, Laurence K., 216n19
Simmons, J. L., 137
Simson, Otto von, 195
Singleton, Charles S., 211n24, 213n40
Southern, R. W., 206n45
Spade, Paul Vincent, 197n2
Spearing, A. C., 136, 213–14n2, 218n13
Spenser, Edmund, 95, 213n41
Squire's Tale, 216–17n1
Stahl, William Harris, 68, 76, 79, 80, 198n6, 207n3, 210–11n19, 211nn21,22, 26, 210n21, 222n1
Statius, 112, 113
Steel, Anthony, 200n18
Stevick, Robert D., 195
Strohm, Paul, 19, 28, 202n31

Tale of Sir Thopas, 30, 40, 76, 216–17n1; as discussed by John Burrow, 76–77; as "rym dogerel," 70
Taylor, A. E., 222n1
Temple of Venus, 67, 89, 98, 109, 112, 119, 127, 189, 190
Thundy, Zacharias P., 34, 202n32
Thynne, William, 8, 24, 25, 29, 198nn4,8, 209–10n17; as editor of 1532 *BD*, the only exemplar

containing lines 31–96, 29–30; paragraph sign at line 1311 in Thynne's *BD* edition, 24–26

Troilus & Criseyde, 1, 4, 20, 30, 63, 98, 114, 120; art of reporting past events in, 145–46; betrayal of Criseyde by Troilus, 179–82; betrayal of Troilus by Criseyde, 177–78; consummation scene, 154–61; Criseyde's formal appeal to Hector, 146–48; Criseyde's rationale for leaving Troy, 183–85; differences between males and females progressing toward love, 150, 157; Diomede in, 137, 164, 178–79, 183–85, 219n5; as double genre, 163–64; "dulcarnoun" in, 141–45; Hector in, 147–50, 153, 164, 169, 179, 184, 219n2; internal dialogue, 4, 167; manipulation of time in, 161–62; mathematics in, 140–45; Pandarus manipulates Criseyde, 169–70; parallel paths of Criseyde and Troilus, 176–77, 185; poet as creator, 3, 173–74, 181; progress revealed in still-life "snapshots," 170–72; Troilus, Boethius, and art's permanence *vs.* life's impermanence, 187; Troilus's and Criseyde's initial glimpse of each other, 150–52; Troilus and Pandarus, proverbial styles compared, 167–68; truth and poetry, 101

Vickery, Gwen M., 9

Virgil (Publius Virgilius Maro) 3, 57, 95, 99, 106, 108, 112–13, 119–20, 131–33, 135, 137, 139, 195–96, 206n47, 213n40, 217–18n7; Aeneas' abandonment of Dido excused by, 133–34; *Aeneid*'s Dido-Aeneas episode and unity of *HF*, 129; *Aeneid* on walls in *BD*, 106; Caesar Augustus/Octavian, patron of, 21, 26; calendar and *Georgics 1* linked by, 95; golden ratio used by, 57; *Georgics 1* as interpreted by LeGrelle, 213n40

Walker, Denis, 19

Wetherbee, Winthrop, 146, 212n30, 214n5, 215n10, 218n10

Wife of Bath's Tale, 125, 219n4, 221n18

Williams, George, 98, 221n19

Windeatt, Barry, 162, 210n18, 217n3, 219n2, 221n15

Yates, Frances, 18

Yeats, W. B., 215–16n17

Edward I. Condren (1934-2020) was professor of English at the University of California, Los Angeles.

www.ingramcontent.com/pod-product-compliance
Lightning Source LLC
Chambersburg PA
CBHW031807220426
43662CB00007B/552